G. K. Chesterton

A Centenary Appraisal

G. K. Chesterton

A Centenary Appraisal

Edited by
JOHN SULLIVAN

Paul Elek
LONDON

First published 1974 by
ELEK BOOKS LIMITED
54-58 Caledonian Road, London N1 9RN

ISBN 0 236 17628 5

Printed in Great Britain
at the St Ann's Press, Altrincham, Cheshire WA14 5QQ.

Contents

Illustrations

Acknowledgement

Editor and publishers express their gratitude and thanks to
Miss Dorothy Collins, not only for her kind permission to
reproduce all except two of the illustrations in this book, but
also for her invaluable help in making this material available
to them. The illustrations showing the cover of the first edition
of *Greybeards at Play* and the 'thank-you letter' to Mrs C. F. G.
Masterman are reproduced by permission of the Editor,

Notes on Contributors

KINGSLEY AMIS. Edited *G. K. Chesterton: Selected Stories* (1972).

W. H. AUDEN. Edited *G. K. Chesterton. A Selection from his Non-fictional Prose* (1970).

DUDLEY BARKER. Novelist and biographer. Author of studies of Galsworthy and Arnold Bennett and of *G. K. Chesterton* (1973).

IAN BOYD. University of Saskatchewan. Awarded doctorate by University of Aberdeen for a thesis on Chesterton's early novels.

PATRICK CAHILL. A Devereux distributist and once secretary of the Central Branch. Compiled *The English First Editions of Hilaire Belloc* (1953), and edited *One Thing and Another* by Hilaire Belloc (1955).

DOROTHY COLLINS. Chesterton's secretary and literary executrix. Edited *The Surprise*, a play (1952); *A Handful of Authors* (1953); *The Glass Walking-Stick* (1955); *Lunacy and Letters* (1958); *Where All Roads Lead* (1961); *The Spice of Life* (1964); and *Chesterton on Shakespeare* (1972).

P. N. FURBANK. Author and critic. *Samuel Butler (1835–1902)* (1948); *Italo Svevo: The Man and the Writer* (1966); *Reflections on the Word 'Image'* (1970).

CHRISTIANE D'HAUSSY. Head of English Department, University of Paris XII-Creteil. Author of *Le Catholicisme en Angleterre* (1970).

G. C. HESELTINE. Worked on *G.K.'s Weekly* (Director) and in the Distributist League (Secretary). Knew Chesterton well. His book, *The Change: Essays on the Land* (1927), has a Foreword by G.K.C.

STEPHEN MEDCALF. Lecturer in English in the School of European Studies, University of Sussex.

PETER MILWARD, S.J. Professor of English, Sophia University, Tokyo. Edited *Orthodoxy* and *Essays on Shakespeare by G. K. Chesterton* for Japanese students.

W. W. ROBSON. Professor of English Literature, University of Edinburgh. Author of *Modern English Literature* (1972), etc.

BROCARD SEWELL. Priest of the Carmelite Order. An early worker for the Distributist Movement and *G.K.'s Weekly*. Author of *My Dear Time's Waste* (1966); *Footnote to the Nineties* (1969); *The Vatican Oracle* (1970).

JOHN SULLIVAN. Author of *G. K. Chesterton: A Bibliography* (1958); *Chesterton Continued* (1968).

Preface

G. K. Chesterton was born in Kensington on 29 May 1874. It must be said at once, however, that this book is neither a pious memorial volume nor just a centenary tribute but a critical assessment. There is need for a comprehensive view of Chesterton, for a consideration of what he actually achieved in his lifetime and why his work is of value to us today. In the introduction to his recent selection of Chesterton's short stories, Kingsley Amis wrote: 'He, or a large part of him, has never been out of favour with me, nor with a high proportion of literates over thirty-five or forty. It is tempting to conclude that the disfavour, if any, must reside among junior age-groups; at the same time, a great deal of Chesterton's work and public personality must be directly antipathetic, for reasons of varying cogency, to the standard liberal intellectual of any generation.' This is true. For many people, Chesterton is a name remembered, but remembered for the wrong things. In the minds of many who have never attempted to read him there lingers a legend of a funny fat man who was anti-semitic, a journalist who wrote many essays and some poems, some detective stories and a great deal of apologetics. It is surely time that the modern reader should become aware of how much of Chesterton's vast output is still worth reading and how much of it is of permanent value.

In this collection of essays specially commissioned for the centenary, modern writers, scholars and critics consider Chesterton's work and its relevance to modern readers. The list of contributors and their subjects indicates the wide range of Chesterton's appeal: the contributions themselves reveal the impact of his personality on those who knew him well, such as Dorothy Collins and G. C. Heseltine, and what his work in prose and verse means to a number of modern writers and critics. Dudley Barker, following his recent book on Chesterton, provides a brief survey of his oeuvre and Stephen Medcalf an elaborate

and well-documented one. W. H. Auden considers the poetry
and rediscovers the forgotten *Greybeards at Play*. Kingsley Amis
casts a shrewd eye over the fiction in general and Ian Boyd and
W. W. Robson treat of special aspects of the fiction in depth.
P. N. Furbank assesses what is generally held to be the period of
Chesterton's best work. Brocard Sewell's account of the early
days of Distributism is complemented by Patrick Cahill's view
of the relation of Chesterton's social thought to the modern
world. From overseas, Christiane d'Haussy and Peter Milward
review Chesterton's position in France and Japan respectively.

When evidence such as this of Chesterton's continuing
vitality is set out, the popular belief that he is played out is
seen at once to be a truly Chestertonian paradox. The truth is
that until recent years serious critical assessment of his work has
been lacking. Much of the writing about him during his lifetime
and since has been popular stuff which perpetuated the legend
of his personality at the expense of his achievement. Chesterton
was pre-war, and in the present age his manifest belief in
good and evil, his sturdy support of many virtues that have
come to be regarded as old-fashioned have made it possible
for him to be thought of as a back number. His political stance,
that of an ex-Liberal, opposed equally to what he called 'the
twin evils of Capitalism and Communism,' has not helped his
reputation either. Above all, perhaps, the kind of writing in
which he excelled, that of 'a superb metaphysical journalist' as
someone has called him, has gone out of fashion as intellectual
debate has shifted from the periodical and the platform to the
TV screen. In all this, Chesterton's characteristically original
novels, his literary criticism and biographies, his poetry have
come to be ignored by the generality of readers.

A reconsideration was due and that is what this book seeks
to provide. The instant and warm response of the contributors
when first invited to write was in itself, I think, a tribute to the
enduring influence of Chesterton's genial personality and to the
lasting value of what he wrote. The men and women who have
written in the pages that follow of the various aspects of this
most various of men, have written freely, some objectively as
critics, others as friends and admirers, all as people who are
interested in what Chesterton has to say to the modern reader
and why it is important.

In the issue of the *Illustrated London News* for June 1, 1907, when he was 33, Chesterton wrote: 'If you or I were told by way of prophecy that we should live (as I shall) until 1957, or (as you will) until 1979, we might feel sensitive about a year or so; but when we are dead we may care about many things but I hope at least we shall no longer care about dates.' Chesterton did not live till 1957 but died, too soon, in 1936. Since his death, eleven books have been compiled from his uncollected writings. In all over thirty books have been written about him and his work. Innumerable references are made to him in a great variety of contexts and he is frequently quoted, with and without acknowledgement. Also in this period there have been two retrospective exhibitions of his work, one in Manchester in 1957 and another in Forty Hall, Enfield in 1971, both of which attracted large attendances. A third exhibition, designed to commemorate the centenary, is to be held under the auspices of the National Book League at their headquarters in Albermarle Street, London W1.

It seems appropriate that the centenary of Chesterton's birth should be marked by a contemporary assessment of the work of this man of original mind who was endowed with a remarkable range of self-expression, an assessment in which the indelible mark that he has made upon our literary consciousness should be demonstrated through some consideration of his thought and literary achievement and of his present real standing among perceptive readers both at home and overseas.

John Sullivan
Strawberry Hill, 1974

The Achievement

A Brief Survey of Chesterton's Work

DUDLEY BARKER

The most obvious feature of Chesterton's work is its quantity. Few men have managed, in a writing life of some forty years, such an immense and immensely varied output. Between 1900 when his first book appeared, and his death in 1936, he published one hundred books—novels, biography, poetry; collections of essays, of short stories, of detective stories; books on religion, on sociology, on politics; travel books, volumes of literary criticism, a couple of plays, polemics, and a history of England. In the last five years of his life he became a famous radio broadcaster, most of his talks being afterwards published. Posthumously came another volume of short stories and one of the most charming autobiographies in the language. Since then, ten more Chesterton volumes have been published, mostly compiled from the vast, unmeasured, perhaps now immeasurable bulk of his essays and verse scattered widely in magazines and newspapers during his lifetime. For alongside his authorship Chesterton never staunched his broad flood of general journalism and his steady stream as columnist; he wrote the weekly 'Notebook' in the *Illustrated London News* from 1905 until the week he died, with only a few breaks because of illness or absence overseas; of his 1,535 'Notebook' essays, more than a thousand have yet to be collected into volumes.

It is astonishing that a man who wrote so much, so quickly, should also often have written so well. Two of his novels seem secure of their place in the literature of twentieth-century England. Half a dozen of his poems are still familiar, as is his fine English epic. At least one of his religious books is still widely read; so are many of his light essays and some of his literary criticism. He is accepted as the best English aphorist of our century. His little priest, Father Brown, ranks among the dozen best-known detectives of fiction. In addition to all that, of course, he wrote a huge amount of ephemeral, tired, worthless prose, and a very great deal of nonsense.

He first emerged as an essayist who had published in periodicals a few short poems which people remembered; notably 'The Donkey' and 'By The Babe Unborn'. He had in fact, in 1900, published two volumes of verse, one of nonsense verses and the other, which his father paid a publisher to put out, a pompous, boring verse play together with the reprinted short lyrics. Few noticed the volumes. Even fewer bought them. This was particularly unfortunate since Chesterton, then working for £1 a week as a publisher's assistant, had hoped for enough money to enable him to marry Frances Blogg, a serious, religious girl from Bedford Park, that first garden-suburb and home of late-Victorian intelligentsia.

However, the money that verse would not provide began to flow from essays. Chesterton's friends among a group of young radicals just down from the Universities, who had bought a failing weekly, the *Speaker*, in which to attack the complacent jingoism of the Liberal Party, introduced him as a writer. His first essays appeared in the *Speaker* and were soon widely noticed.

From them he formed his third volume, *The Defendant*; each essay a defence of something, such as of Penny Dreadfuls, of Nonsense, of Heraldry, of Ugly Things. He omitted the political essays, although his pro-Boer, anti-jingo attitudes show in the Defence of Patriotism: ' "My country right or wrong" is a thing that no patriot would think of saying except in a desperate case. It is like saying, "My mother drunk or sober". . . . The extraordinary thing is that a people who have Shakespeare, Newton, Burke and Darwin to boast of . . . talk as if we have never done anything more intelligent than found colonies and kick niggers.'

But most of the *Defendant* essays are light-hearted, chuckling, showing already Chesterton's superb knack of the neat phrase, and his love of paradox and logic of the absurd. These were the skills that made an immediate reputation in Fleet Street for an unknown publisher's-reader; a reputation that became national when he was invited to write an essay each Saturday for the Liberal *Daily News*. The distinction persists of those journalistic essays. A few tastes: 'The Iliad is only great because all life is a battle, the Odyssey because all life is a journey, the Book of Job because all life is a riddle'; 'A strange idea has infected humanity that the skeleton is typical of death. . . . There is no reason why the living skeleton should not become the essential symbol of life'; 'Bad story writing is not a crime. Mr Hall Caine walks the streets openly'; 'Moral truisms have been so much disputed that they have begun to sparkle like so many brilliant paradoxes'.

His second volume of essays, published in 1902 when he was already married, established in a flat facing Battersea Park, and living from his journalism, was collected chiefly from the *Daily News*. He had been invited at first to write on literary subjects, and these essays, collected as *Twelve Types*, established him as a literary critic and decided the direction of his writing life. His criticism, rarely profound, was remarkably perceptive. His brother Cecil's comment that it was 'the work of a journalist, and a journalist must be readable or perish' misses its essential value. Chesterton could plunge his pen into any hackneyed subject—Charlotte Brontë, say, or Pope, or Scott or Stevenson—and pluck out its core in a few fresh phrases. Charlotte Brontë 'showed that abysses may exist inside a governess and eternities inside a manufacturer.' Of Pope he asked: 'Have we really learned to think more broadly? Or have we only learned to spread our thoughts thinner? I have a dark suspicion that a modern poet might manufacture an admirable lyric out of almost every line of Pope.' About Stevenson's work there is 'a certain clean-cut angularity which makes us remember that he was fond of cutting wood with an axe.' Scott 'arranged his endless prefaces and his colossal introductions just as an architect plans great gates and long approaches to a really large house.'

The freshness of it introduced Chesterton to the literary gaffers of his day—to the deaf, spinsterish Swinburne at Putney; to the deaf, voluble Meredith on Box Hill; to John Morley, then editing the 'English Men of Letters' series. Morley invited him to write the volume on Robert Browning; an act of extraordinary editorial courage (or rashness) since Chesterton at that time had published nothing longer than an essay. Max Beerbohm advised him to accept, since he was still young enough to say something original. Chesterton's *Robert Browning* amplified the remark. As he admitted, with a chuckle, there was not much about Browning in his book; and what there was, was mostly inaccurate. It was chiefly a book about Chesterton's thoughts on poetry, life and religion. The publisher raged when he read the proofs. The firm would be disgraced. The book was intolerably unlike anything else in the series, and grossly careless. Most of Browning's lines were misquoted, and there was one which Browning might well have written in 'Mr Sludge the Medium', but, as it happened, had not. Chesterton always quoted from memory (and often misquoted) because he 'refused to surrender a total and frequent experience of a poem to a false re-encounter with the actual lines'; the true reason, of course, was indolence.

Nevertheless, Chesterton's *Browning* was an immediate and lasting success. It enlarged him from journalist to author, though the journalism flowed merrily alongside. Indeed, the two streams often merged. Essays in the *Daily News* were the nucleus of his book *Heretics*, a couple of years later, attacking the philosophies of contemporary writers, with incidentally a good deal of straightforward literary criticism. The freshness of view persisted. It was worth saying that Kipling 'sings the arts of peace much more accurately than the arts of war'; and that he lacked patriotism. 'He admires England because she is strong, not because she is English.' It was a useful proposition that Shaw was no capering humorist, but a man in deadly earnest, without ideals, and therefore dangerous. And there were splendid knockabout essays deriding Tolstoyan simplicists, the 'dusty egoism' of George Moore, and novelists of smart society.

But the true successors to *Robert Browning* were two more literary biographies. First came a short, vivid account of a great Victorian artist, *G. F. Watts*; then, in 1906, *Charles Dickens*, Chesterton's happiest book. He had been immersed deeply in Dickens's novels since boyhood; he could repeat long sections by heart (doubtless inaccurately). Throughout his life he wrote about Dickens, including prefaces to each novel in the 'Everyman' edition. He frequently lectured on Dickens. His first radio talk was about Dickens and Christmas. He cherished Dickens's chair, which the Dickens Fellowship presented to him.

Part of the value of his *Charles Dickens*, therefore, is that it was written with devotion. But there is much more. Chesterton's ability to probe straight into essentials and illuminate them with a few phrases was never stronger. Of a subject which had been so worked upon he had fresh things to say, and they have formed more of the public image of Dickens, and the public appreciation of his novels. than the writings of many another critic or biographer. He was the first to assert clearly that 'Dickens's work is to be reckoned always by characters, sometimes by groups, oftener by episodes, but never by novels. You cannot discuss whether "Nicholas Nickleby" is a good novel or whether "Our Mutual Friend" is a bad novel. Strictly, there is no such novel as "Nicholas Nickleby". There is no such novel as "Our Mutual Friend". They are simply lengths cut from the flowing and mixed substance called Dickens—a substance of which any given length will be certain to contain a given proportion of brilliant and of bad stuff.' Chesterton's second basic clarification was that 'Dickens did not strictly make a literature; he made a mythology. . . . He did not always manage to make his characters men, but he always managed, at least, to make them gods. They are creatures like Punch or Father Christmas.' And what happier single sentence could there be about the main stream of English narrative literature than: 'Sam Weller would have been a great gain to the Canterbury Pilgrimage and told an admirable story'? Or what neater summary of the phenomenon of Charles Dickens than: 'Dickens stands first as a defiant monument of what happens when a great literary genius has a literary taste akin to that of the community. . . . Dickens did not write what the people wanted. Dickens wanted what the people wanted.'?

The book confirmed Chesterton's standing. It drew appreciation from such diverse men as Bernard Shaw, William James, Swinburne and President Theodore Roosevelt. Moreover its influence persisted. Years later Maurois called it one of the best biographies ever written (above all because it is not a biography), and T. S. Eliot declared, 'there is no better critic of Dickens living than Mr Chesterton.'

Unfortunately, *Charles Dickens* proved the summit of Chesterton's literary criticism. He wrote several more books which could thus be catalogued, and hundreds of essays, articles and prefaces, but nothing ever again so good. Of the books, the one that has lasted best is the extended essay *The Victorian Age in Literature*, still in print and being read after fifty years and some twenty successive editions. It starts brilliantly with an essay on the spirit of England in the nineteenth century, and flows well to the great Victorian novelists and philosophers. Scattered across it like sun-sparkles on a stream are vivid phrases and sentences setting down the essence of a writer: 'There was about John Stuart Mill even a sort of embarrassment; he exhibited all the wheels of his iron universe rather reluctantly, like a gentleman in trade showing ladies over his factory.' 'Matthew Arnold kept a smile of heart-broken forbearance, as of a teacher in an idiot school, that was enormously insulting.' ' "Wuthering Heights" might have been written by an eagle.' '. . . a feeling that the characters in Meredith are gods, but that the characters in Henry James are ghosts.' 'Stevenson seemed to pick the right word up on the point of his pen, like a man playing spillikins.' Then the book goes on to the great Victorian poets, and the sparkle inexplicably vanishes, as though Chesterton, of all men, felt that he had nothing he particularly wanted to say about poets. Or perhaps he was simply tiring.

He wrote only two more books, years later, in which literary criticism was the major factor. His *Robert Louis Stevenson*, containing more an account of Chesterton's youth than Stevenson's, is only, as criticism, a development of an early essay in the *Daily News*. His *Chaucer*, written a few years before his death, is one of the few Chesterton books in which dullness predominates. That he wrote badly about a subject so dear to him was perhaps because the pressures of journalism and an absurd back-to-mediaevalism politics, undertaken as a duty towards his dead brother Cecil, had by then sapped too much of his health and vigour. Or perhaps he was by then too old. For he aged as a writer far more quickly than as a man.

Most of his best work, indeed, was done in little more than the first decade of his writing life. If all that remained were what he published between the appearance of his first volume in 1900 and the performance of his only considerable play in 1913, very little of Chesterton that matters would be lost. In those thirteen years came the literary biographies, his three best novels, most of his essays that are still read, his most important book on religion, his strongest statement of social views, all his poetry, and the earliest (and best) of his 'Father Brown' detective stories. In 1914 he suffered a mental and physical collapse during which he lay in a coma for months, and from which it was feared he might not recover. Had he died during that illness, Chesterton's literary reputation would have been practically the same as it now is, although half of his books were yet to come, as well as the great bulk of his journalism; but of the books, only five are of much consequence, and little of the journalism can compare with that of his Fleet Street decade. And he wrote no more poetry, only occasionally verse.

In that first decade of writing, however, he was brilliantly spontaneous. He started as novelist as suddenly and effectively as he had become essayist. *The Napoleon of Notting Hill* is one of the most unusual first-novels of modern times. Chesterton's tale of war of the future, between the London boroughs which had become separate little states in mediaeval trappings, is amusing enough in itself (and an odd prophecy of urban guerrillas). But it is subsidiary to the theme of conflict between Auberon Quin, the satirical King of England (elected from the Civil Service—and thought to have been modelled on Max Beerbohm) and Adam Wayne, the stern, fanatical Lord High Provost of Notting Hill. It is these two who, when the fighting at last is over and mankind laid low in grief and suffering, come together as two lobes of the same brain, the humorous and the fanatic, finding a philosophical justification for existence clearly derived from the Book of Job, which Chesterton read and pondered upon, year after year. The novel does not deal with human relationships; it contains, for instance, no women. It is rather a statement of political beliefs, and a philosophical allegory. As such it had an instant success, and is still in print, still being read throughout the English-speaking world, still exerting its curious charm.

This first novel was followed by two others, *The Ball and the Cross* and *The Man Who Was Thursday*, written in that order, but the latter published first.

The Ball and the Cross has now largely been forgotten, although it should rank not far below the others. Like them it is an allegory, told in jesting narrative until the closing scenes. An atheist and a devout Catholic swear to fight a duel because the Catholic considers the atheist has insulted the Mother of God. But they are continually thwarted by pursuing police, by newspaper reporters intrigued by men who will kill each other over the question of God's existence, and by other comic characters and mischances. At last they are trapped in the garden of a lunatic asylum, the madness of the world, in which two themes are worked out; on the spiritual plane, the struggle between good and evil; on the political, a prophecy of the authoritarian State which Chesterton clearly saw approaching. A comparison with Kafka is unavoidable, and curious; at that time, of course, Chesterton knew nothing of Kafka. There are the similarities of naturalistic dialogue in a mad setting, of incessant awareness of actual and positive evil and persecution, both spiritual and human. The chief dissimilarities are that Chesterton's surface narrative is light-hearted, often comic; and that he had, by then, emerged from an adolescence of despair and doubt into an unshakeable acceptance of orthodox Christianity.

His adolescent despair, which had been unusually severe and brought him near to mental breakdown, was the origin of his third novel, *The Man Who Was Thursday*, unquestionably his best. The surface narrative of this allegory is melodrama. The man who was Thursday—a detective smuggled on to the inner council of seven anarchists who aim to destroy the world, each bearing as code-name a day of the week (and of the Creation)—is engaged in successive wild combats with the others, only to find, in turn, that each is also a detective in diguise. Only Sunday remains, to be chased madly through London and at last to emerge as the Sabbath, the peace of God. Chesterton said that he did not intend Sunday to represent the Deity, 'but rather Nature as it appears to the pantheist, whose pantheism is struggling out of pessimism.' But this is not the impression that the reader receives by the final chapter, which is, once again, a direct reference to the Book of Job. The Kafka-like method of realistic dialogue and action in irrational circumstances is even more pronounced than in the earlier novels. But the theme is ever more strongly that of faith and optimism.

In the same year, 1908, Chesterton published *Orthodoxy*, in which he stated this faith without a veil of fiction. He insisted that it is not an ecclesiastical treatise, but 'a slovenly sort of autobiography'—his account of how, reasoning from an initial wonderment at the extraordinariness of existence in itself, he raised himself from the despair of his adolescent years

by working out a system of beliefs which he then found already
existed—those of orthodox Christianity. 'It was as if I had been
blundering about since my birth with two huge and unmanageable machines,' he wrote,

of different shapes and without any apparent connection—the world
and the Christian tradition. I had found this hole in the world;
the fact that one must somehow find a way of loving the world
without trusting it; somehow one must love the world without being
worldly. I found this feature of Christian theology, like a sort of hard
spike, the dogmatic insistence that God was personal, and had made
a world separate from Himself. The spike of dogma fitted exactly
into the hole in the world—it had evidently been meant to go there
—and then strange things began to happen. When once these parts
of the two machines had come together, one after another, all the
other parts fitted and fell in with eerie exactitude. Having got one
part right, all other parts were repeating that rectitude, as clock
after clock strikes noon. Instinct after instinct was answered by
doctrine after doctrine.

With elaboration, this book remained his basic statement of
Christian belief throughout his life; that orthodoxy was the
only practical explanation of existence, the key that fitted the
lock.

In the decade of his best novels, literary biographies, essays,
and definitions of his religious and philosophical position,
Chesterton also set out his somewhat odd political theories (in
a book called *What's Wrong With The World*) unduly influenced
by Hilaire Belloc and by his own brother Cecil, and composed
nearly all his poetry. Such exhaustive and varied output
emphasizes the strength of his mind during those years. It also
emphasizes his physical strength, for he was already pictures-
quely stout, consuming immense draughts of wine and beer in
Fleet Street bars, drinking and arguing incessantly in apparent
idleness, yet pouring out, in addition to his books, such a stream
of ephemeral newspaper and magazine journalism as would
keep most men at their desks day long and for much of the
night.

And the poetry. Nobody, I imagine, would call Chesterton a
great poet. Yet there are not a few of his lyrics that somehow
stick in the general memory, poetry that most people have

actually heard or read: old Noah not caring where the water
goes if it doesn't get into the wine; the song against the wicked
grocer; the rolling English drunkard making the rolling English
road; the despised donkey with a shout about its ears and palms
before its feet; the Christ-child lying on Mary's lap; and a few
more. But the songs were by no means all. There was the occasional thrust, such as the famous exhortation to Birkenhead
('Chuck it, Smith!'). There was the epic, especially *The Ballad
of the White Horse.*

This was the only work in his life which he pondered and
drafted over several years. The idea was that King Alfred's
long defeat by the Danes, then his victory at Ethandune—but
victory never complete, always having to be guarded and fought
over again—is a microcosm of the English throughout their
history. With this central idea went that of Alfred as a Christian
king, and Chesterton's love for England of earlier times, 'in the
good time of smaller things,' the England of the dawn, of the
holy kings riding down by Severn side; and his almost mystic
feeling for the white horses cut from the grass of England's
chalk downs by men of unmeasured antiquity. For complicated
reasons in his childhood and marriage, for him the white horse
represented chivalry.

It was perhaps because, in 1909, his wife removed him from
London to a permanent home at Beaconsfield, only some thirty
miles from the Berkshire White Horse Vale, that he was
suddenly stirred to write the poem which he had long incu-
bated. He hired a car and he and his wife were driven west to
Glastonbury and the Isle of Athelney, where he gazed at the
reeds and river grassses where Alfred took refuge. Once he
began writing, he finished the whole epic in a fortnight. In
the circumstances of defeat and victory, it *fits* the English as
perhaps no other poem does. As witness that, on one grey
morning of the second world war, *The Times*'s leading article
consisted only of a plain statement of the defeat in Crete, and
two stanzas from Chesterton's ballad:

I tell you naught for your comfort,
Yea, naught for your desire,
Save that the sky grows darker yet
And the sea rises higher.

> Night shall be thrice night over you,
> And heaven an iron cope.
> Do you have joy without a cause,
> Yea, faith without a hope?

Then, on the morning when the great news came of Alamein, the same newspaper's leading article quoted from the same poem:

> 'The high tide!' King Alfred cried.
> 'The high tide and the turn!'

A familiar comment on Chesterton is that he was a master who left no masterpiece. It may be that, of all he wrote, *The Ballad of the White Horse* is the only possible refutation.

Certainly the work by which he is now best known to a wide readership cannot make claim. Father Brown is a familiar fictional detective. But the Father Brown stories are not a masterpiece in the way that those of Sherlock Holmes are, or those of Maigret, or even of Poirot or Perry Mason. Many have ingenious ideas, particularly those written during Chesterton's prolific decade and published in the first collection as *The Innocence of Father Brown* in 1911. It is an ingenious idea for a mystery story that a man in evening dress at a club dinner, and a waiter serving, differ only in the way in which the one strides and the other shuffles; or that a murderer can walk out of a building carrying the corpse in a sack, without anybody seeing him, because he is the postman, an accepted part of the scene, an 'invisible man'. But even before the end of the first Father Brown volume the basic ideas had grown wild and confusions had arisen. It is not a credible idea for a mystery story that a man on a church steeple could fling a hammer accurately enough to kill a man in the roadway below. The chief criminal opponent of the little detective in one story becomes his chief assistant in another. The detective upon whom Father Brown depends in the first story is disposed of in the second as the murderer whom Father Brown detects. The little priest himself alters considerably in character and conception as the series lengthens. Chesterton's original idea of a priest knowing more about evil than most criminals (because of the confessions of others) scarcely lasted intact through the

first two volumes, *The Innocence* and *The Wisdom*. By the third
volume, *The Incredulity of Father Brown*, twelve years later,
Chesterton was deeply engaged as editor of his *G.K.'s Weekly* (a
laborious task for which he was ill-suited), and in propagating
an impractical political theory called Distributism. Both were
a severe drain, not only upon his time and energy, but upon
his purse; he kept the magazine in existence only by subsidizing
it with money he earned by writing. Father Brown became then
the chief provider, and the rest of the Father Brown stories
were potboilers.

Not much needs to be said, indeed, about most of what
Chesterton wrote after 1914. During the first world war his
books were only war-propaganda pamphlets, and a *Short
History of England* which is chiefly about the delights of mediaev-
alism. The fiction he wrote in the Twenties and Thirties falls
well below his former standards. He collected into volumes
some lively newspaper and magazine articles on his travels to
Ireland, to Palestine, to the United States of America and to
Rome, but these books are essentially sheaves of travel articles,
little more.

His move from the Anglo-Catholic into the Roman Catholic
Church in 1922, however, revived in him some of his earlier
powers. The next book he wrote, a short biography of *St Francis
of Assisi*, is as clear, simple and charming as anything he produced. His picture of St Francis, who had been one of his heroes
since boyhood, is drawn with such affection that it was at once
a success.

His second book of this period was provoked by Wells's
Outline of History. Chesterton attacked Wells's theme of the
steady betterment of mankind in *The Everlasting Man*, essentially
a Christian view of history, centred around the brief life on
earth of Jesus. In a sense it is the sequel to his earlier *Orthodoxy*,
the completion of his journey from non-belief to complete and
immovable religious conviction.

In spite of the vast writing output which Chesterton maintained until the very week of his death in 1936, there is not
much more of his work that needs noting. His two further
literary biographies, *Robert Louis Stevenson* and *Chaucer*, have
already been discussed. But there was one more biography to
come towards the close of his life; a brief account of *St Thomas*

Aquinas, companion to his *St Francis of Assisi* which it matches in length and simplicity, but well exceeds in profundity. To attempt to depict, in so brief a space, the greatest of Christian philosophers, as Chesterton insists that St Thomas is, and to show how he reconciled the Christian with the great pagan philosophies, was daunting indeed. Chesterton achieved it with, as he puts it, only 'a popular sketch of a great historical character who ought to be more popular . . . a rough sketch of a figure in a landscape, not of a landscape with figures.' The sketch is not only a convincing portrait of the saint, but makes clear to an ordinary reader how St Thomas 'did not reconcile Christ to Aristotle; he reconciled Aristotle to Christ.' It was the last book that Chesterton wrote (apart from a few more collections of newspaper essays and magazine stories); it is satisfying and right that it should be so good.

Although Chesterton's *Autobiography* was published shortly after his death, he had written most of it some ten years earlier, and laid it by. Its publication, however, beautifully rounded off his life. For all its inaccuracies (his memory failing him quite often, usually to soften things), and its omissions (such as practically any mention of his marriage and his private life thereafter), it is a book of delights. This kindly, generous, immensely courteous, often stubborn and pig-headed, portly man, so immensely filled with the sense of comedy, and with the certainties of faith, never drew a more agreeable portrait than this of himself.

Chesterton the Edwardian

P. N. FURBANK

It would be fair, I think, to call G. K. Chesterton the archetypical Edwardian writer. 'Edwardian' is not an established
term quite like 'Romantic' or 'Augustan', yet for me at least
it has a fairly precise meaning. It suggests a writer formed by,
and attuned to, the Harmsworth era. Shaw and Kipling were
Edwardian writers in this sense, though not chronologically;
and in saying this one is saying something about the nature of
their imagination. What I mean is, that the imagination of the
'Edwardian' writer is nurtured not so much by the sap of
nature as by printer's ink. It is an *ad hoc* imagination, a product
of the will and of opinion. Everything, even in Kipling, is
there to make a case and can be converted back into a case.

If one accepts this definition, then what one notices about
'Edwardian' writers, as compared with the modernist artists
like Yeats and Joyce who were coming to maturity at the same
period, is that the Edwardians were much more natural men.
To cultivate the true, unconscripted imagination in art, as
Yeats and Joyce did, consumes all the artist's natural humanity
and leaves him a stiff and unnatural monster in real life. Shaw,
Wells and Chesterton, by contrast, splashed about in the
intellectual life in a thoroughly carefree way; perhaps no other
group of writers has ever done so to the same degree. And why
I have called Chesterton the archetypical Edwardian is
because, while possessing as much verve and invention as any
of his contemporaries, he was franker in admitting to himself
that it was all paper and printer's ink. There is a moral good
taste in Chesterton which prevents him, as it does not always
prevent Shaw—think of *St Joan*—from asking you to accept
his impromptus as true imagination. In his fantastic novels you
never for a moment leave the weekly column or the debating-
hall; it is simply that the whole universe becomes a debating-
hall, and the argument happens to be continued on the dome
of St Paul's or the pantomime battlefield of Notting Hill.

How Chesterton became the kind of writer he was makes,

biographically speaking, a curious story. As we learn from
Maisie Ward, he did not reach puberty until he was eighteen or
nineteen—evidently he suffered from some mild glandular
disorder, as one night have guessed from his later fatness. The
fact was clearly important. For to come to puberty so belatedly,
when in most other respects you are in the midst of adult life,
must be a very strange, and perhaps shattering, experience;
and so it proved with Chesterton. He became a victim of
phantasmagoric sexual obsessions, which convinced him of the
close and immediate presence of the devil. And, more to the
point, it gave to the intellectual movements of the day, in which
he had already taken a cheerful debating-society interest, a
sulphurous flavour of diabolism for him. His reaction was to
combat them with the weapons of his childhood—with a toy-
theatre medievalism, pasteboard swords and debating-society
high jinks. It was a reaction of genius, restoring his moral
balance and leaving his intellect untrammelled and free. None
the less it left him with some extremely odd, and rather comic,
misconceptions. It prevented him from having much real
notion of what Ibsenism, or Zolaism, or Symbolism or Schopen-
hauerian pessimism were about. It even left him feeling that
there was something sinister, and metaphysically subversive, in
Impressionist painting—at least, he thought that his own 'black
night of the soul' might partly be laid at its door. The notion
appears at one of the climaxes of *The Man Who Was Thursday*,
as expressing Gabriel Syme's bewilderment when 'The Criminals Chase the Police':

The ex-Marquis had pulled the old straw hat over his eyes, and the
black shade of the brim cut his face so squarely in two that it seemed
to be wearing one of the black half-masks of their pursuers. The
fancy tinted Syme's overwhelming sense of wonder. Was he wearing
a mask? Was anyone wearing a mask? Was anyone anything? This
wood of witchery, in which men's faces turned black and white by
turns, in which their figures first swelled into sunlight and then
faded into formless night, this mere chaos of chiaroscuro (after the
clear daylight outside), seemed to Syme a perfect symbol of the
world in which he had been moving for three days . . . was not
everything, after all, like this bewildering woodland, this dance of
dark and light? Everything only a glimpse, the glimpse always
unforeseen, and always forgotten. For Gabriel Syme had found in

the heart of that sun-splashed wood what many modern painters
had found there. He had found the thing which the modern people
call impressionism, which is another name for the final scepticism
which can find no floor to the universe.

Altogether, his crisis and recovery left Chesterton at a slight
angle to reality. They confirmed him in the chosen role of
innocence and absent-mindedness, and also in the conviction
that all human experience could best be dealt with in the form
of an argument. They were the making of him as a writer. But
of course not the kind of writer who counts most of all—not a
writer like Kafka (I am citing another fantasist) who wrestles
with the full actuality of life. But then, that much is included
in our definition of 'Edwardian'. Shaw prided himself on being,
in person, a realist and a practical man—and by comparison
with Chesterton he was Zola, Mr Bounderby and the Admirable
Crichton rolled into one—nevertheless one murmurs during
his plays, 'Of course, life is not like that . . .'

There is another slight oddity in Chesterton's formation as a
writer. He was a refugee from the *fin-de-siècle*, and yet he
borrowed almost all his equipment as a writer from it. He was
evidently fascinated by Wilde, as all his contemporaries were,
and took over the paradox from Wilde, in order to turn it
against him. In Wilde the paradox was expressive of a quarrel
with nature. It was the emblem of those who lived 'A rebours'—
against the grain, at odds with nature, using the wrong organs
of the body in sex, and so on. Chesterton took it over as a
weapon against just this attitude, as a device for bouncing
oneself into a fresh vision of the ordinary and the natural. And
he wielded it much in Wilde's style. In that alliance of the
fanatic and the joker cemented at the end of *The Napoleon of
Notting Hill*, the joker, Auberon Quin, is, in essentials, Wilde.
His epigram, 'The reversal of the obvious is as near as we can
come to ritual with our imperfect apparatus' echoes Wilde's
philosophy and tone with great fidelity.

Chesterton also took over Wilde's 'impeccable bad taste', the
bedecking of one's prose with gorgeous and gaudy 'artist'
colours. Not uncritically, indeed; for he makes somewhere a
good remark about Wilde's disagreeably caressing tone towards
jewels and precious substances. But his own passion for gaudy

colour is not simply toy-theatre heraldry, it is also Nineties aestheticism. Prose such as this is more or less pure Wilde:

The sealed and sullen sunset behind the dark dome of St. Paul's had in it smoky and sinister colours—colours of sickly green, dead red or decaying bronze . . .

. . . he never saw her again until all his tale was over. And yet, in some indefinable way, she kept recurring like a motive in music through all his mad adventures afterwards, and the glory of her strange hair ran like a red thread through those dark and ill-drawn tapestries of the night.

'Yes, the costume of the nineteenth century is detestable', remarks Lord Henry dreamily in *Dorian Gray*. 'It is so sombre, so depressing. Sin is the only real colour-element left in modern life'. Chesterton, who was equally in arms against the sombreness of modern life, was content here again to use the weapons of Lord Henry's creator.

Likewise Chesterton's idea of the poet, flaming-haired and gorgeous-tongued, is Wildean; it is Swinburne as transmitted by Wilde. And so, again, is his intellectual bravado, his love of impromptu, and—what goes with them—the cheerful ignorance.* Part of the zest for Wilde in his conquest of English society lay in the concealment of the abysses of his ignorance. He succeeded very well. Yeats has recorded his amazement, upon meeting Wilde, that this 'scholar' should also be so perfect a man of the world; yet, so far as one can tell, he only ever read one modern French book, and that was *A Rebours*. Chesterton, of course, did not conceal his ignorance, he announced it blithely. And perhaps one should not call it ignorance, for he read enormously; but whatever it was—say, a beaming disregard for dates and details—it became part of his costume and role. Nevertheless there was a kinship to Wilde here. Wilde loved to allude, in a grand gesture or generalization, to vast tracts of (in his case largely non-existent) knowledge. And with more to support it, this was Chesterton's habit too. It was the Fleet Street method, the method of a thinker

*Jack Worthing has a nice Chestertonism in Act 1 of *The Importance of Being Earnest*. 'I don't really know what a Gorgon is like, but I am quite sure that Lady Bracknell is one. In any case, she is a monster, without being a myth, which is rather unfair'.

living his intellectual life in public. One can see in Wilde, who exercised, and revelled in exercising, such an extraordinary hold over the public imagination, the ancestor of the Fleet Street 'prophet'. This was a new type of prophet, no longer just a teacher or member of the 'clerisy', but a teacher and entertainer combined. He spoke to a new, and to a considerable extent self-taught, audience; and what that audience demanded was not just edification or scholarship but 'ideas', ideas of every description.

Here, I need hardly say, we are at the heart of Edwardianism. Never did ideas so run rampant: in the columns of weeklies and dailies, on the stage, in gas-lit mission halls and salons and model villages and simple-life colonies. It was an inspiriting time, and one feels a nostalgia for it. Though, on the other hand, it was this period which, understandably, produced in modernist writers their distrust of all 'ideas' as the enemy of art. Chesterton, said Eliot, had a mind as full of ideas as a rabbit-warren; 'but I have yet to see evidence that he thinks'. It was a most unfair, and rather Chestertonian, remark; and it has always remained a somewhat dark mystery what Eliot meant by 'thinking', a word with which he sandbagged many opponents. Yet there was some truth in the jibe. The faith in 'ideas' of Chesterton and his fellow-prophets was part of the optimism of that brief post-Victorian moment and perhaps wasn't fitted to survive it. All the same, we should not write off Edwardian polemics as mere mock-battles, or as some kind of indoor game. So much free intelligence playing round fundamental issues could not fail to leave a deposit of truth and to have effect on events. I have a curious anecdote to illustrate this. In 1909 Gandhi read an article by Chesterton on Indian nationalism in the *Illustrated London News*. It was indeed a very sparkling article. 'I do not doubt for a moment that the young idealists who ask for Indian independence are very fine fellows; most young idealists are fine fellows', Chesterton had said in it.

I do not doubt for an instant that many of our Imperial officials are stupid and oppressive; most Imperial officials are stupid and oppressive. But when I am confronted with the actual papers and statements of the Indian Nationalists I feel much more dubious, and, to tell the truth, a little bored. The principal weakness of

Indian Nationalism seems to be that it is not very Indian and not
very national. It is all about Herbert Spencer and Heaven knows
what. What is the good of the Indian national spirit if it cannot
protect its people from Herbert Spencer? I am not fond of the
philosophy of Buddhism; but it is not so shallow as Spencer's
philosophy . . . .

Suppose an Indian said: 'I heartily wish India had always been
free from white men in all their works. Every system has its sins:
and we prefer our own. There would have been dynastic wars;
but I prefer dying in battle to dying in hospital. There would have
been despotism; but I prefer one king whom I hardly ever see to a
hundred kings regulating my diet and my children. There would
have been pestilence; but I would sooner die of the plague than die
of toil and vexation in order to avoid the plague. There would have
been religious differences dangerous to public peace; but I think
religion more important than peace. Life is very short; a man must
live somehow and die somewhere; the amount of bodily comfort a
peasant gets under your best Republic is not so much more than
mine. If you do not like our sort of spiritual comfort, we never asked
you to. Go, and leave us with it.' Suppose an Indian said that, I
should call him an Indian Nationalist, or, at least, an authentic
Indian, and I think it would be hard to answer him. But the Indian
Nationalists whose words I have read simply say with ever-increasing
excitability, 'Give me a ballot-box. Provide me with a Ministerial
dispatch-box. Hand me over the Lord Chancellor's wig. I have a
natural right to be Prime Minister. I have a heaven-born claim to
introduce a Budget. My soul is starved if I am excluded from the
Editorship of the *Daily Mail*,' or words to that effect.

Gandhi was thunderstruck by the article. He immediately
translated it into Gujarati, and on the basis of it he wrote his
book *Hind Swaraj*, his own first formulation of a specifically
'Indian' solution to his country's problems. Thus you might
argue, not quite absurdly, that India owed its independence,
or at least the manner in which it came, to an article thrown
off by Chesterton in half-an-hour in a Fleet Street pub.

So much for Chesterton's formation and role as an 'Edwardian' writer. Now a word about his central belief, which he
evolved—and which, he said, preserved him—when in 'the dark-
est depths of the contemporary pessimism'. I mean the belief
that 'Even mere existence, reduced to its most primary limits,
was extraordinary enough to be exciting'. That 'At the back

G.K.C.——C

of our brains ... there was a forgotten blaze or burst of astonishment at our own existence' and 'the object of the artistic and spiritual life was to dig for this submerged sunrise of wonder'. As we know, the belief did sustain him throughout his career and was the basis for some of his most engaging fantasies—such as that of *Manalive*, in which the hero, to revive his excitment at his own existence, burgles his own house and elopes with his own wife.

One would like to put this belief in perspective; and a name that comes up in my mind is Proust. Not the most obvious of conjunctions you might say, and I don't suppose either would have been too delighted by it. Moreover, it is true, Chesterton's message is an ethical one in a way that Proust's is not; he presents being thankful for one's existence as a *duty*. I will concede that there are other dissimilarities. Yet to make it one's deliberate and systematic task, as both did, to 'dig for this submerged sunrise of wonder' of one's childhood; to approach the task not nostalgically and in yearning for a lost self but in the firm belief that the self was *not* lost, that it was still there, available, if you could dig down to it, and the most serious thing in life—that does constitute a likeness. Many paths lead to that moment in *Time Regained* when, on his stumbling on two uneven paving-stones in the Guermantes' courtyard, all the staleness, lassitude and jadedness drop away from the narrator's vision of the world and he is possessed by 'a joyous certainty sufficient without other proofs to make death indifferent to me'. 'Galvanisez nos pauvres vertèbres' cried Verlaine. The writers of the turn of the century feel benumbed and beaten down by the drabness, and especially the triviality, of existence, and they demand at all costs a vision. They may, like Yeats, set their teeth and construct their own mythologic vision, inventing something to believe in and then believing in it. 'Consequently I rejoice, having to construct something/ Upon which to rejoice' Eliot puts it, with circular syntax (there is something especially of the twentieth century in the heroic cold-bloodedness of the undertaking). They may on the other hand look for their vision and glory in the common world. This is the path which leads on from realism and naturalism, the path taken by Proust and Joyce.

For an English writer of the period, though, there was a

special obstacle barring this second path, an obstacle inherent in the English class-system. Edwardian English writers were obsessed by the problem of the 'suburban'. At heart they despised the suburban, which for them represented triviality rampant; and the gentlemanly presuppositions of literary society and literary prose-style in England encouraged them to despise it. Yet they felt a compunction about despising it: if for no better reason, because they were writing in the Harmsworth era and very much hoped to be read in suburban homes; but also because, in so far as they were the inheritors of the Goncourts and of Maupassant, they felt it their duty to be beyond class-prejudice and impartially to reclaim all kinds of human existence for art. As a result, the characteristic ambition of Edwardian writers may be said to have been *to redeem the suburban*.

Of course, I am using the word 'suburban' in a very loose way and am speaking almost as much of writers' attitude to the *petit bourgeois* generally—small-town life, lower-middle-class life etc. The point is more that the word 'suburban' itself had come into prominence at this period, as a synonym for triviality. It is a complex and peculiarly English word, tendentious rather than descriptive. What is 'suburban' cannot be identified on any map, and its meaning changes from speaker to speaker; for when people use the term they are expressing a fear about their own class-position. The fear prompts a myth, which is that suburban people spend their life imitating gentlefolk—that everything in suburban life is a parody.

'Redeeming the suburban', if the phrase be allowed, became a leading preoccupation of the novelists of this period: of Bennett, of Wells, of Forster and of Chesterton. Bennett, who was in a peculiar situation in this regard, coming from a lower-middle-class background himself, approaches the matter in a rather disagreeable way. He is always asseverating, too loudly, that, looked at rightly and as an artist should, *petit bourgeois* life is 'glorious'.

What had happened? Nothing! The most commonplace occurrence! The eternal cause had picked up a commercial traveller (it might have been a clerk or curate, but it in fact was a commercial traveller), and endowed him with all the glorious, unique incredible attributes of a god, and planted him down before Sophia in order to produce the eternal effect. A miracle performed specially for Sophia's benefit! No-one else in Wedgwood Street saw the god walking along by her side. No one else saw anything but a simple commercial traveller. Yes, the most commonplace occurrence!

(*Old Wives' Tale*)

Wells in *Mr Polly* has, though less disagreeably, much the same tone. He 'glories' in his 'little man's' rebellion against the humdrum in a falsely bonhomous and condescending tone. Chesterton was too nice a man, and too devoid of any allegiance to literary realism, to take such a tone. Yet the same problem hovers about his own 'redeeming of the suburban'. In his *Autobiography* he tells a story which has some bearing on the writing of *The Napoleon of Notting Hill*.

When I was a young journalist on the *Daily News*, I wrote in some article or other the sentence, 'Clapham, like every other city, is built on a volcano'. When I opened the paper next day, I found the words confronting me, 'Kensington, like every other city, is built on a volcano.' It did not matter, of course, but I was a little puzzled and mentioned it to my immediate superior in the office, as if it were some freak of a fanciful compositor. But he glowered at me in a heavy and resentful manner, which would alone be a confession of guilt, if there were any guilt, and said rather sulkily, 'Why should it be Clapham?' And then, as if throwing off the mask, 'Well, I live at Clapham''. And he, knowing that I lived at Kensington, had bitterly transferred to that royal borough what he imagined to be a taunt.

'But I was glorifying Clapham!' I cried pathetically, 'I was showing it as epical and elemental and founded in the holy flame.' 'You think you're funny, don't you?' he said. 'I think I'm right', I said.

The trouble with this, if one is to be literal and pedantic, is that Chesterton thought the name 'Clapham' funny too; and nothing in *The Napoleon of Notting Hill*, no vision of an army for Bayswater or a flag for Notting Hill, no invocation of the 'pastoral chiefs' of Shepherd's Bush or the 'rude clans' of Paddington Green, does anything to contradict this. His 'redeeming of the suburban' in this novel did much for the 'little-England' and anti-Imperialist cause, but it did nothing for Notting Hill. It was too much to hope that it would. It needed

an artist of the stature of Joyce or Lawrence to shake English
literature out of its class-prejudices. Chesterton's intellectual
games with the suburbs, and his exploitation of them in what he
calls his 'vague and visionary revolt against the prosaic flatness
of a nineteenth-century city and civilisation', are only good
because he laid no claims to be a novelist, in the humanistic
sense, at all. One attaches no more literalness to his dealings
with Clapham and Surbiton and Shepherd's Bush than to
Shaw's paradoxical dustmen.

I have been restrictive towards Chesterton so far, and
deliberately, for centenaries must not make us grow pious.
'What we want isn't centenary volumes', someone said to me,
'but just for a few of his books always to be kept in print'. For
myself, I would even say a lot of his books, but no doubt this
won't be. It is, I suppose, the penalty paid for not being,
properly speaking, an artist. I don't suppose that on Orwell's
centenary there will be many of Orwell's books in print. Yet I
should think he might well be in currency still; and so, certainly, is Chesterton today. There are jokes of his, and fancies, and
judgements that you could not get along without. We need
Chesterton; he is so indispensable that we need not make a
cult of him.

Of his novels, I would think *The Man Who Was Thursday* the
best fitted to survive. It is the profoundest and most aerated,
the one springing from the deepest paradox and most completely pervaded and penetrated by its paradox. It is not surprising
that a doctor once told Chesterton that the novel had been a
great help in treating mental patients. As a parable of out-
facing paranoiac imaginings—that classic one, especially, of the
whole world being in a conspiracy against you—the book has
great force and originality. It is a true comedy of psychosis,
exploring that absurd and tireless logic with which the insane
create their own dilemmas and make evil out of what is
innocent. And absurdest and most logical of all, funniest and
most like some theorem of the reversibility of all propositions,
is the duel-scene. Especially I like the passage beginning when
the bogus Marquis, in desperation, interrupts the fighting:

'Please let me speak', he said. 'It is rather important. Mr Syme',
he continued, turning to his opponent, 'we are fighting today, if I

remember right, because you expressed a wish (which I thought irrational) to pull my nose. Would you oblige me by pulling my nose now as quickly as possible? I have to catch a train.'

'I protest that this is most irregular', said Dr Bull indignantly . . .

'Will you or will you not pull my nose?' said the Marquis in exasperation. 'Come, come, Mr Syme! You wanted to do it, do it! You can have no conception of how important it is to me. Don't be so selfish! Pull my nose at once, when I ask you!' and he bent slightly forward with a fascinating smile. The Paris train, panting and groaning, had grated into a little station behind the neighbouring hill.

Syme had the feeling he had more than once had in these adventures—the sense that a horrible and sublime wave lifted to heaven was just toppling over. Walking in a world he half understood, he took two paces forward and seized the Roman nose of this remarkable nobleman. He pulled it hard, and it came off in his hand.

Whether in fact this, or any of the novels, will live I am not sure. What I am surer of is that Chesterton will live as a moralist. If he was weak in aesthetic taste, he was, on the other hand, extraordinarily strong in moral taste. It is this which, for instance, makes him worth listening to as a literary critic. There is nobody one is more ready to allow the use of the word 'vulgarity'. It was he who put his finger on what was true, among all that was false, in the charge that Dickens was a vulgar optimist:

. . . he gave the characters a comfort that had no especial connection with themselves; he threw comfort at them like alms. There are cases at the end of his stories in which his kindness to his characters is a careless and insolent kindness.

Likewise he condemns the insularity of the great Victorians for the right reason, which is that it was a kind of bad taste.

We feel that it *is* a disgrace to a man like Ruskin when he says, with a solemn visage, that building in iron is ugly and unreal, but that the weightiest objection is that there is no mention of it in the Bible; we feel as if he had just said he could find no hair-brushes in Habakkuk. We feel that it *is* a disgrace to a man like Thackeray when he proposes that people should be forcibly prevented from being nuns merely because he has no fixed intention of being a nun himself. We feel that it *is* a disgrace to a man like Tennyson, when he talks of the French revolutions, the huge crusades that had recreated the whole of his civilisation, as being 'no graver than a schoolboy's barring out.'

One feels this same good taste about him in his own life and ideas: one never has to feel profoundly ashamed for him, in the way that, every now and then, one is ashamed for Shaw, the Webbs or Wells, or even such a stickler for good taste as Henry James. The reason, I think, is that the virtue he thoroughly understood and practised was humility, a quality very closely bound up with good taste. I am not persuaded by Chesterton over faith; or over hope (he took too alarmist a view of what a pessimist was); or over charity (philanthropy is not such a mortal sin as he made out); but I am always convinced by him over humility. He has grasped better than anyone the truth that certain things it is not only unbecoming, but a contradiction in terms, to be proud of. This is what gives him such an impregnable position in a book like *Heretics* and makes his critique of imperialism, and the Superman, and 'neo-paganism' there so unanswerable. Here really *is* a book which should be in print, and I cannot end this essay better than by quoting it.

The pride which, proportionally speaking, does not hurt the character, is the pride in things which reflect no credit on the person at all. Thus it does a man no harm to be proud of his country, and comparatively little harm to be proud of his remote ancestors. It does him more harm to be proud of having made money, because in that he has a little more reason for pride. It does him more harm still to be proud of what is nobler than money—intellect. And it does him most harm of all to value himself for the most valuable thing on earth—goodness. The man who is proud of what is really creditable to him is the pharisee, the man whom Christ Himself could not forbear to strike.

Four Fluent Fellows

An essay on Chesterton's fiction

KINGSLEY AMIS

Chesterton's first book of fiction, *The Napoleon of Notting Hill* (1904), is in outline, and on the face of it, a romance about the future. The date indicated is 1984, but this coincidence, though doubtless odd, is unilluminating. Those twin concerns, to diagnose the contemporary world and through doing so to sound a warning about what it may turn into, characterize Orwell's novel and much orthodox science fiction besides; they find no more than a very incidental place in the Chesterton work. This indeed opens with an attack on prophecy and shows us, first, a society 'almost exactly like what it is now', then, later, a creation of pure and free fancy. (We could capture the book for science fiction only by taking what C. S. Lewis called 'the German view' that any and every romance about the future must fall within that category.)

The product of Chesterton's fancy is a London in which, by a kind of reversion to a medievalism that never existed, the various boroughs, while owing ultimate allegiance to the Crown, become independent city-states. Each has its Provost with his attendant group of heralds, its flag, its citizen-soldiery—armed with no more than sword and halberd—in their distinctive uniforms, its manufactured traditions and mottoes, its ambition and honour. Notting Hill, having ignominiously defeated an aggressive coalition of Bayswater and the Kensington boroughs, acquires a twenty-years' hegemony over all London, only to perish by a combined final onslaught, a set battle in Kensington Gardens.

This sounds like a straightforward, if idiosyncratic, chronicle of adventure and action. In fact, it is both more and less than that, a verdict that may prove not quite so hideously dull as it sounds if I amplify it by suggesting that in this first novel are to be found all its author's important concerns as a writer of fiction, concerns at times cumulative and mutually helpful to marvellous effect, now and then disastrously at odds, but concerns that always recur in his tales and give them their unique flavour and place in the canon.

The preludial attack on prophecy mentioned above consists of some sensible and provocative remarks couched in, often buried under, a style that wavers from the jocular to the facetious. Two concerns are at work here, or, to put it perhaps more appropriately, two men: Chesterton the Polemicist and Chesterton the Buffoon.

The Polemicist, thickly or thinly disguised, turns up virtually everywhere in Chesterton's fiction, and it must be said of him at once that he is rarely less than entertaining and often lends argument an elegance and an epigrammatic sting worthy of the best of the author's avowed polemical writing. Here, the argument is about nationalism and politics generally, it is conducted from more than one point of view, and most of it has nothing to do with the rest of the story; indeed, after the principal debate one of its chief participants, Juan del Fuego, a Nicaraguan grandee about as authentic as his name, is reported to have dropped dead. Right at the end of the book, the Polemicist puts in a secondary appearance to advance the not very inflammatory point that the humorist and the idealist, or the clown and the fanatic, are the two essential parts of the whole, sane man.

The clownish half of this synthesis corresponds to the figure I have called the Buffoon, to some tastes a mildly dismaying companion. He is actually incarnated in the character of Auberon Quin, an owlish minor civil servant who finds himself elected King—by what must have been a very arbitrary process. Until then he has been able to do little more than mystify and bore his friends with a string of elaborately pointless anecdotes; now he can mystify and bore all the people of London by decreeing that they build walls round their municipalities and parade in grotesque costumes sounding tocsins. At last—rather late, in fact, there appears a man who takes the whole charade seriously.

This is Adam Wayne, the youthful Provost of Notting Hill, tall, blue-eyed and red-haired. Red hair in Chesterton's men is a badge of unworldliness and chivalry (in his women it belongs to the sedate and serious-minded). Here we have the fanatical half of the synthesis, and at this point, too, a third Chesterton takes a hand in the shaping of the story. Aware of the deficiencies of the title, I dub the newcomer Chesterton the Melodramatist, meaning no disparagement, intending only to allude to that fusion of the grand and the histrionic, the magnificent and the magniloquent, which we find in the poems of Housman or the music of Tchaikovsky, and which we can respond to, even be deeply moved by, without necessarily ranging it alongside the work of Tennyson or Beethoven.

But let the Melodramatist speak: he does much of his work in dialogue, though he also operates through the heroic gesture, the stroke of symbolism, through *coup de théâtre* and *peripeteia* and transformation scene. (Wayne has interrupted a royal audience where the provosts of the Kensington boroughs— Buck, Barker, et al.—are petitioning the King to sanction a new development scheme which will swallow up Pump Street, an unimportant corner of Notting Hill cluttered with dingy toyshops, etc.)

. . . Buck said, in his jolly, jarring voice: 'Is the whole world mad?'
The King sprang to his feet, and his eyes blazed.
'Yes,' he cried, in a voice of exultation, 'the whole world is mad, but Adam Wayne and me . . . He has answered me back, vaunt for vaunt, rhetoric for rhetoric. He has lifted the only shield I cannot break, the shield of an impenetrable pomposity. Listen to him. You have come, my Lord, about Pump Street?'
'About the city of Notting Hill,' answered Wayne proudly. 'Of which Pump Street is a living and rejoicing part.'
'Not a very large part,' said Barker, contemptuously.
'That which is large enough for the rich to covet,' said Wayne, drawing up his head, 'is large enough for the poor to defend.'
The King slapped both his legs, and waved his feet for a second in the air.
'Every respectable person in Notting Hill,' cut in Buck, with his cold, coarse voice, 'is for us and against you. I have plenty of friends in Notting Hill.'
'Your friends are those who have taken your gold for other men's hearthstones, my Lord Buck,' said Provost Wayne. 'I can well believe they are your friends.'
'They've never sold dirty toys, anyhow,' said Buck, laughing shortly.
'They've sold dirtier things,' said Wayne, calmly; 'they have sold themselves.'

'It's no good, my Buckling,' said the King, rolling about on his chair. 'You can't cope with this chivalrous eloquence. You can't cope with an artist . . .'*

Even the couple of intrusions by the Buffoon, even the occasional lapses into the idiom of a lower kind of melodramatic writing, cannot hold back the speed and zest of that exchange, the confidence with which the unvarnished adverbs—proudly, contemptuously—are slapped down, and Buck and Barker are made to toss up their slow lobs for instant, unreturnable despatch. At this stage, the nature of the book changes; a little further on, the King tells Wayne, 'I tried to compose a burlesque, and it seems to be turning half-way through into an epic.' After making every allowance for the fact that novelists move by unanalysable instinct at least as much as by conscious thought, it still remains tempting to hear the author's voice in the King's remark, owning up to a belated change of mind.

The epic admittedly ticks over for a few pages while something is said about Wayne's 'mental condition'; not a great deal, hardly more in quantity than is needed to show what it is and how he attained it. No one doubts that Chesterton was deeply interested in people and their relations with one another, but at least in his fiction—parts of his literary criticism may be a different matter—he does not go in much for 'characterization' as it is normally thought of, for differentiating, developing, showing response to circumstance. Adam Wayne has just got to be extraordinary so that he will speak and act as he does.

He acquired his fanatic's brand of local patriotism as a child, we are told: not in the humdrum sense that it all started early, but in that he was most fully a child when he discovered what Notting Hill meant to him. Chesterton never developed a character who is and remains a child, but his tales are full of insights into childhood, celebrations of it and of the disregarded truth that the adult who has missed or rejected any part of what it is to be a child is a sad, stunted creature. In another novel he speaks of 'that concrete and material poetry which a child feels when he takes a gun upon a journey or a bun with

*I suspect that Chesterton meant to give the first speech quoted to Barker and the fourth to Buck. He might mix up names but he would probably not have given the same character two incompatible voices.

him to bed'. (I can still remember the gentle shock of reading
that sentence for the first time, the flash of realization, not that
you fully understand the author, but, far rarer and more
memorable, that the author knows all about you.) More
directly, Father Brown explains why a naval lieutenant in full
dress, and in suspicious circumstances, was brandishing his
sword.

'. . . He thought he was quite alone on the sands where he had
played as a boy. If you don't understand what he did, I can only
say, like Stevenson, "you will never be a pirate." Also you will
never be a poet; and you have never been a boy.'

Adam Wayne is a poet all right, in fact the poet, as well as
the Napoleon, of Notting Hill: a poet, moreover, not only in the
rather shifty, late meaning of 'one with strong (or refined)
feelings' about this and that. He also, it turns out, once published
a book of actual poems conveying his sense of the beauty and
mystery of his urban surroundings, in the spirit of more conventional poets whose subject is rural nature. The Buffoon has
a finger or two in this pie, but it is another Chesterton who says
of Wayne that 'twenty feet from him (for he was very short-
sighted) the red and white and yellow suns of the gaslights
thronged and melted into each other like an orchard of fiery
trees, the beginning of the woods of elf-land.'
The same Chesterton is at work in an earlier passage, long
before the advent of Wayne:

The morning was wintry and dim, not misty, but darkened with
that shadow of cloud or snow which steeps everything in a green or
copper twilight. The light there is on such a day seems not so much
to come from the clear heavens as to be a phosphorescence clinging
to the shapes themselves. The load of heaven and the clouds is like
a load of waters, and the men move like fishes, feeling that they are
on the floor of a sea. Everything in a London street completes the
fantasy; the carriages and cabs themselves resemble deep-sea
creatures with eyes of flame . . .

Here, obviously, is our fourth Chesterton, one whom, again,
I am chary of labelling. 'Chesterton the Painter' has its
attractions. It does the service of reminding us that the author

started his career not as an author, but as a painter in the proper sense, or at any rate as an art student at the Slade. I wonder very much whether the pictures he produced at that time, if any, show the fascination with the effects of light which can be seen in what I have quoted and which constantly reappears throughout his novels and stories. Every such reappearance seems fresh, different from all the others; we see not only London (though we see London most and perhaps best), not only the town or the village or the castle or the inn, but countryside from the lush to the stark, salt-flat, seashore, estuary, river (light on water, as might be expected, particularly attracted him), at all times of day but with a preference for dusk and dawn, in fog, in rain, in lightning, under snow. Chesterton the Impressionist? That is about the best I can do; the title has thin but legitimate roots in the writing of the 1880s, as a glance at, say, some of Wilde's shorter poems will show.

In *The Napoleon of Notting Hill*, the status of Chesterton the narrator is sufficiently indicated by denying that role an initial capital. There is a story holding at any rate its second half together, there are some fine moments of military action and expectation, but the main job of the narrative is to bridge the gaps between the returns of the various other roles. The closing scene, at the end of which Wayne and Quin set off like—perhaps a bit too much like—Don Quixote and Sancho Panza to roam the world, is right, is a triumph, but it is the triumph of the Melodramatist with some useful support from the Polemicist. No self-respecting, or mere, storyteller would have permitted himself a finale so blatantly implausible; implausible not just by ordinary commonsense standards, but even by the bizarre ones of what has gone before. (A look at the text compels the unanswerable question: Where had everyone else disappeared to?)

There is the sufficiently obvious view that some narrative power must reside in any work of fiction that keeps the reader reading; I cannot decide how far it is vulnerable to the demurrer that readers are kept reading by plenty of things that are not fiction—much of Chesterton's verse, for instance. However, on this view, the Narrator earns his capital letter, and to spare, in the second novel, *The Man Who Was Thursday*, which is the author's fictional masterpiece. To revert to Father

Brown's dictum, and perhaps to take a slightly menacing tone
for the moment, if you are not kept reading by it you will
never be a poet (in any sense I would accept) and you have
never been a boy. At any rate, saying so gives me the chance of
saying too that it would not be in order to add 'or a girl' at the
end of that last sentence. There are no unsympathetic female
characters in Chesterton's tales; there are no developed female
characters either. Sexual love, marriage, domesticity stand high
and firm in the Chestertonian set of values, but they are implied,
invoked, used as unargued motives or goals, not explored.

The solitary girl in *The Man Who Was Thursday* comes in
in the first chapter and on the last page. At the start, she is
doing what Chesterton's women spend a good half of their time
doing: listening to the men talk. The men in this case are two
poets called Gabriel Syme and Lucian Gregory, and they are
talking about anarchism. As might be expected, the Polemicist
gets a good innings here, but by the end of the chapter he has
merged into the Melodramatist. The setting is a suburban
garden transfigured by Chinese lanterns that glow 'in the
dwarfish trees like some fierce and monstrous fruit' and a strange
evening sky that seems to be 'full of feathers, and of feathers that
almost brushed the face'. The Impressionist goes on as he
begins.

What our three collaborators produce, working so closely in
harmony that there are no incongruities, no gaps to be bridged
by orthodox exposition, is of course a story, one of a kind that
eludes categorization, like Chesterton's other novels. *The Man
Who Was Thursday* is not quite a political bad dream, nor a
metaphysical adventure, nor a cosmic joke in the form of a spy
thriller, but it has something of all these. It is *sui generis*.

Syme, besides being a poet who talks against anarchism, is a
policeman with the job of fighting it. His credentials are franked
'The Last Crusade'—I would love to see that emblazoned on
some Whitehall office door. In pursuance of a sort of bet, he
allows Gregory to take him to dinner in a greasy riverside pub
that turns out to serve champagne and excellent lobster
mayonnaise. More surprisingly, dinner-table and diners
presently descend *en bloc* into an underground chamber:
shades, or rather anticipations, of Ian Fleming's *Live and Let
Die*.

Here a secret anarchist meeting is held; not very plausibly, but after some enjoyable and perverse rhetoric, Syme gets himself elected in place of Gregory to the Central Anarchist Council, whose members are named after the days of the week. So the man who has become Thursday sets out by moonlight, in a heavy cloak and bearing a sword-stick, to carry the war to the enemy.

At his introduction to the others on the Council, the novel starts to earn its subtitle, *A Nightmare*. They are not only hateful, they are physically monstrous in a way that seems to body forth the evil in their souls. The eyes of Saturday are covered by black glasses, as if they were too frightful to see. Monday, the Secretary, has a beautiful face with a smile that goes up in the right cheek and down in the left and is wrong. The face of Sunday, the gargantuan President, is so huge that Syme is afraid that at close quarters it will be too big to be possible, like the mask of Memnon he remembers seeing as a child in the British Museum, and he will have to scream. The Melodramatist breaks new ground here.

When the spectacles and the mask of anarchy are removed, however, Saturday is human enough, in fact another paladin of the Last Crusade. One by one the other Days declare themselves, until only the Secretary stands between police and President. But Monday is Sunday's agent, with the power of turning the world itself against the crusaders. The chase sweeps across a France of sturdy peasants and soldierly patriots and cultured men of wealth (more fun to read about, at least, than most real Frenchmen) transformed one after the other, in true nightmare fashion, into fanatical allies of anarchy. At last the only surviving champions of Christendom, and of reason and order, turn at bay.

The end is fantasy on a different level. In a second chase, it is Sunday who is pursued. He is caught up with but not caught; you cannot catch a being that is more than human, that represents what, were it not for Chesterton's well-known abhorrence of Shaw, I would be tempted to call the Life Force. This end sounds less than satisfactory, and it is, though not so unsatisfactory as it sounds. I can swallow it.

What I find indigestible in the closing scenes is the fortunately brief reappearance of the Buffoon in the person of the

fleeing Sunday, who at one point makes off mounted on a
Zoo elephant and who bombards the pursuit with messages of
elephantine facetiousness. I have one further cavil, in that the
Impressionist sometimes gets out of hand. He is itching to
describe a breakfast-party on an open balcony in Leicester
Square and also a snowstorm in the London streets, so the latter
is made to follow the former on the same morning. And chrono-
logy is telescoped, as it often is in Chesterton's tales, just to save
time. He could not be bothered to introduce what we might now
call cut-away material to imply an interim, nor even to throw
in the odd dull but useful sentence merely mentioning a pause
in talk, a couple of hours on the road in which nothing of
interest took place. This is the sort of thing critics mean when
they accuse Chesterton of not being a proper novelist. In a
nightmare, the defect perhaps matters less; at any rate, unlike
other such defects, it seems to matter less as soon as its presence
has been fully noted.

In the later novels, the Melodramatist bows himself out and,
pari passu, the Impressionist is reduced to the status of a scene-
painter: any old time of day and most places will do as background to conversation. It is the Polemicist who comes increas-
ingly to the fore. Part of him is propagandist, the champion of
Roman Catholicism against its various foes, but it is a much
smaller part than people with a sketchy knowledge or recollection of the real Chesterton would have us believe. And those
foes embrace, not any kind of Protestantism, but unreason,
superstition, diabolism, militant rationalism, moral neutralism,
Tolstoyism, anarchism, materialism, mystical cults. To enjoy
the spirited peppering of most of these targets, nothing more
doctrinal than a belief in reason is required. Further, the shots
fly in both directions: if the outcome of the battle is never in
doubt, the enemy is allowed some not always ineffectual return
fire.

This interest in dialogue as against monologue comes out
strongly in the third novel, *The Ball and the Cross* (1910), an
undervalued and, I find, largely overlooked work. Just what
sort of novel it is is once more not easy to tie down. It opens like
a kind of science fiction, in the marvellous flying-machine of
Professor Lucifer; its middle and main part is a blend or
alternation of Polemicist material and a simple but vigorous

action story. Atheist and Christian—the one is made as attractive a character as the other—fight it out in words and, when not prevented by officious interveners, notably police-men, with swords as well. The physical duel is inconclusive; the metaphysical comes out predictably but acceptably.

The final section is as fantastic as its counterpart in *The Man Who Was Thursday*, but this is more overtly theological: Lucifer lives up to his name in the role of superintendent of a gigantic lunatic asylum in which, were he to triumph, the mass of mankind would end up incarcerated. Chesterton's interest in madmen, which pervades his fiction, is at more than first sight surprising in so sane a writer and human being. Some of it serves his love of paradox, furnishing the man whose devotion to rationalism deprives him of his reason, the man whose devotion to reason makes him appear insane in the eyes of the illogical or the incurious. This is not the whole story, the rest of which I confess I cannot for the moment discover. But it must be stressed that Chesterton is not anticipating, would on the contrary have found devilish, current trendy notions that sanity is a relativist or quasi-political label, that there are insane societies but no insane individuals, etc.

By the time of *Manalive* (1912), the novels are in sad case. The hero, Innocent Smith—a name, like the title, that bodes no good—spends his inexhaustible leisure on projects like dropping his wife off at boarding-houses or places of business in order to re-encounter and re-woo her. As a long lecture near the close informs us flatly, this is his way of demonstrating (to whom?) his belief in the perpetual freshness of marriage. The author has to keep telling us that Smith is irrepressible and a harlequin, that 'he filled everyone with his own half-lunatic life.' These assertions are never demonstrated; Chesterton could not create comic incident or write funny dialogue.

The same primacy of the Buffoon—for it is he—disfigures collections of stories like *Tales of the Long Bow* (1925) and *The Paradoxes of Mr Pond* (1937, posthumous). In the first, a group of buffoons conspires to produce as literal facts a series of common phrases habitually used to express unreality or impossi-bility. So Commander Blair builds a castle in the air—a doctored balloon; Owen Hood sets the Thames on fire—or rather ignites a layer of petrol floating on part of its surface;

G.K.C.—D

and what of it? The eponymous narrator of the other book
introduces his yarns with laborious verve, such that his 'paradoxes', far from being the unlooked-for truths of G.K.C. at his
best, are no more than irresponsible and pointless mystifications.

Enough of the Buffoon: significantly, he makes not even the
most fleeting appearance in any of the Father Brown stories.
That incisive little cleric does occasionally and briefly pose as a
simpleton, but always for a dead-serious purpose, and any
full-grown specimen of the type he would have booted off the
stage in short order.

With no more than three or four exceptions, the best of
Chesterton's work in the shorter form is to be found in the
Brown saga. This consists of what are much closer to being
detective stories than most of his other fiction is close to any
accepted category. Before turning to it, I might just remark on
the pertinacity, or desperation, with which he clung to the
detective form in nearly all his short pieces. For a writer with
little interest in, or aptitude for, narration as such, a crime or
mystery plus investigation plus dénouement is a convenient
clothes-horse over which all manner of diverse material can be
draped. So it is with 'The Trees of Pride'*, the sixty-five pages
of which involve a disappearance and a reappearance, but
really describe a glorified nature-ramble.

The Impressionist (to resume) is in top form throughout the
Brown stories, even those written after, say, 1918, when he had
all but disappeared from the novels. In 'The Sins of Prince
Saradine' and 'The Perishing of the Pendragons' and elsewhere
he achieves some of the finest, and least regarded, descriptive
writing of this century. And it is not just description; it is
atmosphere, it anticipates and underlines mood and feeling,
usually of the more nervous sort, in terms of sky and water and
shadow, the eye that sees and the hand that records acting as
one. The result is unmistakable: 'That singular smoky sparkle,
at once a confusion and a transparency, which is the strange
secret of the Thames, was changing more and more from its
grey to its glittering extreme . . .' Even apart from the alliteration, who else could that be?

In these stories, the Polemicist and the Melodramatist are

*From *The Man Who Knew Too Much* (1922). Inexplicably omitted, along with
three shorter stories, in the 1961 Darwen Finlayson reprint of the volume.

often hard to distinguish from the Impressionist and from each other. Between them, the three produce wonderfully organized puzzles that tell an overlooked truth, parables that touch the emotions, syllogisms that thrill the senses. No author ever invented titles that more exactly prefigure what is to follow them—'The Salad of Colonel Gray', 'The Song of the Flying Fish', 'The Point of a Pin', 'The Wrong Shape', 'The Absence of Mr Glass'. There is a glint of alloy there among the pure metal, yet it seems to hold everything together in a way that nothing else could.

Now and again a solution is fudged, the criminal is unbelievably lucky, a witness is unbelievably unobservant, Father Brown sits on a clue. Now and again (a mannerism not uncommon in the other fiction) he pauses pregnantly and a feed-man obligingly throws up a 'By which you mean . . . ?' or a 'But then you knew . . . ?' so that Brown can drop his revelatory blockbuster in a voice like the roll of a drum. I admit to surges of irritation at times like these; they soon die down.

Of Chesterton's seventeen volumes of fiction, seven or eight, with another half-book or so of odds and ends, are worth keeping and re-reading; not a bad score. Very well, he remains a minor master in the genre, but there he remains, in spite of the glaring fact that so much of what interested him was irrelevant or even directly inimical to fiction as we usually think of it. His reader can promise himself, at the lowest count, what Lucian Gregory promised Gabriel Syme near the beginning of *The Man Who Was Thursday*. And that is . . . ? A very entertaining evening.

Philosophy in Fiction
IAN BOYD

It has been generally acknowledged that much of Chesterton's writing is frankly propagandistic both in its aim and its method. His reputation has always been that of a controversialist rather than a literary artist. At the same time, those who have studied his writing are aware of the obvious distinction between his directly controversial work and a considerable body of writing which might be called literature. The fact that the controversial works contain some of his best imaginative writing and the literary works some of his most significant political and religious commentary has of course made the division difficult to justify. But it would not be an unfair comment to describe most of the work in Chestertonian criticism as an effort to distinguish and perhaps to separate the art from the propaganda.

Among critics this division of Chesterton's work into art and propaganda becomes in practice a division between his mind and imagination. Those who prefer the imaginative writings are usually prepared to dismiss the propaganda as ephemeral journalism. Maisie Ward, for example, although she seems willing to defend any of the books which might be described as religious, suggests that politics distracted Chesterton from the literary career he was meant to follow.[1] And C. S. Lewis in defending Chesterton from an attack in *The Listener* by James Stephens distinguishes between the two senses in which an author belongs to his period: the first, the negative sense, is when he deals with things 'which are of no permanent interest but which only seemed to be of interest because of some temporary fashion'; the second is when he expresses matter of permanent importance through forms 'which are those of a particular age':[2]

The real question is in which sense Chesterton was of his period. Much of his work, admittedly, was ephemeral journalism: it is dated in the first sense. The little books of essays are mainly of historical interest. Their parallel in Mr Stephen's work is not his romances but his articles in *The Listener*. But Chesterton's imaginative works seem to me to be in quite a different position. They are, of course, richly redolent of the age in which they were composed. The anti-Germanicism in the Ballad of the White Horse belongs to a silly and transitory historical heresy of Mr Belloc's—always, on the intellectual side, a disastrous influence on Chesterton. And in the romances, the sword-sticks, the hansom cabs, the anarchists, all go back to a real London and to an imagined London (that of *The New Arabian Nights*) which have receded from us. But how is it possible not to see that what comes through all this is permanent and dateless?[3]

On the other hand there is a large group of critics who are willing to jettison the more obviously literary works in order to preserve the more obviously controversial. In fact they value Chesterton more as a thinker than as a writer. Hugh Kenner, for example, defines the essential Chesterton as a meta-physician whose work is chiefly valuable for the insights it provides by way of aphorisms and analogies.[4] Similarly Etienne Gilson speaks of his importance as a philosopher.[5] And T. S. Eliot, although he admires some of the early literary work, particularly the Dickens criticism and what he calls the Stevensonian fantasies, argues that Chesterton's importance is found in 'the place he occupied, the position, he represented during the better part of a generation.'[6] In fact he writes of him as if he were writing about the leader of a religious sect or a political party:

To judge Chesterton on his 'contributions to literature', then, would be to apply the wrong standard of measurement. It is in other matters that he was importantly and consistently on the side of the angels. Behind the Johnsonian fancy-dress, so reassuring to the British public, he concealed the most serious and revolutionary designs—concealing them by exposure, as his anarchist conspirators chose to hold their meetings in Leicester Square. (The real Johnson, indeed, with his theology, politics and morals, would be quite as alien to the modern world of public opinion as Chesterton himself.) Even if Chesterton's social and economic ideas appear to be totally without effect, even if they should be demonstrated to be wrong—which would perhaps only mean that men have not the goodwill to carry them out—they were the ideas for his time that were fundamentally Christian and Catholic. He did more, I think, than any man of his time—and was able to do more than anyone else,

because of his particular background, development and abilities as
a public performer—to maintain the existence of the important
minority in the modern world.[7]

But among critics whose interest in Chesterton is extra-
literary, those who perhaps have done the most serious damage
to his artistic reputation are a group which might be called the
professional Catholics. For them, Chesterton is an institution
to be defended rather than an author to be discussed. A
characteristic which defines their attitude is an aggressive
defensiveness towards him as a writer who needs their protection
combined with an astonishing ignorance and uncertainty about
the writing they are trying to protect. Bernard Bergonzi, who
betrays something of the same attitude himself in his somewhat
exaggerated attempt to avoid it, seems to have them in mind
when he describes the way many of his co-religionists refuse
even to discuss a question such as the anti-Semitic element in
Chesterton's writing.[8] He might have added that the refusal
to evaluate Chesterton as a writer often goes with a refusal to
tolerate any criticism of him as a literary artist. At the first hint
of criticism there is as it were an immediate closing of ranks,
which is followed, as often as not, first by a perfunctory tribute
to his personal qualities, and then by an evident eagerness to
change the subject. This attitude may be explained in terms of
the altogether understandable gratitude which an embattled
minority feels towards a writer whom they regard as their
champion. But whatever its explanation as a cultural phenomenon, there is no doubt that those who share this view have
helped to create an impression of Chesterton which they are
the first to resent. Their preference for what appears to be his
most controversial work and their refusal to discuss it in any
detail has had the effect of fostering an antagonism for him
which is equally unbalanced and uncritical. It is significant,
for example, that Orwell, who shows signs of knowing a
surprising amount about his work, should nonetheless regard
him as the leader of a group which in its discipline and like-
mindedness corresponds almost exactly to the Communist
Party. His description of the later Chesterton as a violent
propagandist is in fact merely a hostile version of the view
popularized by Chesterton's Catholic supporters:

Chesterton was a writer of considerable talent who chose to suppress both his sensibilities and his intellectual honesty in the cause of Roman Catholic propaganda. During the last twenty years or so of his life, his entire output was in reality an endless repetition of the same thing, under its laboured cleverness as simple and boring as 'Great is Diana of the Ephesians'. Every book that he wrote, every paragraph, every sentence, every incident in every story, every scrap of dialogue, had to demonstrate beyond possibility of mistake the superiority of the Catholic over the Protestant or the pagan. But Chesterton was not content to think of this superiority as merely intellectual or spiritual: it had to be translated into terms of national prestige and military power, which entailed an ignorant idealisation of the Latin countries, especially France.[9]

Even more curiously, however, the defence of Chesterton as a Catholic hero is frequently accompanied by an unmistakable note of patronage. Writers as different as Graham Greene and Evelyn Waugh, who agree in their preference for his controversial work, also agree in their somewhat equivocal praise of his 'simplicity'. Waugh confesses surprise at the number of critical studies of Chesterton's work 'in all its ephemeral bulk' and argues that it needs no elucidation: 'he wrote especially for the common man, repeating in clear language his simple, valuable messages.'[10] His tribute to Chesterton's character is a dismissal of his art:

He was a lovable and much loved man abounding in charity and humility. Humility is not a virtue propitious to the artist. It is often pride, emulation, avarice, malice—all the odious qualities—which drive a man to complete, elaborate, refine, destroy, renew, his work until he has made something that gratifies his pride and envy and greed. And in doing so he enriches the world more than the generous and good, though he may lose his own soul in the process. That is the paradox of artistic achievement.[11]

Greene's judgment is very similar. He argues that the simplicity which enabled him to write successful books of religious apologetics made him unable to understand the squalid complexities of political life which he needed to understand in order to beome a successful novelist:

For the same reason that he failed as a political writer he succeeded as a religious one, for religion is simple, dogma is simple. Much of the difficulty of theology arises from the efforts of men who are not primarily writers to distinguish a quite simple idea with the utmost accuracy. He restated the original thought with the freshness, simplicity, and excitement of discovery. In fact, it was discovery: he unearthed the defined from beneath the definitions, and the reader wondered why the definitions had ever been thought necessary. *Orthodoxy, The Thing,* and *The Everlasting Man* are among the great books of the age.[12]

The attempt to divide Chesterton's work into art and propaganda ultimately fails both as a description of what he thought and as a criticism of what he wrote. One is asked to make a choice between books which are supposed to be art, but which on examination turn out to be a kind of propaganda, and books which are supposed to be admirable as propaganda, but which are acknowledged to be generally inartistic. Fortunately, however, this unnecessary dilemma can be resolved if one ignores the false assumptions on which it is based and examines the writing with some care. Among these writings, none offers a better starting-place for a revaluation of Chesterton's achievement than does his fiction. Of all his work, none is more difficult to fit into the familiar and misleading categories of art versus journalism. It presents special problems for those who would claim Chesterton as a purely literary artist, because although quite clearly imaginative work, it also quite clearly points to something which is generally considered as being outside the field of literature. If these books are novels, they are novels only in the loosest sense of the word. If they are propaganda, they scarcely conform to any popular notion of what propaganda is supposed to be. Scattered passages repeat arguments which occur in the books of essays, but the arguments presented in the novels are usually presented in entirely imaginative terms. In fact Chesterton's fiction does not lend itself to any easy description. It consists of works which are a curious blend of literature and propaganda. Their meaning is certainly social and political, but it is usually expressed through the imaginative pattern which each of them reveals. And although they are books which can be easily related to Chesterton's social and political philosophy, they very frequently qualify this philosophy with independent and unexpected nuances of their own. Without fulfilling precisely the definition of any of the terms, they may be described as political fables, parables, and allegories, or more simply and conveniently as novels. But whatever name one gives them, they invite enquiry. For they stand in the strange and largely unexplored borderline region of Chestertonian studies which lies between art and propaganda, in which meaning is shaped and expressed by imagination and in which fiction is used as a means of accomplishing the twofold educational task which Chesterton called 'training the minds of men to act upon the community' and 'making the mind a source of creation and critical action'.[13]

It is true that Chesterton's own comments on his novels would seem to discourage their serious consideration. Not only does he insist that none of his stories are true novels, but he also claims that he at no time attempted to be a novelist.[14] He speaks of the ideas which he wished to express through these books, but adds that the books represent good ideas which have been spoiled.[15] There is of course no need to accept an author's self-criticism as a necessarily fair or final judgment of his work. In one of the Dickens prefaces, Chesterton himself anticipates a commonplace of modern criticism by warning readers of the dangers of the intentional fallacy in criticism.[16] Nonetheless his comments must be taken into account. What is particularly interesting is that in the same passage in which he deprecates the value of his novels as works of literature he makes a claim for their serious value as journalism. The fiction to which he refuses the name of art is described as being part of a larger effort in which writing is used as a means of bringing about social change. The context of the passage is also significant. It comes at the beginning of the large chapter in the autobiography in which he pays tribute to Belloc both as friend and as a writer.[17] And by identifying the aims of his own work with those of Belloc, as he does at the conclusion of the passage, he is perhaps allowing for the possibility that someone may make the claim for his own work which he makes for Belloc but is unable to make for himself:

But it was not the superficial or silly or jolly part of me that made me a journalist . . . In short, I could not be a novelist, because I really like to see ideas or notions wrestling naked, as it were, and not dressed up in masquerade as men and women. But I could be a journalist because I could not help being a controversialist. I do not even know if this would be called mock modesty or vanity, in the modern scale of values; but I do know that it is neither. It occurs to me that the best and most wholesome test, for judging how far a legitimate liking for direct democratic appeal, has prevented me from being a real literary man, might be found in a study of the man of letters I happen to know best; who had the same motives for producing journalism, and yet has produced nothing but literature.[18]

There are moreover two important elements in the statement which provide valuable insights into the meaning of the kind of fiction Chesterton wrote. The first is his insistence that in his imaginative work, as in his other writing, his chief concern is with the conflict of ideas. In novels written according to this plan one would expect to find what one does in fact find, characters who are primarily types representing conflicting political and social points of view. Secondly the passage also suggests that the novels are directly related to the political and social preoccupations of their author. The 'direct democratic appeal' of which he speaks suggests that his fiction is an extension of the journalism which he wrote in order to bring about the political and social changes which he thought necessary, his novels being political allegories written as a kind of political propaganda. In an essay published in *G.K.'s Weekly* he speaks of his desire as a writer to 'awaken the imagination':

. . . and especially that extreme and almost extravagant form of imagination that can really imagine reality. The true aim of art is to awaken wonder, whether the wonder takes the form of admiration or anger. It is natural for us to say in the ordinary way of speech, that monopoly is monstrous; but a certain mystical clarity of light is needed in which to see it actually as a monster. . . . we can hardly avoid having, in propaganda like this, a considerable element of fable and fantasy and all that the serious may call nonsense. Believe me, it is not half so nonsensical as what they call sense. If we have included a great many burlesques and travesties along the same lines of satire, it is for the perfectly practical reason mentioned above. It is that men must be made to realise, if only by reiteration, how utterly unreal is the real state of things.[19]

What Chesterton meant by allegory is never clearly expressed in his writing, but there is some evidence that he associated it with an almost platonic view of life. Abram's definition of allegory as the simple conversion of a doctrine or thesis into a narrative 'in which the agents, and sometimes the setting as well, represent general concepts, moral qualities, or other abstractions' describes only a part of what he meant by the term.[20] Similarly the definition of a parable as a short narrative 'presented so as to bring out the analogy, or parallel, between its elements and the lesson that the speaker is trying to bring home to us' is also unsatisfactory as a complete description of what Chesterton meant.[21] For one thing, there is no indication that he made any distinction between allegory and parable. When he uses these terms, he uses them as though they were interchangeable. In his study of William Blake, he defines the ordinary meaning of allegory ('taking something that does not exist as a symbol of something that does exist'),[22] and he then goes on to say that this definition must be reversed if one is to understand Blake's poetry. Writing of the lamb as a symbol of innocence, he comments, 'he meant that there really is behind the universe an eternal image called the Lamb, of which all living lambs are merely the copies or the approximation. He held that eternal innocence to be an actual and even awful thing.'[23] It is this view of allegory which Chesterton makes his own:

But the main point here is simpler. It is merely that Blake did not mean that meekness was true and the lamb only a pretty fable. If anything he meant that meekness was a mere shadow of the ever-lasting lamb. The distinction is essential to anyone at all concerned for this rooted spirituality which is the only enduring sanity of mankind. The personal is not a mere figure for the impersonal; rather the impersonal is a clumsy term for something more personal than common personality. God is not a symbol of goodness. Goodness is a symbol of God.[24]

The implication of Chesterton's view is that the whole of human life is made up of an unending series of hieroglyphs which it is the business of the allegorist to select and interpret. There is no question of a thesis which can be presented alternatively as a symbolic narrative or as a discursive argument. A parallel argument can indeed be constructed which expresses partly at least the truth which is expressed imaginatively by the allegory, but the allegory is in no way a translation of a discursive argument into symbolic terms. There is a sense in which the meaning does not exist apart from the allegory which reveals it. This may be why Chesterton speaks of the artistic mind as one that 'sees things as they are in a picture.'[25] And finally, this may be why in one of the later novels, the central character makes a claim for an entirely symbolic view of life: 'I doubt,' Gabriel Gale says, 'whether any of our action is really anything but an allegory. I doubt whether any truth can be told except in parable.'[26]

This notion of allegory helps to illuminate what Chesterton meant by fiction as a kind of propaganda. The novels are political in the general sense that they are directed towards an illumination of the political and social questions which he believed to be of central importance. Occasionally, too, one is able to recognize what seem to be topical political issues in the background of the novels, whether it is the Boer War in *The Napoleon of Notting Hill* or the General Strike in *The Return of Don Quixote*. But although the novels sometimes have their beginnings in particular political or social problems, their allegorical form gives these incidents a more general significance. Adam Wayne and Juan del Fuego are far more important as types of the small nation's doomed heroism than they are as representatives of the Boer resistance which gave Chesterton the idea for their creation. And Michael Herne and Douglas Murrel have clearly more to do with the dangers of a particular kind of political detachment than they have to do with the incipient Fascism and ironic Conservatism which they also illuminate.

The direct democratic appeal of which Chesterton speaks has in fact little resemblance to the kind of political fiction which for example the later fiction of H. G. Wells may have taught us to expect by that phrase. In Wells's case, the novels which he began to write after 1910 were characterized by endless discussions about the social questions of the day and the increasing reliance on characters as commentators. Chesterton very seldom expresses his social philosophy in fiction of this kind. There are occasional passages of topical satire, but the allegorical quality of the novels always remains sufficiently strong to prevent any of them becoming political essays cast in the form of fiction.

What one actually finds is something very like the kind of literature which John Holloway examines in *The Victorian Sage*. It is fiction used as a way of mediating imaginatively a particular political view of life. As Holloway remarks, this prophetic and seer-like quality cannot be explained entirely by rhetoric, since it can be achieved at least as successfully in the form of a novel as it can in the form of a discursive essay. Indeed Holloway's description of what the sage sets out to do in his writing might be applied equally well to what Chesterton sets out to do in his fiction:

. . . the sage has a special problem in expounding or in proving what he wants to say. He does not and probably cannot rely on logical and formal argument alone or even much at all. His main task is to quicken his reader's perceptiveness; and he does this by making a far wider appeal than the exclusively rational appeal. He draws upon resources cognate, at least, with those of the artist in words. He gives expression to his outlook imaginatively. What he has to say is not a matter of "content" or narrow paraphraseable meaning, but is transfused by the whole texture of his writing as it constitutes an experience for the reader.[27]

There are two general conclusions which may be drawn from a careful study of the fiction. The first concerns the somewhat unexpected political view which an analysis of the novels reveals, and the second the correlation between the political meaning of the fiction and its literary value.

It is of course true that the fiction does to an extent mirror fairly accurately the political thought which one finds in Chesterton's other writing. Early novels such as *The Napoleon of Notting Hill* and *The Ball and the Cross* and pre-World War One novels such as *Manalive* and *The Flying Inn* again and again echo essays written at the same time. The preoccupation with Distributism which characterizes the post-War essays is also characteristic of the post-War novels and short stories. In 'The Resurrection of Father Brown', for example, the priest-detective makes a somewhat improbable appearance as a kind of Distributist reformer in South America. And in one of the last and most melodramatic of the stories, the action is almost entirely concerned with the familiar Distributist argument against revolutionary Socialism and modern Capitalism as being essentially the same phenomenon.[28] Ronald Knox, in making a selection of the stories, found that the didactic purpose sometimes crowded out the detective interest: '. . . have we not good reason to complain of an author,' he asks, 'who smuggles into our minds, under the disguise of a police mystery, the very solicitude he was under contract to banish?'[29] It is also true that in a number of the stories one finds evidence of the same allegorical imagination which gives Chesterton's best fiction its remarkable power. A story such as 'The Chief Mourner of Marne' is perhaps more successful as a sermon on the sacrament of penance than as the story about an unusual duel, and a story such as 'The Dagger with Wings' probably fails equally as a detective story and as a political tract. But there remains a considerable group of stories in which the didactic purpose is brilliantly fulfilled by purely literary means. And although the general reader may miss the social or political point which is at the centre of stories such as 'The Invisible Man' and 'The Queer Feet', they are stories which deserve Frank Swinnerton's description as fables that mesmerize.[30] Often the very settings have a symbolic value. The Dantesque imagery of bitter cold in 'The Sign of the Broken Sword' is altogether relevant in a story which deals with the theme of treason.

But the most interesting and important feature which a study of the fiction reveals is its treatment of the theme of medievalism. The common view of Chesterton's social philosophy is that it expresses a longing for a literal return to medieval times. A careful study of the fiction indicates the falsity of such an interpretation. The shortest summary of what the novels have to say about the restoration of a medieval social order is that it is a dangerous political dream. In *The Napoleon of Notting Hill*, Adam Wayne's neo-medievalism brings back poetry and pageantry to modern life, but it also creates a neo-Imperialism which is as oppressive as the Imperialism it was supposed to replace. In *The Ball and the Cross*, which was the second novel he wrote, MacIan's dream of a medieval theocracy turns out to be a nightmare of authoritarian terror and repression. Even a later novel such as *Tales of the Long Bow*, which corresponds most closely to the popular view of Chesterton's medievalism, has in fact surprisingly little to do with a return to a medieval past. What the successful revolution achieves is the protection of an agrarian social system.

The most subtle and ironic treatment of the medieval theme is found in the novel which was serialized in *G.K.'s Weekly*, which was the organ of the Distributist League. *The Return of Don Quixote* is perhaps the best example of the way in which the best fiction works. The medieval experiment which the hero introduces does little to alter the realities of modern political life, except to the extent that it distracts the people from the existence of the real social problems which it leaves unaltered. The restoration of pageantry and colour to political life, which delights Herne and his followers, is also a means of deceiving them. The criticism which Chesterton makes about State Socialism and Capitalism is now followed by a criticism of Distributism itself. Nothing that has been written about the folly of romantic medievalism goes as far or hits as shrewdly as the criticism that one finds in what is ostensibly his most flamboyantly medieval novel.

The illusion which medievalism represents is also associated with the unreality of the medieval world which is actually restored. The medievalism of Notting Hill depends ultimately on the improvisations of Auberon, who claims no special knowledge of history and in fact regards the entire project as a joke. The medievalism of *The Ball and the Cross* is equally bogus. And *The Return of Don Quixote* invites the same kind of doubts. There is no reason to believe that Herne's few days of anti-quarian research really qualify him as a medieval specialist, and the result of his hastily conducted research shares something of the theatrical quality of the amateur play-acting with which it begins.

At the same time the ironical treatment of medievalism does not imply the rejection of 'medieval' values. The dream of restoring a medieval social order may be a dangerous illusion, but there is a sense in which the illusion is necessary. It has in fact the qualities of a myth. Those who mistake it for a reality destroy the society they are trying to reform, but those who recognize it as an ideal possess a valuable means of under-standing and judging the modern world. Perhaps the best example of the way in which medievalism becomes a way of understanding modern political life is found in *The Man Who*

Knew Too Much. The medieval pageant in which Horne Fisher, a kind of secular Father Brown, takes part provides him with the historical prospective he needs in order to understand the squalid charade of modern politics in which he is involved. Sometimes those who misunderstand the function of the medieval myth and those who understand it are the same people. Adam Wayne and Evan MacIan learn eventually from the romanticism which at first deludes them. And in *The Return of Don Quixote* Herne's superficial studies finally provide him with the principles which enable him to condemn his own medieval political experiment.

Another way in which the novels reveal an unexpected side of Chesterton's political and social philosophy is more directly related to their allegorical quality. This has to do with the use of opposed but complementary characters who help to define a complete and balanced political point of view. The success with which this method is used varies greatly from novel to novel, and indeed is used fully only in the early novels and in a certain number of novels which were published in the early and mid Twenties. The elements involved in the balance remain remarkably constant. The main conflict is always between a kind of idealism on the one hand and a kind of irony on the other. And the resolution of a conflict always involves an affirmation of the political forces which have been previously opposed. In *The Napoleon of Notting Hill*, Auberon's irony and Wayne's fanaticism are finally revealed as the two essentials of political sanity which achieve their equilibrium in the Chestertonian common man. In *The Ball and the Cross*, the quarrel between MacIan and Turnbull dramatizes the conflict between romantic Christianity and revolutionary Socialism, and is finally resolved by an affirmation of the values which each one represents. In the other pre-War novels little attempt is made to create a political synthesis in this way. Nonetheless in *Manalive*, Innocent Smith derives a kind of cumulative wisdom from the various political types whom he meets in his journey around the world, and in *The Flying Inn*, Humphrey Pump represents a complete expression of what Chesterton meant by the common man.

It is in the early post-War novels, however, that the use of political and social typology achieves its most interesting form.

In *The Man Who Knew Too Much*, Horne Fisher makes a far more detailed case against the corruptions of parliamentary government than one finds in *The Flying Inn*. Admittedly the emphasis is generally negative, but in a story of almost unrelieved political disaster, some attempt is made to understand the motives of the people who bring the disaster about. In *Tales of the Long Bow*, a series of marriages illustrates the pastoral side of Distributism. The most successful use of typology is found in *The Return of Don Quixote*. Themes which were treated individually in the earlier novels are now brought together as the first complete expression of the Distributist political and social viewpoint. The political forces which are reconciled in the final synthesis are various and unexpected. Instead of the familiar opposition between characters representing idealism and irony, the novel introduces three central characters, each of whom possesses valuable political insights and dangerous political limitations. Herne, a romantic idealist in the tradition of Wayne and MacIan, is ostensibly the directing force of the novel's action. Braintree, who has affinities with Turnbull and Lord Ivywood, is at once the embodiment of the revolutionary spirit which demands social justice and the doctrinaire spirit which ignores the variety and complexity of real life. Murrel, who recalls the ironic detachment of Auberon, also represents a kind of Tory scepticism about the possibility of political improvement, which was characteristic of Horne Fisher.

The kinds of women these men fall in love with and the part played by women add a further complexity to the novel. Herne's impersonal idealism turns into a kind of neo-Fascism under the influence of the strong-minded Rosamund Severne; whereas Braintree's Syndicalism is eventually humanized under the influence of Olive Ashley's romantic idealism. Murrel undergoes a rather different transformation. His attempt to find the lost illumination colour becomes a romantic quest during which he falls in love and discovers an instance of the social injustice which is the real subject of the book. There is little in Chesterton's other writing which prepares one for the surprising resolution of this many-sided conflict. The resolution involves first of all a sharp distinction between religion and politics. The idealism which leads to political disaster also leads to religious conversion. But the movement of disillusioned

romantics to medieval religion involves a corresponding affirmation of the Syndicalist solution of worker-control for the social
problem which romantic medievalism has been unable to solve.

It is also important to note that this grouping and re-
grouping of political types is achieved not by the mechanical
manipulation of characters but by purely literary means. The
action is developed by an imagery which changes as the story
proceeds. The pageant which becomes a real-life drama, and
the quest for colour, which brings the pageant to an end, are
symbolic as well as literal events. The broken monument in the
park represents the vague romanticism which inspires much of
the action of the novel, but it also represents the tragic separa-
tion of religion and idealism, which is one of the novel's central
themes. In a novel which Chesterton called a parable for social
reformers,[31] the monument of the dragon standing alone without
the angel that destroys it is an emblem of the need for a balance
between the ideal and the practical sides of life. And the crimson
illumination-paint which Olive Ashley seeks is at once the colour
of the stained-glass window, which represents the religious
values that are absent from modern life, and the colour of
Braintree's revolutionary red tie, which represents the political
solution of modern problems.

The way in which the fiction sometimes fails to use imaginative means is best illustrated perhaps by the final group of
novels which Chesterton wrote. The chapters which make up
The Poet and the Lunatics might be random illustrations of a
central theme, but they are illustrations which do little to
advance the main action. The order of events is entirely
haphazard, and the chapters seem to be merely a way of mark-
ing time until the conclusion is reached. Even the elaborate and
ingenuous attempt to unify *Four Faultless Felons* does not quite
disguise the dissimilarity of the four stories which are supposed
to be unified. And in *The Paradoxes of Mr Pond* the breakdown
in unity is complete: and instead of a novel one is left with a
series of loosely related short stories. The defects of the earlier
fiction are also present, and present in an exaggerated form.
The intrusive symbolism which occasionally mars some of the
earlier novels is also found in the later fiction, where the
heavy-handed symbolic details have little relevance to the
action they are supposed to illuminate: every garden is an

ironic Eden and every sunrise and sunset the symbolic background for a trivial event or a minor climax.

More significantly the literary decline is a political decline
as well. The definition of social sanity in *The Poet and the Lunatics*
is as vague and confused as the manner in which the hero's
adventures are narrated. It is also difficult to say what coherent
political meaning emerges from the bewildering mixture of
social and political themes which one finds in *Four Faultless
Felons*. It is significant that the themes which are treated in the
later fiction are themes which have received their successful
and definitive treatment in the early fiction. Indeed much of the
repetitiousness and sense of fatigue which characterize the
literary decline can be explained in terms of an almost parasitic
dependence on political concerns of the earlier fiction. This
reworking of old material may also explain why so much of the
action of the later fiction is set in an indeterminate period of the
past and why so much of the political background is concerned
with the politics of Edwardian rather than contemporary times.

It would not be difficult to multiply examples of the new
vagueness of outlook and new lack of imaginative grip. The
effect is not always an unhappy one. The rather confused
tolerance which is now expressed for Imperialism is balanced
by a new tolerance which is extended towards the Jews, who
for the first time are represented in something like a favourable
light. The old hostility towards Germany is also modified, and
in *The Paradoxes of Mr Pond*, the very effective Polish propaganda of 'Three Horsemen of Apocalypse' includes a defence of
German romanticism, and 'A Tall Story', the final chapter of
the book, may be read as a kind of apology for Chesterton's
contribution to anti-German hysteria during World War One.
But the most important example of what the new blandness
and loss of imaginative power involves is provided by the treatment of kingship in the final novels.

It is of course true that the exploration of this theme provides
a partial exception to the general absence of contemporary
politics in the late novels. To some extent, at least, the treatment of this theme represents Chesterton's last attempt to come
to imaginative terms with a political force which he recognized
as genuinely modern. But the treatment of the theme owes as
much to the earlier fiction as it does to a new awareness of

contemporary politics. The king, who makes his appearance in *Four Faultless Felons* as Clovis the Third of Pavonia, and in Mr Pond's imaginary republic as the Unmentionable Man, derives his real interest from being a member of the group of monarchs which begins with Auberon Quin in *The Napoleon of Notting Hill* and ends with Michael Herne in *The Return of Don Quixote*. In relation to these figures from the earlier fiction, the king of the later fiction is a new and somewhat disquieting version of a very familiar Chestertonian type. At first the change in his role seems to be an improvement. Instead of the ineffectual romantic who releases political forces he can neither understand nor control, he is now a practical statesman standing above party politics but ready to intervene in them when the interests of the nation require. Saving the people from a corrupt parliament seems to be his favourite occupation. In Pavonia, he prevents a revolution by championing the policy of reform which the politicians have neglected, and in Mr Pond's anonymous republic he succeeds in reconciling the conflicting values of revolutionary Socialism and Liberal idealism. In a word, he represents an easy solution to the difficult problems of modern politics.

But these very un-Chestertonian virtues of efficiency and success are the qualities which make the king a somewhat ominous figure. In one of the late essays, Chesterton calls monarchy 'the mood of the hour'.[32] What is disturbing about the expression he gives to this mood in his final novels is the apparent lack of awareness of how dangerous it could be. The political role which he imagines for the king is perhaps harmless enough. And since he is supposed to represent genuine authority, it is perhaps unfair to call him a Fascist figure. But the way in which he combines contempt for parliamentary government with a fondness for authoritarian action does suggest the kind of Fascist solution which some of Chesterton's followers were accused of advocating after his death.

Thus what at first seems to be the one important imaginative development of a major political theme in the late novels is in fact a final indication of failure in political imagination. The greatness of the failure can only be measured by a comparison between what the king had been with what he has now become. The comic subtlety which gave an unexpected meaning to medievalism, and the delicate balance between a multitude of political types which gave an extraordinary power to the best of Chesterton's fiction have disappeared, and one is left instead with the grim and humourless figure of a king whose negative qualities make him an Auberon who has lost his wit and a Herne who has learned nothing from experience.

Father Brown and Others*

W. W. ROBSON

Chesterton himself did not attach great importance to the Father Brown stories. Ordered in batches by magazine editors and publishers, they were written hurriedly for the primary purpose of helping to finance his Distributist paper, *G.K.'s Weekly*. And though they have proved to be the most popular of Chesterton's writings, critical attention to them has been casual. This is partly because they are detective stories; and the detective story is commonly dismissed, without argument, as a very low form of art. That it is also a very difficult and demanding form, in which many clever writers have failed, is not regarded as relevant. Nor is there much respect for the innovators in this genre, or much comment on their remarkable rarity. If there were, Chesterton's reputation would stand very high; for his detective stories, while they may not be the best ever written, are without doubt the most ingenious. But to show ingenuity and originality in the detective story is for the superior critic merely to have a knack for a particular sort of commercial fiction. It is not the sort of thing he takes seriously. And Chesterton himself, it seems, would have agreed with him.

I shall try to give reasons why these stories should be taken seriously. But I must admit at the start that there are two (sometimes overlapping) classes of reader whom I cannot hope to convince. The first consists of those who loathe detective stories; the second, of those who are so prejudiced against the Roman Catholic Church that they cannot read stories in which a priest is presented sympathetically. All I can say to these readers is that the Father Brown stories are much more than detective stories, and if they can overcome their repugnance to the genre they will find a good deal that might interest them in another context; and secondly, that the element of strictly Roman Catholic propaganda in the stories is small. Furthermore, Father Brown is neither a realistic nor even an idealized

*This essay is based in part on my article in the Summer 1969 issue of *The Southern Review*.—W.W.R.

portrait of a priest. Chesterton is not competing with *Morte d'Urban*, or with Bernanos; nor is he competing with Robert Hugh Benson. Anti-clericalism is irrelevant.

What is Chesterton saying in the Father Brown stories? Their meaning must be understood in terms of their genre. Whatever else these stories may turn out to be, they are certainly, on the face of it, light fiction, in a recognizable genre. And this genre was invented by Poe. Scholars have found remote antecedents and forbears for Poe's detective tales, but there can be no doubt that the modern detective tale derives from him. His tales of the Chevalier Auguste Dupin are magazine fiction. But they are also offered as moral fables. The virtue they ostensibly celebrate is Reason. Dupin is not concerned with the legal consequences of crime, like Inspector Maigret, nor is he concerned with its moral and religious implications, like Father Brown. For him, a crime is nothing but an intellectual problem. When that is solved, his interest lapses. Poe makes a great show of the rigorous deductions and inexorable logic of Dupin. He is inhumanly patient, penetrating, and clear-headed. But this show of rationality is largely bluff, part of the game that Poe plays with his readers. It is notable that 'The Mystery of Marie Roget,' which to all appearances is the most dully realistic and scientific-looking of the three Dupin stories, based on a real life case, is in fact the most impudently fraudulent. Dupin's solution does not emerge from his reasoning: his reasoning, indeed, leads him in quite another direction. But Poe, surprised, no doubt, by a belated development in the real life case, cunningly inserts the suggestion here and there that Dupin was all the time on the right track. At the end all that the bemused reader is clear about is that the rabbit has been produced from the hat. *How*, is nobody's business. And the classical detective story, created by Poe, is not a triumph of reason, but a conjuring trick. This is evident in the most famous, and the best, of the three Dupin stories. 'The Purloined Letter'. Everyone remembers the motif of this story: that some things are too obvious to be noticed. And this is the secret of successful conjuring. The simple suppose that 'it must be up his sleeve.' But it isn't: it's in front of your nose. The successful conjurer, like George Orwell, knows that the hardest things to see are the things that are in front of your

nose. Those who are prepared to enjoy a classic demonstration
of this, in a detective story which is nothing but a detective
story, should read John Dickson Carr's novel *The Black
Spectacles*.

Chesterton, like all detective story writers, derives from Poe.
Indeed, it might be said that he derives from a single story
of Poe: many of the Father Brown stories can be regarded as
ingenious variations on the theme of 'The Purloined Letter'.
The suggestion of realistic police work, which we have in 'The
Murders in the Rue Morgue' and 'The Mystery of Marie
Roget', did not attract him. Father Brown keeps away from
the secular authorities:

> 'The Coroner has arrived. The inquiry is just going to begin.'
> 'I've got to get back to the Deaf School,' said Father Brown. [He
> has just solved the mystery.] 'I'm sorry I can't stop for the inquiry.'

There are no chemical analyses or careful checking of alibis in
these stories. Nor is there the dry intellectuality of Dupin. For
between Poe and Chesterton comes Conan Doyle. It is, of
course, Sherlock Holmes who humanized the figure of the Great
Detective, the symbol of reason and justice. The Sherlock
Holmes stories are in some ways inferior as literature to the
Dupin stories. Holmes has a less distinguished mind than
Dupin. But Dupin is a colourless character, and his confidant
is even dimmer. It is the personalities of Holmes and Watson
that we remember, the Baker Street 'atmosphere', in those
rooms where it is always 1895, the inimitable blend of exotic
excitement and reassuring cosiness.

As a conjurer, Doyle must rank low. The card often emerges
patently from Holmes's sleeve. In that excellent tale 'The
Bruce-Partington Plans,' the solution turns on Holmes's
realizing that the dead man's body was on the roof of an underground train. But this is a mere guess. Often Doyle does
not even *pretend* to play fair with the reader. However, this does
not matter. Doyle was the master of something rarer than
conjuring: magic. It may be, indeed, that magic is not compatible with conjuring. At any rate, Doyle rose to a high rank
among literary magicians when he invented Dr Watson. For
it is Watson, not Holmes, that is responsible for the magic. It is

only when we see the great man through his eyes that the whole conception reveals its unique triumphant blend of absurdity and sublimity. It is he who possesses the secret, more than Stevenson does in the *New Arabian Nights*, of evoking romance from the prosaic. London place names like 'Norwood' and 'Blackheath' will for some readers of Dr Watson's memoirs always retain overtones of mysterious romance.

All this was naturally congenial to the author of *The Napoleon of Notting Hill*. Chesterton was fascinated by the romance of the prosaic.

His dubious eye roamed again to the white lettering on the glass front of the public-house. The young woman's eyes followed his, and rested there also, but in pure puzzlement.

'No,' said Father Brown, answering her thoughts. 'It doesn't say "Sela", like the thing in the psalms; I read it like that myself when I was wool-gathering just now; it says "Ales" '.

This slight example may serve to illustrate how much all these writers—Chesterton, Stevenson, Doyle—are disciples of Dickens, the great master of the unfamiliarity in the familiar. But Chesterton was perhaps the closest of them all to the detective story side of Dickens. The novel of Dickens that has most in common with Chesterton is *The Mystery of Edwin Drood*. It will be said that this is not merely a detective story, that it has imagination and moral seriousness. All the same, it *is* a detective story, and as such it is genuinely mysterious. And this is not only because it is unfinished. Neither *Barnaby Rudge* (*pace* Poe) nor *Bleak House*, which are both *inter alia* detective stories, would have been hard to solve if they had been left unfinished at a point comparable to the point where *Edwin Drood* breaks off. The quality of Chesterton's work at its best, in the Father Brown stories, is comparable to that of *Edwin Drood*. It is true to its genre: it is full of suspense, sensation, genuine clues, red herrings, 'atmosphere', real mystery and spurious mystery. But Chesterton, though he might talk light-heartedly about batches of corpses despatched to the publisher, is serious, as Dickens is serious in *Edwin Drood*. In these stories murder is murder, sin is sin, damnation is damnation. Every imaginative writer must choose his genre, and every genre has limitations.

Those of the detective tale are obvious, and the most serious is this: no character can have depth, no character can be done from the inside, because any must be a potential suspect. It is Chesterton's triumph that he turned this limitation of the genre into an illumination of the universal human potentiality of guilt and sin. No character in the stories matters except Father Brown. But this is not a fault, because Father Brown, being a man, epitomizes all their potentialities within himself. 'Are you a devil?' the exposed criminal wildly asks. 'I am a man,' replies Father Brown, 'and therefore have all devils in my heart.'

This ability to identify himself with the murderer is the 'secret' of Father Brown's method. Some readers have misunderstood Chesterton's intention here. They suppose that Father Brown is credited with special spiritual powers, pertaining to his rôle as a priest. They see him as a thaumaturgic Sherlock Holmes. One adverse critic saw in Father Brown's ability to divine the truth, where plodding mundane detectives fail, a typical dishonest trick of the Catholic apologist. But it is made quite clear that Father Brown owes his success not to supernatural insight but to the usual five senses. He is simply more observant, less clouded by conventional anticipations and prejudices, than the average man. The kind of clue he notices is not cigar ash or footprints, but something like this:

'I am sorry to say we are the bearers of bad news. Admiral Craven was drowned before reaching home. . . .'
'When did this happen?' asked the priest.
'Where was he found?' asked the lawyer.

A moment later the priest realizes that the lawyer has murdered Admiral Craven. If you are told that a seaman, returning from the sea, has been drowned, you do not ask where his body was 'found'. Admiral Craven was found in a landlocked pool; Father Brown realized that Mr Dyke could only know that because he had put him there. Most of the clues in the stories are of this kind. It is true that at the end of this story ('The Green Man') Father Brown does show some knowledge which, in the terms of the story, he could not have acquired by natural means; he knows that Mr Dyke committed the murder because his client, the Admiral, discovered that he had been robbing him. This is a fault in the story. But the same sort of fault can be found in greater writers when they are winding up the plot. Shakespeare makes Iago confess that he dropped Desdemona's handkerchief in Cassio's chamber. Surely a man like Iago would never have confessed anything. The essential discovery that Father Brown makes in this story is the identity of the murderer, not his motive.

Chesterton takes pains to emphasize that Father Brown has no supernatural powers, by frequently contrasting him with false images who claim them. (Examples are to be found in stories like 'The Song of the Flying Fish' or 'The Red Moon of Meru'.) Their characteristic sin is spiritual pride. They are quite happy to be accused of crimes which they have not committed, if the crimes are thought miraculous. For contrast, we have a story like 'The Resurrection of Father Brown', in which Father Brown is subjected to the overwhelming temptation to claim credit for a false miracle: that he has risen from the dead. Without hesitation, dazed as he is, he discredits the story.

Father Brown is, then, not a thaumaturge. But it must be granted that, apart from his powers of observation, he has exceptional moral insight. It is well known that Chesterton conceived the idea for this character after meeting a priest whose 'unworldliness' proved to be compatible with an inside knowledge of crime and wickedness. His 'innocence' was of a kind that would have shocked the would-be sophisticated young men whom Chesterton soon afterwards heard patronizing the clergy for their ignorance of the world. Chesterton makes a good deal of play with the contrast between Father Brown's appearance, moonfaced, blinking, dropping his umbrella, and the reality of his insights into men's minds and hearts. But Chesterton's aim is not really a psychological study of such a man. Almost at once Father Brown becomes largely a mouthpiece for Chesterton's own wit and wisdom. Here are a few examples:

'There is a limit to human charity,' said Lady Outram, trembling all over.

'There is,' said Father Brown dryly, 'and that is the real difference between human charity and Christian charity.'

'He's a pretty rotten fool and failure, on his own confession.'

'Yes,' said Father Brown. 'I'm rather fond of people who are fools and failures on their own confession.'

'I don't know what you mean,' snapped the other.

'Perhaps,' said Father Brown wistfully, 'it's because so many people are fools and failures without any confession.'

'There is one mark of all genuine religions: materialism.'

'The quality of a miracle is mysterious, but its manner is simple.'

'And can you tell us why,' he asked, 'you should know your own figure in a looking-glass, when two such distinguished men don't?'

Father Brown blinked even more painfully than before; then he stammered: 'Really, my lord, I don't know . . . unless it's because I don't look at it so often.'

'Now, in my opinion that machine can't lie.'

'No machine can lie,' said Father Brown, 'nor can it tell the truth.'

'If you convey to a woman that something ought to be done, there is always a dreadful danger that she will suddenly do it.'

'I agree that the woman wants to kill the co-respondent much more than the petitioner does.'

'Yes,' said Father Brown, 'I always like a dog, so long as he isn't spelt backwards.'

These could all have been starting-points for Chestertonian essays. The artistic reason for Father Brown's powers of repartee, and his wittiness in general, is that we look straight at him as we do not look at Sherlock Holmes, who is reflected in the—sometimes exasperated—admiration of Dr Watson. Chesterton has dispensed with a Dr Watson; and so Father Brown has to seem brilliant to *us*. And the only way this can be done is by making him brilliant. The remarks I have quoted are only a small selection. Father Brown by himself has no solidity. He is not a credible priest; he seems to be away from his parish as often as Dr Watson was away from his practice. He comes and goes from nowhere. The temptation to make him a semi-symbolic figure must have been great. Agatha

Christie succumbed to a similar temptation in her stories about *The Mysterious Mr Quin*. But this is false to the genre. Chesterton's stories, though often fantastic, are not fantasies. Again and again it is emphasized that Father Brown in himself is an ordinary man: an extraordinarily ordinary man.

But Father Brown's ordinariness is ordinariness *à la* Chesterton. He shares his creator's aesthetic sense. Indeed, his detective powers are closely connected with his aesthetic sense. He knows what is the 'right' crime for the 'right' criminal. The whole of the story called 'The Wrong Shape' is built around this aesthetic criminology. The reformed criminal Flambeau, hunted and converted by Father Brown in the early stories, has similarly an aesthetic sense about his crimes. He chooses the right sort of crime for the right setting, as in 'The Flying Stars'. (Some memories of the fabled exploits of Vidocq, who fascinated Balzac, must have gone into Flambeau's creation.) It is an aesthetic sense that sometimes provides Father Brown with an essential clue; as in 'The Worst Crime in the World,' where his perception of the balanced arrangement of a hall enables him to spot that one suit of armour, out of what must have been a pair, is missing. And Chesterton, as often, notes the curious and sometimes topsy-turvy relationship between aesthetic fitness and moral fitness:

'It's a wonder his throat isn't cut,' said Mr Smart's valet Harris, not without a hypothetical relish, almost as if he had said, in a purely artistic sense, 'It's a pity.'

The 'hypothetical relish' explains a good deal of our pleasure in the fantasies and atrocities of the stories.

Finally, Father Brown's detective skill owes much to that linguistic sensitivity which he shares with his creator. He finds himself thinking of foreign voyages in a house in Cornwall.

Besides the butler, the Admiral's only servants were two negroes, somewhat quaintly clad in tight uniforms of yellow. The priest's instinctive trick of analysing his own impressions told him that the colour and the little neat coat-tails of these bipeds had suggested the word 'Canary', and so by a mere pun connected them with Southward travel.

Other characters share it at times.

He was a man with more literary than direct natural associations;
the word 'Ravenswood' came into his head repeatedly. It was partly
the raven colour of the pine-woods; but partly also an indescribable
atmosphere almost described in Scott's great tragedy; the smell of
something that died in the eighteenth century; the smell of dank
gardens and broken urns; of wrongs that will never now be righted;
of something that is none the less incurably sad because it is strangely
unreal.

Such things show the literary critic in Chesterton, the power of
verbal analysis which we associate with a critic of our own day
like William Empson, and which Empson himself has praised
in Chesterton. But sometimes this linguistic sensitiveness is
employed in the interests of logical clarity. Chesterton has a
feeling for the niceties of idiom, and their conceptual implications, which recalls a philosopher like the late Professor Austin.
Here are a few examples:

'I said it was his hat. Or, if you insist on a shade of difference, a
hat that is his.'
'And where is the shade of difference?' asked the criminologist,
with a slight sneer.
'My good sir,' cried the mild little man, with his first movement
akin to impatience, 'if you will walk down the street to the nearest
hatter's shop, you will see that there is, in common speech, a
difference between a man's hat and the hats that are his.'

'Hang it all,' cried Simon, 'a man gets into a garden, or he
doesn't.'
'Not necessarily,' said the priest, with a faint smile . . .
'A man gets out of a garden, or he doesn't,' he cried.
'Not always,' said Father Brown.
[The whole story—'The Secret Garden'—must be read for the
explanation.]

'Have you ever noticed this—that people never answer what you
say? They answer what you mean—or what they think you mean.
Suppose one lady says to another in a country house, "Is anybody
staying with you?" the lady doesn't answer, "Yes; the butler, the
three footmen, the parlourmaid and so on," though the parlour-

maid may be in the room, or the butler behind her chair. She says
"There is *nobody* staying with us".' [A nice glimpse here of the
Edwardian scene, which is indeed the point of the well-known
story from which this comes, 'The Invisible Man.']

Father Brown, then, is represented as at the same time an
ordinary man, of simple tastes, who enjoys simple pleasures, and
a clever, shrewd person, with observation and sensitiveness
beyond the ordinary. But he is not a mystic. He remains true
both to traditional theology, and to the genre of the detective
story, in never decrying reason. It is when Flambeau, disguised
as a priest, does this that Father Brown is certain he is a fraud.
Of course, Father Brown is represented as a religious man. It is
not by accident, and not merely to find a new twist to the
Sherlock Holmes formula, that Chesterton makes him a priest.
But once again Chesterton is at pains to dissociate him from
anything exotic, any suggestion of the allegedly subtle lures of
Rome. What he means us to feel about Father Brown is what he
makes an American Protestant feel, in one of the stories which
is set in South America:

He could hardly be expected to sympathize with the religious
externals of Catholic countries; and in a dislike of mitres and
croziers he sympathized with Mr Snaith, though not in so cocksure
a fashion. He had no liking for the public bowings and scrapings of
[the clericalist] Mendoza. . . . The truth was this: that the only
thing he had ever met in his travels that in the least reminded him
of the old wood-pile and the provincial properties and the Bible
on his mother's knee was (for some inscrutable reason) the round
face and black clumsy umbrella of Father Brown.

Again and again in these stories Chesterton shows how much
the common dislike of Catholicism is (or was) due to dislike of
'religious externals'. But the deeper religious meaning of these
stories is to do with something more important then cultural
considerations. The abundance of quacks, mystagogues, sorcer-
ers in them is not only due to the desire to point a contrast
with Father Brown. It is to illustrate, in terms proper to the
genre in which Chesterton is writing, his belief that what
Christianity has shown is that the age-old effort of man to grasp
the Divine is bankrupt. Man cannot come to God. Christianity

says that God came to man. This was what Chesterton was
saying over and over again, in different tones and with varying
degrees of humour or earnestness. Orwell claimed that writers
like Chesterton seem to have only one subject: that they are
Catholics. One might as well retort that Orwell's only subject
seems to be that he was not one. Either the Catholic faith is
relevant to the whole of life, or it is relevant to none of it. That,
at any rate, was Chesterton's position.

In the end, then, the priest's 'steady humble gaze' owes its
power to more than observation. When he realized that the
doctor did the murder, he 'looked him gravely and steadily in
the face'; and the doctor went away and wrote his confession.
He is an atheist, and he begins his confession: '*Vicisti, Galilaee!*'
But he goes on at once 'In other words, damn your eyes, which
are very remarkable and penetrating ones.'

The religious meaning is central in the best of these stories.
But some of them contain a good deal of effective social satire
also. I have already mentioned 'The Invisible Man', that
ingenious fable of the people who 'don't count'. Wells, we know,
had another idea of the 'invisible man'; and Ralph Ellison has
another. Seeing the invisible in Chesterton's story means what
Ellison means: discovering human brotherhood. Some of the
incidental themes in this story are interesting, especially considering its date. We note that the victim Isidore Smythe is a
characteristically modern man, who not only has a fast car, but
more remarkably, a complete staff of robots to wait on him.
Another parable, with a keen edge of social satire, is another
well-known story, 'The Queer Feet'. The point of this story, as
a detective story, is that a gentleman's coat looks the same as a
waiter's; but the stratagem of Flambeau, the owner of the
'queer feet' which now saunter like a gentleman and now scurry
like a waiter, is possible only because of the great gulf fixed
between gentlemen and waiters. It is the 'outsiders', first of all
Death (the dead waiter at the beginning of the story), then the
crook Flambeau, and finally the shabby Father Brown, who
point the satire on the Twelve True Fishermen. Chesterton,
like Kipling, vividly describes the ritualism of English upper-
class life; but he sees it more ironically than Kipling. The
members of the select club The Twelve True Fishermen parody
the twelve apostles, who were fishermen, and fishers of men

like Father Brown, who can bring the reformed criminal back from the ends of the earth with 'a twitch upon the thread'. Light and amusing as the story is, it is an exposure not only of social class, but of plutocracy employing the traditions of social class, to eliminate brotherhood. Yet all the Fishermen are very likeable, and the story ends with an amusing touch. After their silver has been recovered, thanks to Father Brown, their first thought is to invent a new addition to their ritual by way of commemorating its recovery. The members will in future wear green coats, to distinguish them from waiters.

But the most memorable of the stories are not witty parables like these, but imaginative fairy tales. What some readers remember most in the Father Brown stories is Chesterton's powers of description. His liking for a twilight setting—dawn or dusk—has been noted; and so has the constant sense we have that the action is taking place in a toy theatre, where the weird and wonderful backcloth dominates everything, and the tiny puppets that gesticulate in fight or dance in front of it seem faceless and featureless. And these backcloths have a décor which links Chesterton to Swinburne and the Decadents. His moral and religious outlook could not be more different from theirs; but his imagination has been formed on their work. Lurid, or fanciful, or grotesque decoration dominates stories like 'The Wrong Shape' or 'The Dagger with Wings'. Of course this decoration is there in part to distract us. A classical detective story exists to fool the reader; and Chesterton likes to avert our attention from the 'simple centre' to the 'rococo excrescences'. These are Chesterton's own expressions, which come from an incidental brief discussion of *Hamlet* in 'The Queer Feet'. Every successful crime, he says, like every successful work of art, has at its centre something simple. It is Chesterton's task as conjurer to arrange this scene, with bizarre figures in a bizarre setting, so that we shall miss the explanation of the mystery, which always turns on some straightforward, mundane motive. (In more than half the stories the motivation for the crime is nothing more metaphysical or *outré* than greed.)

However, I think the unforgettable descriptions of gardens, houses, landscapes, and the effects of *light* in these stories are not mainly there for camouflage, or merely for scene painting. I think they have something to do with the meaning of the stories;

and this in turn has something to do with the attraction of the
detective story, as a genre, both to Chesterton himself and to
his readers. But first of all let us note that, even at the level of
the plot, the descriptions are highly relevant. This passage from
'The Hammer of God', read in its context, contains the
explanation of the mystery. Two men look down from the top
of a church.

Immediately beneath and about them the lines of the Gothic
building plunged outwards into the void with a sickening swiftness
akin to suicide. There is that element of Titan energy in the architecture of the Middle Ages that, from whatever aspect it be seen, it
is always running away, like the strong back of some maddened
horse. This church was hewn out of ancient and silent stone,
bearded with old fungoids and stained with the nests of birds. And
yet, when they saw it from below, it sprang like a fountain at the
stars; and when they saw it, as now, from above, it poured like a
cataract into a voiceless pit. For these two men on the tower were
left alone with the most terrible aspect of Gothic; the monstrous
foreshortening and disproportion, the dizzy perspectives, the
glimpses of great things small and small things great; a topsy-
turvydom of stone in the mid-air.

This is the sort of passage that we feel is 'too good' for a detective
story. Yet it is surely an artistic virtue, if only a minor one, that
the height of the church and the way the landscape below it
looks like 'a map of the world' should, for the attentive, explain
both the crime's motive, and the method of its commission.

But my main reason for quoting the passage is to call attention to the phrases about 'monstrous foreshortening and disproportion', 'dizzy perspectives', 'glimpses of great things small
and small things great'. These are clues to Chesterton's imagination. First of all, it was intensely visual. He began as a painter,
and we can find the painter's eye in all his descriptions. But—
more important—it was child-like. Passages like this, from 'The
Sins of Prince Saradine', abound in his writings:

A large lemon moon was only just setting in the forest of high grass
above their heads, and the sky was of a vivid violet-blue, nocturnal
but bright. Both men had simultaneously a reminiscence of childhood, of the elfin and adventurous time when tall weeds close over
us like woods. Standing up thus against the large low moon, the

daisies really seemed to be giant daisies, the dandelions to be giant
dandelions. Somehow it reminded them of the dado of a nursery
wall-paper.

This child-like quality in Chesterton attracts some readers and
repels others. Those whom it repels dislike the association he
makes between childish fantasies about winged daggers and
flying vampires, and serious themes of good and evil. They feel
that the former degrade the latter. This sort of criticism has
been levelled against a later writer, Charles Williams, who also
attempted to use thriller material as a means of saying something serious. I cannot answer this objection, except by saying
that Chesterton himself seems to have been aware of it, and
tries to answer it in his story 'The Dagger with Wings'. Here
the real mystery of nature is contrasted with the spurious
mystery, the 'white magic', which the criminal mystagogue
exploits. Father Brown, as usual, appears as the agnostic: 'I do
believe some things, of course, and therefore, of course, I don't
believe other things.' The wickedness of the mystagogue and
murderer Strake is explained as the perversion of a good thing:
his power as a story-teller. He enjoys his masquerade as the man
he has murdered. 'He enjoyed it as a fantasy as well as a
conspiracy.' The monistic mumbo-jumbo with which he tries
to deceive Father Brown is recognized by Father Brown as 'the
religion of rascals'. In contrast, the cold of the air, as Father
Brown walks home after the exposure and arrest of Strake,
'divides truth from error with a blade like ice.' Crime and
insanity in this story are associated with changing colours,
pantheistic unities, mixed-upness; goodness and innocence with
the whiteness of snow, the dualism of black and white, truth
and error, artifice and nature. The villain Strake has the wilful-
ness, the perversity, the distortions, of a naughty child. It is the
normal imagination of the child that shows him up.

We might say, then, that Father Brown is imagined by
Chesterton as a child whose vision is undistorted. The psychological critic will no doubt see in the contrasting distortions of
perspective, the 'wrong shapes', the murderous yet strangely
unheated fantasies of the stories, some relationship to the child's
bizarre notions of the behaviour of adults. For reasons of
temperament, period, and literary mode, Chesterton avoids

overtly sexual themes in the Father Brown stories. Yet it was presumably the real Father Brown's knowledge of sexual depravities that shocked Chesterton. And in 'The Secret of Father Brown' the priest confides to his interlocutor that he 'acted out' in his imagination all the crimes that he had investigated. What renders Father Brown invulnerable is precisely this anterior playacting.

The main critical problem posed by these stories, as by Chesterton's work as a whole, is how to distinguish between the child-like and the childish. Some of his books of stories, in a vein similar to the Father Brown series—*Four Faultless Felons*, *The Paradoxes of Mr Pond*, *The Poet and the Lunatics*—seem often childish in a bad sense. (The best of them is perhaps an early one, *The Man Who Knew Too Much*, in which Horne Fisher is a kind of 'political' counterpart to Father Brown.) These inferior stories offer the illustrated working-out of a verbal conundrum, rather than a mode of exploring the world. But Chesterton's passion for paradox cannot be wholly reduced to that. It lies at the heart of his genius, as well as of his tiresomeness. Hugh Kenner's able work on *Paradox in Chesterton* needs supplementing with a study which will discriminate between the profound and the shallow in Chesterton's wit. At least it can be said of Chesterton that his paradoxes, if sometimes they lack profundity, are never merely silly and flashy, as Oscar Wilde's can be, because they reflect a consistent view of life. And when Dean Inge describes him, with a note of animosity Chesterton rarely provoked in his opponents, as 'that obese mountebank who crucifies truth head downwards', an admirer of Chesterton might be moved to retort with the words of the painter in 'The Fantastic Friends' (*The Poet and the Lunatics*):

'The world is upside down. We're all upside down. We're all flies crawling on a ceiling, and it's an everlasting mercy that we don't drop off. . . . We were talking about St Peter. You remember that he was crucified upside down. I've often fancied his humility was rewarded by seeing in death the beautiful vision of his boyhood. He also saw the landscape as it really is: with the star-like flowers, and the clouds like hills, and all men hanging on the mercy of God.'

The Gift of Wonder
W. H. AUDEN

All lovers of poetry, I imagine, would rather quote from poems they admire than talk about them. Once read or listened to, their merits should be immediately apparent. One feels this all the more strongly in the case of a poet whom, like Chesterton, one suspects to be out of fashion and little read. Aside from a few stock anthology pieces, like 'The Donkey' and 'Lepanto', how many of his poems are known to the contemporary reading public? Not very many, I fear. Editorial footnoting, as distinct from aesthetic judgment can, however, sometimes be essential. *The Divine Comedy*, for example, is full of references to the names of persons and places with which the contemporary reader, even if he is Italian, is unacquainted, and he needs to be informed of the facts. When Chesterton is obscure, this is usually because the stimulus to his poem came from some public event with which he assumed his readers were familiar, but which has now been forgotten. 'A Song of Swords' is prefaced from a newpaper cutting: 'A drove of cattle came into a village called Swords, and was stopped by the rioters.' But, since I know nothing about this incident in Irish history, I cannot make head or tail of the poem. With the help of a footnote, perhaps I could. I know a little more about the history of World War One, but the meaning of 'The Battle of the Stories' (1915) eludes me and I would welcome editorial assistance. In only one of his poems, 'The Lamp Post', do I feel that my lack of comprehension is Chesterton's fault. It seems to be based upon some private mythology of his own, which neither I nor any other reader can be expected to decipher.

Consciously or unconsciously, every poet takes one or more of his predecessors as models. Usually, his instinct leads him to make the right choice among these, but not always. In Chesterton's case, for example, I think that Swinburne was a disastrous influence. That he should ever have allowed himself to be influenced by Swinburne seems to me very odd, when one thinks how utterly different their respective views about Life, Religion and Art were, but he was and always to his harm. It is due to Swinburne that, all too often in his verses, alliteration becomes an obsessive tic. In Anglo-Saxon and Icelandic poetry where the metrical structure is based upon alliteration, its essential function is obvious. In modern verse, based upon regular feet and rhyme, alliteration can be used for onomatopoeic effects, but only sparingly: in excess it becomes maddeningly irritating. The other vice Chesterton acquired from Swinburne was prolixity. Too often one feels that a poem would have been better if it had been half the length. 'Lepanto', it seems to me, exhibits both faults.

> He sees as in a mirror on the monstrous twilight sea
> The crescent of his cruel ships whose name is mystery;
> They fling great shadows foe-wards, making Cross and Castle
>   dark,
> They veil the plumèd lions on the galleys of St Mark;
> And above the ships are palaces of brown, black-bearded chiefs,
> And below the ships are prisons, where with multitudinous
>   griefs,
> Christian captives, sick and sunless, all a labouring race repines
> Like a race in sunken cities, like a nation in the mines.
> They are lost like slaves that swat, and in the skies of morning
>   hung
> The stairways of the tallest gods when tyranny was young.
> They are countless, voiceless, hopeless as those fallen or fleeing
>   on
> Before the high Kings' horses in the granite of Babylon.

In the case of his longest and, perhaps, greatest 'serious' poem, *The Ballad of the White Horse*, I do not, however, I am happy to say, find the length excessive. When, for example, Elf the Minstrel, Earl Ogier and Guthrum express in turns their conceptions of the Human Condition, what they sing could not be further condensed without loss. Here Guthrum.

> 'It is good to sit where the good tales go,
>   To sit as our fathers sat;
> But the hour shall come after his youth,
> When a man shall know not tales but truth,
>   And his heart shall fail thereat.

'When he shall read what is written
   So plain in clouds and clods,
When he shall hunger without hope
   Even for evil gods.

'For this is a heavy matter,
   And the truth is cold to tell;
Do we not know, have we not heard,
The soul is like a lost bird,
   The body a broken shell.

'And a man hopes, being ignorant,
   Till in white woods apart
He finds at last the lost bird dead;
And a man may still lift up his head
   But never more his heart.

'There comes no noise but weeping
   Out of the ancient sky,
And a tear is in the tiniest flower
   Because the gods must die.

'The little brooks are very sweet,
   Like a girl's ribbons curled,
But the great sea is bitter
   That washes all the world.

'Strong are the Roman roses,
   Or the free flowers of the heath,
But every flower, like a flower of the sea,
   Smelleth with the salt of death.

'And the heart of the locked battle
   Is the happiest place for men;
When shrieking souls as shafts go by
And many have died and all may die;
Though this word be a mystery,
   Death is most distant then.

'Death blazes bright above the cup,
   And clear above the crown;
But in that dream of battle
   We seem to tread it down.

'Wherefore I am a great king,
    And waste the world in vain,
Because man hath not other power,
Save that in dealing death for dower,
He may forget it for an hour
    To remember it again.'

Guthrum's pessimistic conclusions about the nature of the
internal and invisible life are based, it should be noticed, upon
his observations of objects in the external and visible world,
clouds and clods, flowers, a dead bird, etc. Chesterton, however
different his conclusions, does the same. Both in his prose and
in his verse, he sees, as few writers have, the world about him as
full of sacramental signs or symbols.

Wherein God's ponderous mercy hangs
On all my sins and me,
Because He does not take away
The terror from the tree
And stones still shine along the road
That are and cannot be.

Men grow too old for love, my love,
Men grow too old for wine,
But I shall not grow too old to see
Unearthly daylight shine,
Changing my chamber's dust to snow,
Till I doubt if it be mine.

I would not call him a mystic like Blake, who could say:
'Some see the sun as a golden disk the size of a guinea, but I
see a heavenly host singing Holy, Holy, Holy.' Chesterton
never disregards the actual visible appearance of things. Then,
unlike Wordsworth, his imagination is stirred to wonder, not
only by natural objects, but by human artifacts as well.

Men grow too old to woo, my love,
Men grow too old to wed:
But I shall not grow too old to see
Hung crazily overhead
Incredible rafters when I wake
And find I am not dead.

Drawing by G.K.C. at the age of seven

I am akin to all the earth
Linked in the vast design ——
The Aged Pig will often wear
That strange sweet smile of mine

My niece the Barnacle has got
My piercing eyes of black
The Elephant has got my nose.
(I do not want it back)

And I, who loved the Octopus
Since we were boys together —
Who have no secrets from the shark:
Shall I then fear the weather?

I love to bask in sunny fields
But when that hope is vain
I go & bask in Baker Street
All in the pouring rain.

The snow, where fly, try some strange
Hard snowballs without —law
noise
On streets untenanted, except
By good unconscious boys —
O Rain & Hail & thunderbolt,
Snow, fire & general Fuss
Come to my arms — come
—all at once
O photograph me thus!

From the Publications of the Encouragement
of Rain Society: Vol CCCXI.

Page from illustrated nonsense poem in manuscript (1898); a later version appeared in Greybeards at Play (1900)

Cover of the first edition of Greybeards at Play, *designed by G.K.C.*

Pen and ink drawings (1893)

Probably most young children possess this imaginative gift, but most of us lose it when we grow up as a consequence, Chesterton would say, of the Fall.

> They haven't got no noses,
> The fallen sons of Eve;
> Even the smell of roses
> Is not what they supposes;
> But more than mind discloses
> And more than men believe . . .
>
> The brilliant smell of water,
> The brave smell of a stone,
> The smell of dew and thunder,
> The old bones buried under,
> Are things in which they blunder
> And err, if left alone . . .
>
> And Quoodle here discloses
> All things that Quoodle can,
> They haven't got no noses,
> They haven't got no noses,
> And goodness only knowses
> The Noselessness of Man.

In verses such as these, there is little, if any, trace of Swinburnian influence. Behind them one detects the whole tradition of English Comic Verse, of Samuel Butler, Prior, Praed, Edward Lear, Lewis Carroll and, above all, W. S. Gilbert. It was from such writers, I believe, that Chesterton, both in his verse and his prose, learned the art of making terse aphoristic statements which, once read or heard, remain unforgettably in one's mind. For example:

> Bad men who had no right to their right reason,
> Good men who had good reason to be wrong . . .
>
> God is more good to the gods that mocked Him
> Than men are good to the gods they made . . .

> And that is the Blue Devil that once was the Blue Bird;
> For the Devil is a gentleman, and doesn't keep his word.

> But Higgins is a Heathen,
>   And to lecture rooms is forced,
> Where his aunts, who are not married,
>   Demand to be divorced . . .
>
> For mother is dancing up forty-eight floors,
> For love of the Leeds International Stores,
> And the flame of that faith might perhaps have grown cold,
> With the care of a baby of seven weeks old.

I cannot think of a single comic poem by Chesterton that is not a triumphant success. It is tempting to quote several, but I must restrain myself. Instead, I recommend any reader unacquainted with them to open *The Collected Poems* (Methuen) and sample 'The Shakespeare Memorial' (p.156), 'Ballade d'une Grande Dame' (p.190) and 'A Ballade of Suicide' (p.193). His parodies of other poets are equally good, especially those of Browning and Kipling.

I shall, however, now quote from a volume called *Greybeards At Play* originally published in 1900, reprinted in 1930, not included in the Collected Poems and now, I believe, out of print. Until it was sent me by John Sullivan, Chesterton's bibliographer, I had never heard of its existence. I have no hesitation in saying that it contains some of the best pure nonsense verse in English, and the author's illustrations are equally good.

> The million forests of the Earth
>   Come trooping in to tea.
> The great Niagara waterfall
>   Is never shy with me . . .
>
> Into my ear the blushing Whale
>   Stammers his love. I know
> Why the Rhinoceros is sad,
>   —Ah, child! 'twas long ago . . .
>
> Come fog! Exultant mystery—
>   Where, in strange darkness rolled,
> The end of my own nose becomes
>   A lovely legend old.

Come snow, and hail, and thunderbolts
  Sleet, fire, and general fuss;
Come to my arms, come all at once—
  Oh photograph me thus! . . .

The Shopmen, when their souls were still,
  Declined to open shops—
And Cooks recorded frames of mind
  In sad and subtle chops . . .

The stars were weary of routine:
  The trees in the plantation
Were growing every fruit at once,
  In search of a sensation.

The moon went for a moonlight stroll,
  And tried to be a bard,
And gazed enraptured at itself;
  I left it trying hard.

Surely, it is high time such enchanting pieces should be made
readily available.

By natural gift, Chesterton was, I think, essentially a comic
poet. Very few of his 'serious' poems are as good as these. (His
one translation from Du Bellay makes one wish he had done
many more.) But here is a poem of his which any poet would be
proud to have written.

The Sword of Surprise

Sunder me from my bones, O sword of God,
Till they stand stark and strange as do the trees;
That I whose heart goes up with the soaring woods
May marvel as much at these.

Sunder me from my blood that in the dark
I hear that red ancestral river run,
Like branching buried floods that find the sea
But never see the sun.

Give me miraculous eyes to see my eyes,
Those rolling mirrors made alive in me,
Terrible crystal more incredible
Than all the things they see.

Sunder me from my soul, that I may see
The sins like streaming wounds, the life's brave beat:
Till I shall save myself as I would save
A stranger in the street.

The Achievement of G. K. Chesterton*

STEPHEN MEDCALF

'I also dreamed that I had dreamed of the whole creation. I had given myself the stars for a gift; I had handed myself the sun and moon. I had been behind and at the beginning of all things; and without me nothing was made that was made. Anybody who has been in that centre of the cosmos knows that it is to be in hell.'[1]

This speech of his character Gabriel Gale reflects what Chesterton says about himself in his *Autobiography* and elsewhere. He was haunted by a constant fear of discovering that there is no real link between our selves and things: or that there is no world external to our selves, that only our selves exist. The strongest case against him is the claim that knowing such a condition painfully, he simply revolts from it before understanding what it might mean. For (one might say) the feeling that nothing else may *be*—the thirst for outside things—may itself be an adolescent defence against things happening in the back of the mind. It would be significant—if this is the case—that it is precisely in adolescence that most people have gulped down Chesterton in great thirsty swallows. Significant again would be his declaration that he became a Roman Catholic 'to get rid of my sins'[2] and even the actual innocence which makes the remark surprising. For the innocence itself is suspect as a defence against the shadowland of one's mind and against representing oneself accurately to oneself: while the danger of sacramental confession is precisely that one acknowledges the darkness without understanding it, fitting one's complicatedly guilty self into a too easy and too public objective framework. This kind of shrinking might explain why so many of the characters in his novels are not three-dimensional but flat: why

*This essay is part of a conversation of more than eighteen years' standing with Mr A. D. Nuttall, more of which may be found in his *A Common Sky* (London, 1974). It is also in debt to Mrs Gillian Cross, whose thesis *G. K. Chesterton and the Decadents* is, I hope, destined for publication. I owe further debts to the conversation and advice of George Craig, Peter Stallybrass, Gamini Salgado, Anthony Thorlby, Robin Milner-Gulland, Jill Mesher, Hazel Iliffe, Melissa Lipkin and Prudence Baker—S.M.

the love-affairs and the women happen at the edges of his
stories: why his style is so recurrently verbal and rhetorical
(the manic quality of Joyce's wit without the point about
consciousness which Joyce is making): and why he spoilt his
style further by pugnacity and compulsively extravert activity
in journalism, as if in a kind of escape.

It is important to see the exact nature of the charge. It is not
of lack of awareness of the back of the mind, nor even of lack
of interest in it. Chesterton was remarkable in his willingness
to consider such things in his theology and his ethics. Visiting
the Dead Sea in which Sodom and Gomorrah are drowned, he
reflects that 'in all our brains, certainly in mine, were buried
things as bad as any buried under that bitter sea, and if He
did not come to do battle with them, even in the darkness of
the brain of man, I know not why He came.'[3] And of *Dr Jekyll
and Mr Hyde* he observes that people 'think the book means that
man can be cloven into two creatures, good and evil. The whole
stab of the story is that man *can't*: because while evil does not
care for good, good must care for evil. Or, in other words, man
cannot escape from God, because good is the God in man; and
insists on omniscience.'[4]

The case against him is that he knew his shadow side if
anything too well, adopted an arbitrary set of explanations to
avoid going too deep into it, and wrote therefore in a kind of
bad faith. Borges for example praises him for the monstrous
nature of his fantasy, for the kind of terror which he spends so
much of his best writing rejecting, like the terror experienced
by Syme in the Council of Days:

He could only fancy, as in some old-world fable, that if a man went
westward to the end of the world he would find something—say a
tree—that was more or less than a tree, a tree possessed by a spirit;
and that if he went east to the end of the world he would find
something else that was not wholly itself—a tower, perhaps, of
which the very shape was wicked. . . . The ends of the earth were
closing in.[5]

But to praise him for this is to praise him for failing in what
he intended to do—for letting in the nightmares which he
thought it his vocation to dispel. Borges observes that 'Each

story in the Father Brown Saga [as also in *The Poet and the Lunatics*] presents a mystery, proposes explanations of a demoniacal or magical sort, and then replaces them at the end with solutions of this world. . . . Each . . . undertakes to explain an inexplicable event by reason alone.'[6] 'And this, he thinks, is a symbol of Chesterton's life and beliefs. Father Brown himself would retort that the Unknown God's name is Satan: 'the true God was made flesh and dwelt among us. . . . Wherever you find men ruled merely by mystery, it is the mystery of iniquity. . . . If you think some truth unbearable, bear it.'[7] All the same, perhaps it is true that—not Father Brown but Chesterton—sometimes dispels his mysteries too easily to account for their initial horror.

A similarly laudatory condemnation may be made of Chesterton's language. He is acute in observing; but (it may be said) he does not attempt to convey in his style the quality of what he observes. Thus he begins a story:

A thing can sometimes be too extraordinary to be remembered. If it is clean out of the course of things, and has apparently no causes and no consequences, subsequent events do not recall it; and it remains only a subconscious thing, to be stirred by some accident long after. It drifts apart like a forgotten dream. . . . The thing [Harold March] saw . . . simply slipped past his mind and was lost in later and utterly different events; nor did he even recover the memory, till he had long afterwards discovered the meaning.[8]

The part played by this extraordinary thing in the story (it may be remarked without betraying the plot) supports Borges' formula. But there is a further point. T. S. Eliot, perhaps remembering this passage, has something very like it in *The Dry Salvages*:

> We had the experience but missed the meaning,
> And approach to the meaning restores the experience
> In a different form, beyond any meaning
> We can assign to happiness.[9]

The contrast makes very clear the difference between a style like Eliot's, which by obliqueness and omission conveys the very quality of an elusive mental experience, and Chesterton's univocal style, which confines itself to statement or at most to rhetoric.

Chesterton himself defends such a style. Once more, it is not that he is insufficiently aware of the deficiencies of univocal language, but that he is too thoroughly sceptical of the capacities of any kind of language to attempt to refine it. In his first full-length book, he says that any man who believes in the perfection of language 'knows that there are in the soul tints more bewildering, more numberless, and more nameless than the colours of an autumn forest . . . . Yet he seriously believes that these things can every one of them, in all their tones and semi-tones, in all their blends and unions, be accurately represented by an arbitrary system of grunts and squeals . . .'[10]

This passage in its context—it is part of an argument that pictorial allegory, such as Watts' pictures labelled Hope or Mammon, are not to be explained by such *words* as Hope and Mammon, since the pictures are symbols equally expressive of the things the words represent—may explain a great deal of the vivid visual and oral symbols expressed in slovenly language which recur in Chesterton's prose and poetry. But the slovenliness remains slovenly.

Against the charge of bad faith in style he says:

We cannot understand the eighteenth century so long as we suppose that rhetoric is artificial because it is artistic. We do not fall into this folly about any of the other arts. We talk of a man picking out notes arranged in ivory on a wooden piano "with much feeling", or of his pouring out his soul by scraping on cat-gut after a training as careful as an acrobat's. But we are still haunted with a prejudice that verbal form and verbal effect must somehow be hypocritical when they are the link between things so living as a man and a mob. . . . As with any other artist, the care the eighteenth-century man expended on oratory is a proof of his sincerity, not a disproof of it. An enthusiastic eulogium by Burke is as rich and elaborate as a lover's sonnet, but it is because Burke is really enthusiastic, like the lover.[11]

This does very well as an account of the kind of writing in which Chesterton can be impeccable. Wherever he is using language like a musical instrument, wherever there is no question of that odder use of language in which there seems

to be no gap between what one says and the words in which
one says it, he can approach perfection. He can convey collective emotion in a great hymn: in his satirical verse every word
hits the target: he was a perpetual fount of aphorisms; and a
most brilliant parodist. Of one of his translations George Steiner
observes appositely: 'In the no-man's land between du Bellay's
Heureux qui comme Ulysse and Chesterton's English sonnet, so
nearly exhaustive of the original, we seem to hear *"encore
l'immortelle parole"*, Mallarmé's expression for the notion of a
universal, immediate tongue from which English and French
had broken off.'[12]

This is particularly apt because in this translation of du
Bellay Chesterton strikes one as being aware both of what
du Bellay might have wanted to say in English and of the gap
between what one can do with French and what one can do
with English. It is poignancy that he finds in du Bellay: but he
feels that the austere classicism of

Plus que le marbre dur me plaist l'ardoise fine

may sound only frigid in English: so he gives it

More than immortal marbles undecayed,
The thin sad slates that cover up my home.[13]

Chesterton was much embarrassed by the disjunction between
his public self and his real person: but the disjunction is presumably connected with his ability to impersonate.[14] And it
is this ability to impersonate, modified by his awareness of a
strong system of values to judge what he is impersonating, that
makes his literary criticism and his biographies so good.
Robert Browning, Charles Dickens and *The Victorian Age in Literature*
(especially the descriptions of Rossetti and Swinburne in this
last) are all in some degree combinations of impersonation of and
judgment on the authors who had done most to form Chesterton's own art and personality, and on the Victorian compromise
which he loved and attacked. After the war and his conversion
to Rome, the studies—*St Francis of Assisi, Cobbett, Robert Louis
Stevenson, Chaucer* and *St Thomas Aquinas*—are less biographical
and literary, are less about the authors who had formed

Chesterton and more about the Church and its ideals towards which he hoped to be transformed. But they are still impersonations. In all he balances between giving us the books of these people as they would have been if he had written them, or the actions as they would have been if he had done them, on the one hand, and on the other, giving us himself as he would have been if he had written those books or done those things. In all he holds the balance by reference to the scheme of values which he called Orthodoxy. In *Heretics* and in *George Bernard Shaw*, the element of impersonation vanishes, to be replaced by a sense of conversation between personal friends. But the sense of balance remains.

Chesterton does not, however, remain so steady when he is writing immediately from himself. The trouble is, not that he writes a perfect rhetoric to which it is indifferent whether he intended what he says, but that the rhetoric itself goes astray. In his less good verse and even in his best (*The Ballad of the White Horse*, in particular) marvellous writing will suddenly become too knotted for any clear meaning to be discovered at all, or lapse into an unconvincing frenzy. Or he will spoil a fine description with a lame joke.

The description of a horse which gives the keynote of *The Everlasting Man* is a clear example:

Out of some dark forest under some ancient dawn there must come towards us, with lumbering yet dancing motions, one of the very queerest of the prehistoric creatures. We must see for the first time the strangely small head set on a neck not only longer but thicker than itself, as the face of a gargoyle is thrust out upon a gutter-spout, the one disproportionate crest of hair running along the ridge of that heavy neck like a beard in the wrong place; the feet, each like a solid club of horn, alone amid the feet of so many cattle; so that the true fear is to be found in showing not the cloven but the uncloven hoof.[15]

Most of this gives the horse as one might see it freshly and for the first time, as a man with no concept of a horse might see it. The prose is as good as that of William Golding's tour de force *The Inheritors* in giving us the world of a man who does not conceptualize, and promises a style as generally revelatory as Golding's or William Mayne's. But halfway through a sentence

Chesterton spoils the description with a joke about the cloven hoof—entirely conceptual and verbal, in quite a different mode from the passage up till then, and not a very good joke anyway. Imagination in Coleridge's sense has been abruptly replaced by fancy. The passage suggests two faults: first, an inability to leave well alone, a compulsive need for verbal wit, and secondly an uncertainty in Chesterton about what he is doing. Is the description mere verbal fancy, a trick to alter your picture of the horse, or is it real recognition?

For both the uncertainty and the compulsive resort to word-play there are two possible explanations: first, that Chesterton has really felt a remote tremor of fear at the monster he has seen, and secondly that he felt a fear, or at least an unwilling-ness to contemplate that in himself which has enabled him to see it. For this ability raises the one question which haunted him: 'Is there a world of clearly distinguished external objects apart from someone's consciousness of it, or not?'

Perhaps there is no great distinction between the two explanations, the one about Chesterton's subjectivity, and the other about a queerness in objects which his subjectivity revealed to him. He regarded with horror the abandonment of clear outlines; twice he renders this fear by the image of a fog—in *Manalive*[16] and at the opening of *The Ball and the Cross*, where he comments that 'the world of science and evolution is far more nameless and elusive and like a dream than the world of poetry and religion; since in the latter images and ideas remain themselves eternally, while it is the whole idea of evolu-tion that identities melt into each other as they do in a nightmare.'[17]

Chesterton in fact calls his primitive picture of the horse 'something very like a mad vision',[18] and is inclined to say that 'the traditional grasp of the truth' about horses—or about anything—is better. But because, as he often points out, in our present stage of civilization we seem to be in a condition 'of mere fatigue and forgetfulness of tradition',[19] he offers a technique of shock for beginning to grasp again the sane vision. And when he evolves a similar primitive picture of primitive man, he suggests that what we find is a being who saw in a way surprisingly similar to the way in which we see now.

The contrast with Golding's *Inheritors* is instructive here.

Both authors are in reaction against the Whiggish view which they find in H. G. Wells' *Outline of History*: the view that the further we look back at the past of man the more simply crude and violent we see him, until he becomes indistinguishable from the animals. Both agree that there was from the beginning some radical strangeness about *Homo sapiens*. 'Alone among the animals', says Chesterton, 'he is shaken with the beautiful madness called laughter; as if he had caught sight of some secret in the very shape of the universe hidden from the universe itself. Alone among the animals he feels the need of averting his thoughts from the root realities of his own bodily being; of hiding them as in the presence of some higher possibility which creates the mystery of shame.'[20] Both seem to think that this quality should be described as if man were at once fallen and a new creation.

But Golding imagines a man before *Homo sapiens*, man unfallen and innocent in his instincts, without guilt because without self-consciousness: a man who, not being self-conscious, would conceptualize very little and therefore would perpetually see the world as Chesterton offers it, in the shock of newness. *The Inheritors* tries to imagine consistently what this world would be like.

Chesterton does not adventure on imagining a different kind of consciousness: it is probable that he would have thought this an impossible endeavour. He describes nothing beyond the earliest man of whose mind we have any knowledge, the man who painted the cave pictures, man already an artist, whose pictures of stag and cattle already show 'that love of the long sweeping or the long wavering line which any man who has ever drawn or tried to draw will recognise.'[21] The pictures mean, he says, that already 'a new thing had appeared in the cavernous night of nature; a mind that is like a mirror. . . . It is like a mirror because in it alone all the other shapes can be seen like shining shadows in a vision.'[22]

Golding, like the romantics and most of their successors, envisages consciousness as like a lamp whose projection on to the world one could imagine changed. Chesterton, as he here makes clear, thinks of it as a mirror. His scepticism about modern ambitions to represent the nature of consciousness emerges when, commenting on different kinds of obscurity, he

says that Browning is so eager to get to the point that he will
smash a sentence and leave only bits of it, whilst Henry James—
refusing to accept on the mere authority of Euclid that the
point is indivisible—tries to divide it 'by a dissection for which
human language (even in his exquisite hands) is hardly
equal.'[23]

To divide the point—to analyse experience into constituents
which lie only just within the brink of consciousness—to extend
consciousness, and language with it, to a fineness of definition
never before achieved—Chesterton is right in saying that this
was what Henry James aimed at, and would perhaps have been
right in adding that this marks the chief difference not only
between Browning and James, but between most Victorian
and most twentieth-century writers. Underlying this aim is a
wish to divide the point in a further sense—to discover the
point where our consciousness of the world begins—the point
where our lines of perspective converge, at the back of our
minds and in the beginning of our wills—because we know that
our world is partly created from that point like a projection on
a screen, and we *must* know what happens there.

About this aim in using language, and this wish about thinking, Chesterton himself is divided. It is very characteristic of
him that he should choose an image, that of dividing the point,
which shows both that he understood profoundly what
twentieth-century writers want, and that he thought it un-
achievable.

One of his finest feats of historical imagination is that in
which he argues that the early middle ages were ascetic towards
nature, because awareness of nature in the classical world had
been thoroughly defiled. The centre of a Roman garden was
the statue of Priapus. 'It was no good telling such people to
have a natural religion full of stars and flowers; there was not a
flower or even a star that had not been stained. They had to go
into the desert where they could find no flowers',[24] before they
could afford—or even have—the exultant passion for nature of
St Francis of Assisi.

This passage was perhaps in T. S. Eliot's mind when he
wrote his own study of purgation by abstinence in *Ash
Wednesday* and may account for the presence in *Ash Wednesday* of
the garden god and the desert,[25] But Eliot, because he senses

an unreliability in self-consciousness and its projection on the world, tries to explore the nature of purgation, penitence and self-consciousness in themselves. Chesterton envisages instead a change of relation to the external world—centuries of abstinence, then rebirth. And the nature which he envisages St Francis seeing again has its own inherent and not projected meaning. The Franciscan birds and beasts were like symbols, 'like heraldic birds and beasts; not in the sense of being fabulous animals, but in the sense of being treated as if they were facts, clear and positive and unaffected by the illusions of atmosphere and perspective.'[26] Chesterton senses the unreliability of consciousness as much as Eliot: but his remedy was not to investigate the nature of that unreliability, to build his language out of an awareness of it, but to draw attention, even with violence, to the external world.

A great deal of Chesterton's best writing—a second area where he can be almost impeccable—describes the external world, but not in its primitiveness. He describes (in this sort of writing) things conceptualized—as understood by an innocent man's mind but still by a mind that conceptualizes—and argues that this is the way the world is. His description of St Francis's world is developed when he says of some medieval illuminated manuscripts in the John Rylands Library that they possess

a quality that belongs to the simplest and the soundest human feeling. Plato held this view, and so does every child. Plato held, and the child holds, that the most important thing about a ship (let us say) is that it is a ship. Thus, all these pictures are designed to express things in their quiddity. If these old artists draw a ship, everything is sacrificed to expressing the 'shipishness' of the ship. . . . If they draw a flower its whole object is to be flowering. Their pencils often go wrong as to how the thing looks; their intellects never go wrong as to what the thing is.[27]

In accordance with this ideal, Chesterton is at his best as a descriptive writer when he is dealing with sharply distinguished objects which have clear significance. Some of his lovingly-drawn light effects seem as if he is describing not light but a painting of light.

All the heaven seemed covered with a quite vivid and palpable plumage; you could only say that the sky was full of feathers, and of

feathers that almost brushed the face. Across the great part of the
dome they were grey, with the strangest tints of violet and mauve
and an unnatural pink or pale green; but towards the west the
whole grew past description, transparent and passionate, and the
last red-hot plumes of it covered up the sun like something too good
to be seen.[28]

It is as if he were talking of brushwork. Indeed, when he
describes either man-made or natural objects, he often returns
to his experience as painter and draughtsman, as if asking,
'What was going into this as it was made?'
    He is skilful therefore in depicting anything designed by man
(Jerusalem, for example, in *The New Jerusalem*), but especially
paintings themselves, as when he says that Gainsborough
'painted ladies like landscapes, as great and as unconscious
with repose, and . . . gives to a dress flowing on the foreground
something of the divine quality of distance.'[29] But the em-
pathetic quality of his writing on art extends to his descriptions
of landscapes, when they can be seen as responsive to man.
When he talks of the South Downs in *A Piece of Chalk* he carries
his own account of Gainsborough, so to speak, through to
describing landscapes like living beings.
    The first volume of the Father Brown stories, furthermore,
The Innocence of Father Brown, has much of its impact, both in
individual stories and in its air of cohering as a single book,
from a consistent use of symbolic landscape (this occurs in later
Father Brown stories, but less consistently through a volume).
The landscapes or interiors are nearly always convincing and
familiar (seven are set in London, four in the English or
Scottish countryside and one in Paris). But they are also (very
much as in Stevenson) settings of dream, objective correlatives
of something allied to or contrasted with the inner weather of
the mind which (rather than the crime itself) is the real subject
of each story—the dark hotel cloakroom where Father Brown
threatens Flambeau with hell, the Christmas party of Flambeau's last crime, or the huge and lonely setting on Hampstead
Heath where Father Brown tells him that the universe is 'only
infinite physically . . . not infinite in the sense of escaping from
the laws of truth.'[30] The effect is at its height in *The Sign of the
Broken Sword*, the story which most clearly escapes Borges'

charge of an inadequate shift from mystery to reason. It escapes the charge because the moral defect at the end really outdoes in shamefulness the air of nameless evil at the beginning (as is made clear by Flambeau's two failures to guess the answer—a brilliant structural device): and the nature of this defect, prepared for by the description of the frozen woods in which the story is told, is brought home when Father Brown suddenly points at 'a puddle sealed with ice that shone in the moon.' 'Do you remember whom Dante put in the last circle of ice?' he says and Flambeau replies 'The traitors.'[31] The uncompromising condemnation, made by a reference to Dante's iron system of ethics, is expressed in a realization of Dante's symbolic landscape.

It might be said that like his own Adam Wayne in *The Napoleon of Notting Hill* Chesterton tends to describe all the world as if it were made by man because his childhood was spent in Kensington. His attempts to transform our vision of the world are at their most intense when he works on something urban. One might further say of him what Eliot says of Baudelaire: 'It is not merely in the use of imagery of common life, not merely in the use of imagery of the sordid life of a great metropolis, but in the elevation of such imagery to the *first intensity*—presenting it as it is, and yet making it represent something much more than itself—that Baudelaire has created a mode of release and expression for other men.'[32]

Only the words will not mean exactly the same thing when used of Chesterton as of Baudelaire. For one thing, though Chesterton does describe the chaotic and sordid side of his London, he prefers a different kind of intensity: and for another he does it (following perhaps Dickens) with a kind of humour which is also poetry. Thus he observes that people 'talk as if this claim of ours, that all things are poetical, were a mere literary ingenuity, a play on words. Precisely the contrary is true. It is the idea that some things are not poetical which is literary, which is a mere product of words. The word "signal-box" is unpoetical. But the thing signal-box is not unpoetical; it is a place where men in an agony of vigilance, light blood-red and sea-green fires to keep other men from death.'[33] The wit of this appears when one's first reaction—(that this defence against verbalism is itself only a fantastic firework of words)—

surrenders as word by word the sentence proves to be merely true. The only sense of excess is in the word 'agony'. Even that may not have seemed an exaggeration to Chesterton: it is worth remembering the advice of the doctor who towards the end of his schooldays said that Chesterton 'must be preserved from mental shock or strain', since it was 'even chances whether he became a genius or an imbecile.'[34] But this explanation would probably over-emphasize the possibility in him of real madness.

But even in such intense passages as this, the language is still being used like a musical instrument. What is happening is less a fresh sight of a thing than a rearrangement of concepts. There is no assurance here that Chesterton has thought through and defeated the misgivings about consciousness which he certainly felt: only that he has found a refuge from them in intensifying traditional words and traditional feelings, and in recognizing and causing us to recognize their appropriateness in untraditional surroundings.

However, the passage about the signal-box comes from one of Chesterton's earliest books. At the other end of his career he knew what kind of style might achieve this assurance. He adumbrates it when he says that in reading the philosophy of Aquinas, he finds it makes

a very peculiar and powerful impression analogous to poetry. Curiously enough, it is in some ways more analogous to painting, and reminds me very much of the effect produced by the *best* of the modern painters, when they throw a strange and almost crude light upon stark and rectangular objects, or seem to be groping for rather than grasping the very pillars of the subconcious mind. It is probably because there is in his work a quality which is Primitive, in the best sense of a badly misused word. . . . Perhaps the impression is connected with the fact that painters deal with things without words. An artist draws quite gravely the grand curves of a pig; because he is not thinking of the *word* pig. There is no thinker who is so unmistakably thinking about things, and not being misled by the indirect influence of words, as St Thomas Aquinas.[35]

The contrast here is very striking with his early passage relating the limits of language to the symbolic painting of G. F. Watts. Then, he thought both language and painting parallel attempts to symbolize something beyond adequate expression, and chose the genre of symbolic painting to illustrate his point. Now, he chooses a genre and a style which suggest that one can after all make a certain contact with the essences of things. The point of the analogy becomes clearer when we find him saying elsewhere that the angles and jagged lines of Picasso and the Cubists suggest something that 'seems to happen and not merely to exist.'[36]

For the primitive quality in Aquinas's style is due, Chesterton says, to 'the intense rightness of his sense of the relation between the mind and the real thing outside the mind. That *strangeness* of things, which is the light in all poetry, and indeed in all art, is really connected with their otherness, or what is called their objectivity. . . . They are strange because they are solid.' The object becomes a part of the mind, or the mind becomes the object, according to Aquinas; but because the object exists in itself 'it enlarges the mind of which it becomes a part.' The mind responds to objects, eats the meat of reality because 'this feeding upon fact *is* itself.' 'The external fact', according to the Thomist Maritain, '*fertilizes* the internal intelligence, as the bee fertilizes the flower.'[37]

Something like this does appear to be true of Aquinas's style and its queer movement from an intense abstraction to a brilliant concrete realization. Something like it is also true of Chesterton's own style at its best, as for example in the description of the horse and elsewhere in *The Everlasting Man*. 'Look', these styles say, 'this is the way things are: look how they stand out.' They depart strangely from the ideal of language as symbolizing, towards that of language as pointing out.

In the depictions of landscape and sunset already mentioned, Chesterton could plausibly be accused of describing the world as if it were created by an allegorical painter, and perhaps even of carrying his technique of impersonation into the very mind of God. This is not just a trope, but the very thing which he regarded as his greatest temptation and most dreadful nightmare, Gabriel Gale's fear of finding oneself to be the centre of creation. But in other, and on the whole later descriptions, his style, as he says in his essay on the Book of Job of the speech of God, insists 'that if there is one fine thing about the world, as far as men are concerned, it is that it cannot be explained'. It is a style whose main object is wonder: a world whose maker, if one *could* imagine him, would appear 'astonished at the things He has Himself made.'

Thomism, although it embodied Chesterton's sense that the world is utterly other than anything he could have imagined, insists on the intelligibility of things. Chesterton's exposition allows this, but with a peculiar stress. For although he speaks with admiration of a language that deals with things, he makes clear that what he is primarily interested in is not the things distinct among themselves but their otherness from the self perceiving them. He says of a child looking at grass: 'Long before he knows that grass is grass, or self is self, he knows that something is something.'[38]

This emphasis, this interest in the simple being or even happening of things, may go with, but is not the same as, an interest in their essential singularities. The latter interest, which Aquinas perhaps reveals more in his style than Chesterton does, will go with comparing and contrasting things with things, and will issue in a style like Aquinas's in which things, ideas, and things analysed by ideas, stand out stark and primitive. The former, which Chesterton tends towards, goes with expression, not necessarily of any particular detail of the concrete thing, but of its overall weight and impact, especially its unexpectedness.

This stress may account for the worst (and sometimes inexcusable) defect in Chesterton's writing: his swashbuckling carelessness about factual accuracy. His historical and theoretical writing—for example, the discussion of primitive religion in *The Everlasting Man*—is seriously marred by a refusal to give precise accounts, together with the commission of actual inaccuracies. The paradoxical consequence is that while Chesterton professed to speak to plain men, only a man as learned as himself could safely read these parts of his work. And since Chesterton, despite his preference for being a plain man, was phenomenally well-read and in an unsystematic way profoundly learned, these writings are shut off from being useful.

His criticism too is careless of accuracy. There is no excuse for a man who makes detailed close criticism of a quotation which he prefaces (as Chesterton habitually does) 'I quote from memory and probably wrong.'[39] And he quotes violently

out of context when he attacks Kipling for admiring England
without loving her.

In a very interesting poem he [Kipling] says that:

> 'If England was what England seems'

—that is weak and inefficient; if England were not what (as he
believes) she is—that is, powerful and practical—

> 'How quick we'd chuck 'er! But she ain't!'[40]

Even the full version of the refrain

> If England was what England seems
> An' not the England of our dreams
> But only putty, brass an' paint
> 'Ow quick we'd drop 'er! *But she ain't!*[41]

shows what the rest of the poem bears out: Kipling means 'If
England were only powerful and efficient, and all the other
things that go with putty, brass and paint, we could not love
her; but we find an almost inexplicable love of her, bound up
with our dreams, has grown up as we have fought and watched
our friends die for her.'

Chesterton did not verify his references. And yet with all
this, how sensitive he is to the use of language. His discussions
of Othello's

> I know not where is that Promethean heat

and of how it differs from saying 'I do not know how I am to
bring her to life again'[42]—of Milton's

> Dying put on the weeds of Dominic

and its 'certain unexpected order and arrangement of words . . .
like the perfect manners of an eccentric gentleman'[43]—or of
the 'earthquake ellipsis' in Blake's

> How the Chimney-sweeper's cry
> Every black'ning Church appals[44]—

are both good in themselves, and parts of excellent studies of the nature of poetry. Here Chesterton is saying 'Look! notice!' with wisdom and effect. And he does this even with what few critics can disentangle enough from prejudice to touch at all: the Bible. His remarks on the Book of Job and the Gospels make one read those books, perhaps for the first time, as books.

One must give similar praise, in spite of all their inaccuracies, to his treatments of anthropology. The anthropology popular in his own day he accuses of 'a trick of making things seem distant and dehumanised merely by pretending not to understand things that we do understand.'[45] In contrast, his own approach anticipates in many ways that since particularly associated with Professor Evans-Pritchard. As we have already seen, he insists that the most primitive men of whom we know have had an inner life essentially like our own. He not only points out how like sophisticated man primitive man may be, but how primitive sophisticated man remains. 'Creative expression like art and religion'[46] was distinct from the beginning from natural experiences and natural excitements: folklore does not deal with 'stupid and static superstition'[47] but, like the metaphors of poets, with something that 'stirs in the subconscious',[48] and was created and believed in with the same shades 'of sincerity—and insincerity'[49]—as daydreams. A sacrifice to Pallas Athene might have the same seriousness as Dr Johnson's touching all the posts in the street, or a deeper and more religious sentiment, though perhaps never the seriousness with which Dr Johnson reached towards the Cross.

This insistence on the uniformity of human awareness, which suffered under the charge of externality when we considered Chesterton's analysis and expression of his own consciousness, works like his impersonations of Browning and Dickens towards interiority when he deals with the consciousness of other men. He insists on looking at myths 'from the inside', asking how one would tell the story oneself,[50] and on knowing what totems, or loyalties, or religion 'meant in the mind of a man, especially an ordinary man.'[51]

When he deals with the external world, the predominance in his concern of thereness over quiddity allows lapses into verbal wit and a thousand unnecessary hyperboles. But all the same he is interested in pointing out the nature of things, and specially the inward nature of things. At times his methods work together towards a real uncovering: for example—

> When fishes flew and forests walked
>   And figs grew upon thorn,
> Some moment when the moon was blood
>   Then surely I was born.
>
> With monstrous head and sickening cry
>   And ears like errant wings,
> The devil's walking parody
>   On all four-footed things.
>
> The tattered outlaw of the earth,
>   Of ancient crooked will;
> Starve, scourge, deride me: I am dumb,
>   I keep my secret still.
>
> Fools! For I also had my hour;
>   One far fierce hour and sweet:
> There was a shout about my ears,
>   And palms before my feet.[52]

The first verse is well-devised rhetoric: a piece in the tradition of the *impossibilia* which goes back through Horace and Virgil to Archilochus: not used here (as normally in earlier writing) to feed in fancy a delight in the grotesque, but, as Chesterton says of the grotesque in *Robert Browning*, 'to touch the nerve of surprise and thus to draw attention to the intrinsically miraculous character of the object itself.'[53]

The fourth verse is equally good in a quite different way: it reads like pure feeling: as if a chink opens in the donkey's memory (he remembers only what a donkey might, the immediate physical sensations seen in front and heard on all sides, with a vague sense only of something important)—a window on something which gives sense to the world. The allusiveness has a further meaning: what gives sense to a creature's world cannot itself be given a further sense, and therefore must lie, half-expressed, at the edge of that creature's world. But the palms and the shout are concrete and real too: the connection of value with detail and concreteness is very characteristic of Chesterton. 'The personal is not a mere figure for the impersonal; rather the impersonal is a clumsy term for something more personal than common personality. God is not a symbol of goodness. Goodness is a symbol of God,'[54] he says.

But the intermediate verses are more puzzling. The structure is clear and neat: the third verse leading from the donkey's tattered insignificance to his possession of a secret, and suggesting his pains that need some atonement, and the second verse describing a real thing, the donkey himself, in the light of the fantasy of the first verse. But it is possible to feel that under the influence of the what-might-have-been of the first verse, the poem has turned slightly loose from the donkey. If one is supposed to be looking freshly at the actual, a donkey's bray may be sickening but is his head really monstrous, his ears really like errant wings? And did the devil really create him as a parody on, among other beasts, the hippopotamus? In fact, has the devil much place in this verse, even if we allow him his presence as the cause of the donkey's outlawing in the third verse (although the notion that the donkey looks like a creation of the devil is important still in that verse, and still hyperbolic)? And even if one allows the poem to remain grotesquerie, and ignore the real donkey, is it quite consistent with itself? Is the loud diabolic monster of the second verse the same as the maltreated meditative animal of the end? The pathos and sublimity of the end depend on one's mind shifting to the small beast one sees in fields—the patient ass with mild eyes, 'a companion and not a monstrosity' whose ears, admittedly 'unduly developed', Dorian Wimpole scratches in *The Flying Inn*—the animal which is the first he loves because it is 'like a man'.[55]

The charge is the general one against Chesterton: able at grotesquerie, inspired with religion, he is too irresponsible to deal with fact, will beat it any way he likes, so that finally doubt is cast on his religion also. One could defend the poem against internal inconsistency by saying that it is about redemption— one's mind should shift from a diabolic creature to a sweet and meditative one because that is the effect of Christ's riding on it. But one cannot thus defend Chesterton against the charge of remoteness from real donkeys, or against rhetorical inconsistency in making donkeys whatever suits his context.

Another reading would carry the clangour and grotesquerie

through to the end; perhaps Chesterton means one to think of
Christ riding on the devil's parody with its wing-like ears and
monstrous head. The grotesquerie then would not be the device
used, as we suggested earlier, to stand the world 'on its head
that people may look at it', but would be what Chesterton
distinguishes from it in *Robert Browning*, 'the element of the
grotesque [which] in nature means, in the main, energy, the
energy which takes its own forms and goes its own way.'[56] He
might even have in mind in 'The Donkey' the passage which he
quotes from *Mr Sludge, the Medium* in which God is revealed
'close behind a stomach-cyst'.[57]

But, although this may be the right reading of the second
verse, it strains the last verse. The word 'Fools!' introducing the
last verse seems to reflect back on the whole poem hitherto;
and the poem seems then to shift indeed in sense from verse to
verse. We begin by seeing the donkey at its most grotesque as
part of a fantastic background; then for a moment the donkey
described in more detail seems to fit the violence of the background. But it will not do: donkeys are not quite like that, and
as in the third verse we focus more accurately on the derided
beast we find its dumb donkeyness pointing beyond itself to
something transcendent.

This fourfold motion—from fantasy (imagined transcend-
ency) through a fact whose primitive essence is realized by
being set in fantasy, and then, after a new attitude of the mind
has been set up, to a transcendence found in the fact—is the
essence of Chesterton's thought. Its expression in a movement
of style from discordant imagery and clangour to something
subtle and still recurs in both his poetry and prose. The second
and third terms of the motion seem to correspond to Hopkins'
inscape and *instress*. In the imagery that expresses these ideas—
the vivid colours, the detailed patterning, the storm and violence
—Chesterton and Hopkins have much in common. The huge
difference in syntax and rhythm corresponds, as one would
expect, to Chesterton's contrast of Browning and James.
Chesterton cares less than Hopkins about the motion of his
mind in relation to the fact, more about pointing to the fact
itself. He is altogether more careless, more public, forensic,
and argumentative. Yet he reaches at times a stillness while
Hopkins remains in the storm. It is not too far-fetched to say

that Chesterton uses the late Victorian and Edwardian violence and grotesquerie which he shares with Kipling, Swinburne and even Hopkins, as Herbert used the metaphysical conceit: to reach simplicity.

But though we may allow that Chesterton does persuade us of his capacity, and mankind's, to reach the objective, the comparison with Hopkins only emphasizes the charge that in doing this the public nature of his style is covering up something in the subjective world, and that therefore his religion and his treatment of psychology are external and uncomprehending. The earliest of his books in which these charges are seriously at issue is *The Napoleon of Notting Hill*. The theme of this book seems at first sight to be the poetry of cities, and in particular the survival of heroism and love of locality in the deadest megalopolis. It begins with a polemic against prophets of the future which suggests that what we are to have is an attack on scientific Utopianism like Forster's *The Machine Stops*, but in a comic mode.

If this were all, it would be enough to say that after the brilliant debunking of the preliminary essay, the book soundly thrashes the futurology of its time by giving a prophecy— remarkably funny throughout—that London in 1984 will be first concerned (under a government of civil servants and business men) with the solution of traffic problems by driving roads through unwilling communities, and then with antagonism to 'the vast machinery of modern life' breaking out in violence.[58] As a prediction, this is impressive: but if the book were only that, it probably would support the charge of externality.

But in fact Chesterton, realizing that this first theme is both comic and tragic, transforms his subject into the antagonism of humour and tragedy themselves. It is as if Blake, having written

> The fields from Islington to Marybone,
> To Primrose Hill and St John's Wood,
> Were builded over with pillars of gold,
> And there Jerusalem's pillars stood.[59]

had known that this was capable of being comic as well as of being sublime. Humour at the beginning of *The Napoleon* undercuts everything else (perhaps the genesis of Auberon Quin, who was partly a portrait of Beerbohm, is in Chesterton's remark on Victorianism in *George Frederic Watts*: 'Mr Max Beerbohm waves a wand and a whole generation of great men and great achievement suddenly looks mildewed and un-meaning'[60]): 'I have never been to St John's Wood. I dare not', says Quin. 'I should be afraid of the innumerable night of fir trees, afraid to come upon a blood-red cup and the beating of the wings of the Eagle. But all these things can be imagined by remaining reverently in the Harrow train.'[61] And it is only a joke.

But humour itself is undercut when Adam Wayne says flatly: 'Notting Hill is a rise or high ground of the common earth, on which men have built houses to live, in which they are born, fall in love, pray, marry and die. Why should I think it absurd?'—at which Auberon feels as he makes his friend Barker feel by saying 'Why trouble about politics?'—'as if the floor of his mind had given way.'[62]

But Wayne is not thereby proved right. He is undoubtedly slightly mad, in precisely the ways in which Chesterton usually defines madness: he is obsessively logical and 'only laughed once or twice in his life.'[63] His whole tragic enterprise remains threatened for the reader, until the last dialogue, by the sheer comedy of the book, and by the sense that Quin—through whose eyes we mostly see—watches it with 'a sense of detach-ment, of responsibility, of irony, of agony'[64]—knowing that it is all a joke. There is a threat of total nihilism.

But in the last dialogue, when the division between Wayne and Quin becomes overtly an image of human life, Wayne answers the notion that a derisive omnipotence might look at the world in Quin's way with an argument not unlike that of Bertrand Russell's *A Free Man's Worship*:

'Suppose I am God, and having made things, laugh at them'.
'And suppose I am man,' answered the other. 'And suppose that I give the answer that shatters even a laugh. Suppose I do not laugh back at you, do not blaspheme you, do not curse you. But suppose, standing up straight under the sky, with every power of my being, I thank you for the fools' paradise you have made. . . . If we have taken the child's games and given them the seriousness of a Crusade, if we have drenched your grotesque Dutch garden

with the blood of martyrs, we have turned a nursery into a temple. I ask you, in the name of Heaven, who wins?'[65]

Satisfying as this is as a note on values in a universe of chance, it is not the book's final answer. When Wayne is persuaded that his life has been in fact Quin's joke, he realizes and makes Quin realize that they are both mad. The final appeal is beyond both their mad worlds, to the being who can both laugh and love: ordinary common man.

The book is as purely agnostic as it can be: the last dialogue is wholly humanist. Remaining on that ground it successfully challenges and defeats nihilism. It is a philosophical ballet rather than a novel: but it is a very good philosophical ballet.

Chesterton's next novel *The Man Who Was Thursday* moves on from the ground which *The Napoleon of Notting Hill* captured. The seriousness of man's life is taken for granted: the question is raised 'Does that give us any guarantee that the world in which man lives makes sense?' The book's subtitle is *A Nightmare*, and its most remarkable passages embody the terror of being trapped in a dream from which one cannot escape: Syme in the presence of the Council of Days, the pursuit in snow by Professor de Wurms, the blank faces of the Professor and Dr Bull next day, the duel with the Marquis de St Eustache who cannot be wounded, and the moment on the pier when the world seems to be ending. In most of these, as in *The Napoleon of Notting Hill*, the thing to hold on to is the thought of 'common and kindly people'[66]; especially the girl Rosamund whom Syme met before the nightmare began. Once there is something else: the snowy cross on St Paul's against a sickly sky suggests that 'The devils might have captured heaven, but they had not yet captured the cross.'[67] But there is neither of these supports during the passage in which nightmare extends to the physical world, Chesterton's most intense statement of the fear of solipsism. Even the story's recurrent device, that apparent evil is shown to be good, adds to the insecurity:

The inside of the wood was full of shattered sunlight and shaken shadows. . . . Now a man's head was lit as with a light of Rembrandt, leaving all else obliterated; now again he had strong and staring white hands with the face of a negro. . . . This wood of witchery, in which men's faces turned black and white by turns, in which their figures first swelled into sunlight and then faded into formless night . . . seemed to Syme a perfect symbol of the world in which he had been moving for three days, this world where men took off their beards and their spectacles and their noses, and turned into other people. That tragic self-confidence which he had felt when he believed that the Marquis was a devil had strangely disappeared now that he knew that the Marquis was a friend. He felt almost inclined to ask after all these bewilderments what was a friend and what an enemy. Was there anything that was apart from what it seemed? The Marquis had taken off his nose and turned out to be a detective. Might he not just as well take off his head and turn out to be a hobgoblin? Was not everything, after all, like this bewildering woodland, this dance of dark and light? Everything only a glimpse, the glimpse always unforeseen, and always forgotten. For Gabriel Syme had found in the heart of that sun-splashed wood what many modern painters had found there. He had found the thing which the modern people call Impressionism, which is another name for that final scepticism which can find no floor to the universe.[68]

The sight of a peasant in a forest clearing, the common man again, rather unsatisfyingly enables Syme to recover from this mood, but it recurs in the chase of Sunday, and the goonish or even Beckettian humour of the notes he hurls back at his pursuers, as he begins to appear to be incomprehensible Nature itself. (He is incidentally the most medieval of Chesterton's creations, of a middle ages less stable and stylized than Chesterton thought them: his nearest relation is the Green Knight of *Gawain and the Green Knight*.) At the end and suddenly nature turns round and shows its face. The six friends have argued about Sunday in a way confined, like the last dialogue of *The Napoleon*, to human experience. But this book adds revelation: 'I am the Sabbath,' says Sunday, 'I am the peace of God.'[69]

The movement of the dream persuades us that this is true: he is 'contentment, optimism . . . an ultimate reconciliation.'[70] But this discovery does nothing to remove the nightmare. 'We wept, we fled in terror, the iron entered into our souls—and you are the peace of God', says the Secretary, 'Oh, I can forgive God His anger, though it destroyed nations; but I cannot forgive Him His peace.'[71]

As in the Book of Job, a possible answer is given by the irruption of an accuser who denounces Syme and the rest (as Syme at the comic beginning of the book denounced a policeman) for being safe. Their isolation and heroism in face of nightmare has earned them the right to answer 'You lie'. But though this may give a reason for their fate, it does not answer the Secretary's denunciation of God's peace. The dream ends as Sunday's face fills the universe and a voice picks up what was implied by the snowy cross on St Paul's: 'Can ye drink of the cup that I drink of?'[72] But this is a moment of nightmare, as if the pain of God answering the accusation against His peace merely surrounds us with horror. There is a further twist and a further answer: a particular physical detail, the red hair of the accuser's sister, the girl Rosamund. It several times breaks like reality into the trapped world of the dream, and the ending of the book after the dream is a still scene in which Syme sees 'the sister of Gregory, the girl with the gold-red hair, cutting lilac before breakfast, with the great unconscious gravity of a girl.'[73]

There is a sense in which the whole book is about Syme's realizing that he is in love with Rosamund. The agony of aloneness in the dream, the pursuit of reality, is perhaps the reluctance of commitment to someone one loves: and the reconciliation in the book with the fact of being and the nature of the universe is grounded in the physical detail of the beauty and strangeness of her hair. Since the hair may be Frances Chesterton's, it may be thought that the book provides a very good answer to the accusation that Chesterton ignores some reluctance or defect in himself in his fear of the non-existence of the external world. The only defect about *The Man Who Was Thursday* is Chesterton's suggestion in his *Autobiography* that it was *only* a nightmare.[74] That is precisely to treat cheaply the fear that the world is nightmare which it was the book's business to challenge and defeat. Chesterton's fiction (especially, except for *The Poet and the Lunatics*, the post-war fiction) does seem to wane in force in proportion as he fails to do justice to nightmare.

His remaining major novel, however, *The Ball and the Cross*, again challenges a kind of nightmare: not this time that the world is chaotic, but simply that it is hollow: the enemy is still a kind of relativism. In the story, so to speak, Quin and Wayne go on the wanderings begun on the last page of *The Napoleon of Notting Hill*. Wayne, as Ewan MacIan, is little changed, still heroic, still a little mad: only he is now a Catholic and wishes to fight not for his birthplace but for the Virgin Mary. James Turnbull differs more from Quin: he is an atheist of the Victorian tradition, and although the book is again in a sense about the breakdown of what Chesterton called the Victorian compromise, the breakdown comes about not because humour challenges its greatness, but because the two parties to it, commonsense ethics and Christian dogma, can no longer be held back from fighting. The book is vitiated by slightly too many dialogues in which too often MacIan as a Catholic tends to get the better of Turnbull. But he is unable to convince Turnbull, and the *story* makes it clear once again that both are wrong. Turnbull has no reason for his ethics: but MacIan is a man of superstition, who identifies a universal religion with a particular society and particular phenomena. He sees a world in which everything is transparent, such as is 'figured in the coloured windows of Christian architecture':[75] a red cloud seems to him the bloody hand of Heaven pointing at Turnbull's death. His religion is bound up with the feuds of the highlands and with respect for the chieftain, even with the return of the Stuarts. Chesterton has been accused (wrongly, in terms of this story) of the defects of MacIan: with confusing the church militant with the church triumphant, symbol with reality. MacIan believes only in the Cross, in Christianity as religion: there is no point of contact between him and Turnbull who believes only in the Ball, in the secular world, except that they both take their beliefs and their conflict seriously, and are therefore totally isolated in the modern world. They rouse against themselves a series of representatives of the modern world's determined indifference to their quarrel and find themselves in the end in the lunatic asylum provided by complete relativism, docketed as suffering from (respectively) religious mania and Eleutheromania.

They are not wrong in relation to relativism, but they are wrong. In visions in the asylum, when they see respectively the King come back and the Revolution accomplished, they reject their own dreams because both find them inconsistent with justice for real and individual human beings. Still helpless to escape or to convince one another, they find everyone they have ever met confined in the asylum with them for various psychic disorders which cause the belief that one has met Turnbull and MacIan. Their combat has merely persuaded the nation into believing that insanity is present in everybody. The story almost ends in mere destruction like the conflict of Naphta and Settembrini in Thomas Mann's *The Magic Mountain*: there is no other escape from the deadlock. In fact the end is more like the outbreak of the 1914 war in that book. Turnbull and MacIan have decided that physical combat will not settle their differences: but one of their fellow mad men, a French bourgeois, having decided that the asylum represents an intolerable society, burns it down 'in accordance with the strict principles of the social contract.'[76] It is the only possible escape.

But this is not the whole story. It is framed in a story with a slightly different theme, whose first episode is perhaps the heart of everything Chesterton ever wrote. It is a kind of war in heaven between Michael (a Bulgarian monk) and Lucifer (inventor of a flying machine). As they fly through a London fog which images chaos, in a diabolic heaven like that behind St Paul's in *The Man Who Was Thursday*, Lucifer assures Michael of the truth of what MacIan and Turnbull are to find in the asylum: 'Since our science has spoken the bottom has fallen out of the universe.'[77] During the controversy that follows, Lucifer pushes Michael out to swing from the Cross of St Paul's.

In a magnificent description of what it would be like to climb down the dome of St Paul's, Michael after a spasm of clarity and a spasm of terror experiences some state which is not hope, nor faith, nor knowledge, but complete and of the present, positive, a satisfaction: 'It seems almost as if there were some equality among things, some balance in all possible contingencies which we are not permitted to know lest we should learn indifference to good and evil, but which is sometimes shown to us for an instant as a last aid in our last agony.'[78]

When he steps out of the infinity in which he experiences this on to Ludgate Hill, Michael sees a new universe, because in that one moment there has been for him a new creation. 'Everything his eye fell on it feasted on, not aesthetically, but with a plain, jolly appetite as of a boy eating buns. He relished the squareness of the houses; he liked their clean angles as if he had just cut them with a knife.'[79] This impression—this solid world—is repeated at the end when Turnbull and MacIan find Michael in a sealed cell at the asylum whose master is Lucifer: a cell of porcelain tiles such as they have been confined in, with one spike sticking out in a way which they have found they loathe. Michael tells them he is in a good place, with tiles to count. ' "But that's not the best . . . Spike is the best," said the old man, opening his blue eyes blazing; "it sticks out." '[80]

It is Michael before whom, as he comes miraculously out of the blazing asylum, Turnbull kneels as before a saint. Michael's experience can be appealed to beyond the duel of the Ball and the Cross, and is a resting place beyond relativism. The spike sticking out and the clean cut corners are exact symbols for a universe that is not hollow: which is satisfying because it is and has characteristics. They are like the Donkey, or Rosamund's hair, or the world of *St Thomas Aquinas* or even of Picasso and the Cubists. But in *The Ball and the Cross* there is something added: this glory of finitude is the obverse of the infinite, still moment outside ordinary experience which preceded it. As Chesterton said later of St Francis's love for finite things, 'the mystic who passes through the moment when there is nothing but God' sees both everything and 'the nothing of which everything was made.'[81] He sees, like Michael, the act of creation.

Michael's experience (not perhaps quite one of God) is the same as that which is the centre of *The Ballad of the White Horse*. That is a poem of extraordinary heights and depths, from an inevitability like that of the sayings of Christ in

I tell you naught for your comfort[82]

to the appalling self-parody of

the hands of the happy howling men
Fling wide the gates of war[83]

It is partly about despair, and partly about battle. But its centre is a confrontation with despair: first the despair of Alfred at circumstances, at unceasing defeat, and secondly the radical despairs which he confronts in the Danish leaders. Of the four barbarian leaders, one is a straightforward thief, a consumer of civilization: but the other three are given speeches accorded a kind of convincingness which Chesterton does not accord, for example, to the arguments of Turnbull. They seem to be feelings that he recognized in himself: Elf's song of the fallenness of the world:

> There is always a thing forgotten
> When all the world goes well . . .
> The thing on the blind side of the heart,
> On the wrong side of the door . . .[84]

Ogier's choking, destructive rage (a rage which, justified or not, almost kills the man who feels it, and which one might be surprised at Chesterton's knowing, if it were not for some of his political writings) and Guthrum's proclamation that death is everywhere:

> And a man hopes, being ignorant,
> Till in white woods apart
> He finds at last the lost bird dead . . .[85]

but most distant in battle, when 'we seem to tread it down'. And that does seem to be part of the point about Chesterton's own frenetic activity, and in particular about his imaginative obsession with violence and the dreadful lapses of aesthetic and moral judgment which he commits in writing about it: he fights to forget misgiving. One thinks of the 'happy howling men' already quoted, or of the curiously disgusting as well as implausible description in *The Napoleon of Notting Hill* of blood, 'running, in great red serpents, that curl out into the main thoroughfare and shine in the moon.'[86] The very worst example comes in *The Ballad of St Barbara*, in which Chesterton attempts to rewrite the *White Horse* in terms of the Battle of the Marne and comes out with the line

Blast of the beauty of sudden death, St Barbara of the batteries![87]

That is a most significant line, because rhetorically it is a good one: Chesterton's penchant for noise transmitted into poetry,

both sense and sound. And it is one of his most univocal lines:
first because it is so wicked a line, with its saint made into a
goddess of destruction, that one can only believe that Chesterton had lost all contact with the reality of which he is talking,
the bloodied flesh. It is like the blood he speaks of in *Treasure
Island*, which he can bear in quantities (and he is not sure
whether this is because the blood is only crimson lake or
because 'a child is not wicked enough to disapprove of war')[88]
but is terrified by when it is the few drops of blood drawn from
the apoplectic Billy Bones' arm. But secondly the mention of
'sudden death' is univocal in the sense that it deliberately
excludes an overtone: St Barbara, as the poem's subtitle
declares, is 'the patron saint of artillery and of those in danger
of sudden death'.[89] The line therefore ought to have the overtone, 'Barbara, protectress of those killed by the batteries'. But
it does not: in the poem Barbara protects only Frenchmen,
not Germans ('*They* are burst asunder in the midst')[90] and here
'sudden death' means only that she kills. The poem is like that
section of the Aeneid which deals with the battle of Actium,
in which Virgil forgets what in almost every other line is the
very quality of his poetry: that both sides in a conflict have
feelings. Chesterton picks on this passage as demonstrating
Virgil's 'moral sanity'. 'Nobody can doubt his feelings when the
demons were driven in flight before the household gods.'[91]
Chesterton's pugnacity, which took very moving form in his
dying words in 1936 ('The issue is now quite clear. It is between
light and darkness and everyone must choose his side.'[92]) at
other times in his life so possesses him with the meaning of a
conflict that he both forgets the complexity of issues and
transmutes the physical reality of wounding which he never
saw, into a hard, bright allegory.

Nevertheless mere pugnacity (as opposed to definiteness of
choice) is only peripheral in him. When battle is joined,
Alfred's captains go down in succession before the three evils:
every quality in which Chesterton ordinarily trusted, first
English common kindliness before Elf's eerie misgiving, then
law, thought and Rome, which defeat Elf, before mere rage,
and finally romantic paradoxical Irish heroism before the full
rush of the Danes. Against these despairs stands 'the ultimate
moment of despair and its transmutation.'[93] In the stillness

which follows, Alfred finds like Michael a point altogether
outside ordinary feeling, and, like a child rebuilding a sand-
castle, determines to fight again. It recalls the first quietness in
Athelney in which his memory gave him a small image of his
childhood; and in it, smaller again, a manuscript illumination
of the Virgin and Child: and then suddenly the world became
solid:

> All things sprang at him, sun and weed,
> Till the grass grew to be grass indeed . . .[94]

and the picture existed in front of him. As with 'The Donkey'
the essence of a thing reveals a transcendent presence: Mary's,
who gives a message again beyond ordinary feeling.

As with Michael the infinite moment is the obverse of thanks-
giving for finitude. And Chesterton's rhetoric is employed at its
best in the defiance which Alfred gives Elf, Ogier and Guthrum:

> For our God hath blessed creation
> Calling it good. I know
> What spirit with whom you blindly band
> Hath blessed destruction with his hand;
> Yet by God's death the stars shall stand
> And the small apples grow.[95]

The words, which normally move quickly at the speed
appropriate to a narrative poem, become still and slow, so that
the effects of each word can be noticed—the opposite senses of
blessed, the surprising justice of *death* after *destruction*, and the
startling stop on a detail.

It is this combination of emotions in Alfred (a plausible
guess at the historic Alfred who wrote in the words quoted on
the original title-page of the *Ballad*: 'I say, as do all Christian
men, that it is a divine purpose that rules, and not Fate') which
justifies Chesterton's lines on the White Horse itself, left to fade
and darken by the Danes:

> it is only Christian men
> Guard even heathen things.[96]

The enemy is the forgotten growth, like that in Elf's song, which quietly devours the Horse

> the little sorrel, while all men slept,
> Unwrought the work of man.[97]

In this evil stillness the poem almost ends except that in one last verse Alfred properly ends it, defiant.

Chesterton tried to repeat the effects of the *White Horse* not only in the disastrous *St Barbara* but also in *Lepanto*. That is one of Chesterton's impeccable poems: the noise, and the contrast between gallant and sick colours, work perfectly, and the rhetoric is so perfect that anyone paying due attention to the lines while reading aloud has difficulty with tears at the sudden shift

> And he finds his God forgotten, and he seeks no more a sign—
> (But Don John of Austria has burst the battle-line!).[98]

The defiance of fate is there too, and two moments of stillness against the noise—Cervantes' ironic stillness at the end, and the Pope's in

> The hidden room in a man's house where God sits all the year.[99]

All the same, it is less lovable than the immensely flawed *White Horse*: too univocal, too forgetful that the Turks may have had human beings among them, and that the Christians certainly used galley-slaves.

The image of the hidden room, too, seems better used in the prose of *The Everlasting Man*, when Chesterton says that the story of Bethlehem 'surprises us from behind, from the hidden and personal part of our being . . . as if a man had found an inner room in the very heart of his own house which he had never suspected; and seen a light from within . . . it is the broken speech and the lost word that are made positive and suspended unbroken . . .'[100]

Once again, one cannot help suspecting that something of this went into *Ash Wednesday*, in the lines immediately following those quoted earlier about the garden:

The token of the word unheard, unspoken

and the first lines of the next section:

If the lost word is lost, if the spent word is spent
If the unheard, unspoken
Word is unspoken, unheard,[101]

But this time, Chesterton's effect does compare with Eliot's, not univocal but evocative, and subtly moving.

There is in fact in Chesterton's writing a centre which escapes the criticisms gathered under the head of externality. It is apparent again and again in the three major novels and in *The White Horse*, although, except in *The Man Who Was Thursday*, not without being muffled up in defects.

The doctrine at this centre he exposed in the comparably good apologetic books, *Orthodoxy* and *The Everlasting Man*. *Orthodoxy* in particular succeeds in the difficult feat of expounding a total and objective philosophy while always preserving the pressure and involvement of one man's concern. Christianity in the twentieth century is normally presented as claiming the whole of experience and yet as being explicitly about only a part of experience—the religious and the more difficult parts of the ethical. In that part however it presents doctrines which transcend experience. Christians have tried to reconcile this paradox in three principal ways: by reducing the transcendent element to the secular, by reducing the totality of experience to the religious, and by claiming that there are implicit elements in Christianity and the secular which make them coincide without reduction of either. The third, the only one which escapes the charge of dishonesty, is also the most difficult: it is always liable therefore to collapse into one of the other two. Chesterton (whose temptation is to the second course) in *Orthodoxy* keeps substantially to the third. 'Things', he said, 'can be irrelevant to the proposition that Christianity is false, but nothing can be irrelevant to the proposition that Christianity is true.'[102]

The centre of this relevance is 'the fact that one must somehow find a way of loving the world without trusting it': Chesterton's way is the belief that 'God was personal and had made a world separate from Himself.'[103] The most moving passage in the book is that in which Chesterton asserts the extremity of this relation of God to the world, in Gethsemane and in Christ's cry of dereliction. He tells us that if the atheists should wish to choose a god 'They will find only one divinity who ever uttered their isolation: only one religion in which God seemed for an instant to be an atheist.'[104]

This is clearly the same as the final assertion of *The Man Who Was Thursday* and involves the same theodicy: that omnipotence makes God incomplete, that God to be wholly God must know what to be a rebel is like, and what courage is—'that the soul passes a breaking-point—and does not break.'[105] Paradoxically, here and throughout *Orthodoxy* Chesterton's appeal is, as in the novels, to the idea of a complete man. He develops first the idea of obsessive madness as a limitation, and points the likeness to it of various philosophies alternative to Christianity. Then, asking for an idea which does justice to the opposite good qualities in man, he develops a notion of sanity and a generous ethic which find their fulfilment in the magnificence and meekness of Christ.

Behind the particular demands which Chesterton makes of a philosophy that is to fit the universe, he says, lie fairy-tales. His defence of fairy-tales is an important part of the tradition which runs from George MacDonald (and ultimately Coleridge) through himself to C. S. Lewis and J. R. R. Tolkien: and undoubtedly the peculiar quality of fairy-tale is important to the queerly magical quality of some of his best writing, and to the question whether one likes or even understands his work as a whole. His critical writing anyone can admire; but of his more personal works Auden is right in saying 'There are, I know, because I have met them, persons to whom Grimm and Andersen mean nothing: Chesterton will not be for them.'[106]

The quality in question is not what is ordinarily associated with fairy-tale: it does not involve belief in magic, and has nothing to do with superstition, fancifulness or unreality. It is not anarchistic nor irrational. It is a vision of something perpetually fresh: always a new heaven and a new earth, which are quite certainly the old ones. 'All the fire of the fairy-tales'[107] is derived from a primal vision of the world, perhaps the first vision of childhood, 'an almost prenatal leap of interest and amazement.'[108] It is a vision that we have forgotten, in which the common world was as wonderful as a fairy-tale. 'All that we call common sense . . . and positivism only means that for certain dead levels of our life we forget that we have forgotten.'[109] But fairy-tales, Chesterton says in the same phrase that he used to describe Browning's grotesquerie, 'touch the nerve of the ancient instinct of astonishment',[110] and for the same reason—'to draw attention to the intrinsically miraculous character of the object itself.'[111] 'These tales say that apples were golden only to refresh the forgotten moment when we found that they were green.'[112] The arbitrariness of physical fact in fairy-tales partly reflects this. The only satisfactory words for describing nature are 'charm', 'spell', 'enchantment':[113] all physical fact is contingent, everything is fresh because it might have been something else.

But there is a further consequence of this arbitrariness. Seen against this background, what remains constant (in fairy tales and in the world as seen in their light) are the laws of logic and morality. Chesterton's most vivid statement of these beliefs is in the first of the Father Brown stories, already quoted for the appropriateness of the symbolic landscape in which Father Brown tells Flambeau that the universe is not infinite in the sense of escaping from the laws of truth. 'Look at those stars', he goes on, 'Don't they look as if they were single diamonds and sapphires? Well, you can imagine any mad botany or geology you please. . . . On plains of opal, under cliffs cut out of pearl, you will still find a notice-board "Thou shalt not steal".'[114]

This pattern of a fairy setting which sheerly emphasizes the essential truth of daily experience is the pattern of a great deal of Chesterton's poems and stories: that of 'The Donkey', for example, is a special form of it. The Father Brown stories, in particular, though their apparent genre is detective fiction, have much more the quality of fairy-tales. The early ones, as we saw earlier, concentrate their effect on a landscape and an atmosphere at once symbolic and real. The later ones seem often to be deliberate attacks on the conventions of realistic fiction, defences such as Iris Murdoch and John Bayley have written since of the openness of human character. But they always have some clue to a stable interpretation in the human power of imaginative sympathy, 'The Secret of Father Brown'.

Of all Chesterton's best fiction, what he says of George MacDonald's novels holds true.

The commonplace allegory takes what it regards as the commonplaces or conventions necessary to ordinary men and women, and tries to make them pleasant or picturesque by dressing them up as princesses or goblins or good fairies. But George MacDonald did really believe that people were princesses and goblins and good fairies, and he dressed them up as ordinary men and women. The fairy-tale was the inside of the ordinary story and not the outside. One result of this is that all the inanimate objects that are the stage properties of the story retain that nameless glamour which they have in a literal fairy-tale.

The fairy-tale pattern seems to be the inward reason for Borges' formula for Chesterton's stories. Seen in this light they do not 'undertake to explain an inexplicable event by reason alone': rather they surround 'solutions of this world' with mystery.[116] This attempt of course is compounded with the other attempt to combat nightmare. Partly because of this mixed aim, and partly because (as Arthur Machen observes of his own similar stories), it is too easy to translate 'awe . . . into evil',[117] Chesterton's stories sometimes fail. But they succeed often enough to give the lie to the criticism of Chesterton's beliefs which underlies Borges' formula. They bear witness to a religion which is not fundamentally a rationalizing escape from nightmare: it is wonder and worship.

Although, then, the charge of externality, and even of a flight from the inner, holds against a great deal of Chesterton's work, anyone who makes it against his major writings is almost certainly missing their real inner quality. Charles Williams observes that poetry does not communicate emotions or belief, but knowledge of our capacity for an emotion or a belief.[118] Chesterton's inner quality is to communicate knowledge of our capacity for believing in God as creator and of enjoying our position as creatures. Ultimately this knowledge is based on the still, infinite moment, the experience of which he perhaps rather points to than communicates. Ultimately, that is, what he says is based on a faith or experience not of art but about the universe. But what he communicates could be understood and enjoyed short of accepting this experience.

It is possible to hate God as understood by Judaism and Christianity; to hate Him not because of any aberrations of theologians about Hell or the Atonement, but because of something essential to the idea of a God who is at once creator of the world and fountain of moral demand. We have seen something of Chesterton's dealings with the problem of the existence of external evil in a world created by the Good. We have seen that his belief in a personal Creator is actually the direct result of his apprehension of a world that is at once overwhelmingly good—whose very existence demands a loyalty and love that outweighs any particular defect—yet desperately horrible. Particularly in the chapter of *Orthodoxy* called 'The Flag of the World' we find his demand for 'a fiercer delight and a fiercer discontent' with the world satisfied *only* by belief in a Creator who makes moral demands of His creation.[119]

But there is a more radical hatred of God, for which the issue is not about any removable defect of the world, but about any possible state of being of an intelligent creature who is constrained by his own identity and laid under demand by moral law. Chesterton, in an attack on Milton's treatment of the Fall, argues that Adam fell by 'that profoundly inartistic anarchy that objects to a limit as such. It is not indicated [in the Bible] that the fruit was of attractive hue or taste: its attraction was that it was forbidden. . . . The finest thing about a free meadow is the hedge at the end of it. The moment the hedge is abolished it is no longer a meadow, but a waste, as Eden was after its one limitation was lost.'[120]

As this would suggest, Chesterton's strongest philosophical antipathy is to the Nietzschean tradition which denies God, constraint of identity and moral law at once. He represents the position not unfairly with another analogy from painting, in the conversation between Dorian Wimpole, Joan Brett and Lord Ivywood at a gallery of 'Post-futurist' abstract art:

'If you wake up tomorrow and you simply *are* Mrs Dope, an old woman who lets lodgings at Broadstairs . . . in what way have *you* progressed? . . . Don't you see this prime fact of identity is the limit set on all living things?'

'No! ... I deny that any limit is set upon living things. ... I would walk where no man has walked; and find something beyond tears and laughter. ... And my adventures shall not be in the hedges and the gutters; but in the borders of the ever-advancing brain. ... I will be as lonely as the first man. ... He discovered good and evil. So are these artists trying to discover some distinction that is still dark to us.'

'Oh ... then you don't *see* anything in the pictures yourself?'

'I see the breaking of the barriers ... beyond that I see nothing.'[121]

Very interestingly, it is in this novel (*The Flying Inn*) that Chesterton displays great skill in analysing radical changes of character: Dorian Wimpole's seven moods when he is left alone in a wood with a donkey, Joan Brett's decision between Patrick Dalroy and Lord Ivywood, and Ivywood's transition from gentleman to fanatic—of which the last is most impressive. It is as if he were trying to satisfy himself of what are the limits of change in human personality before the culminating event of the book—when Lord Ivywood, declaring himself 'above the silly Supermen', goes mad.[122]

About Chesterton's insistence on accepting identity as a limit, two things must be said. First, in conscious contrast with the decadents, he makes a demand for commitment at the heart of man's shifting unpredictable openness, which corresponds to his preference for clear outlines and enduring essences in the external world. In his exploration of the conditions for having an enduring self he closely resembles Kierkegaard. *Orthodoxy* insists on the necessity to living of real commitment with a real risk:[123] and in one light essay—'A Defence of Rash Vows'— he says most of what Kierkegaard says in *Either/Or* of the difference between the 'ethical' and the 'aesthetic'. 'The man who makes a vow makes an appointment with himself at some distant time or place.' But in modern times the 'terror of one's self, of the weakness and mutability of one's self, has perilously increased, and is the real basis of the objection to vows of any kind. ... And the end of all this is that maddening horror of unreality which descends upon the decadents. ...'[124] Throughout *The Everlasting Man* he argues that this difference of commitment exists between Christianity and paganism: polytheists do not believe in their gods in the same way as Christians believe in God, but as one believes in daydreams.

Christians believe in God, on the other hand, with the same seriousness as both they and polytheists believe in ethics.[125] The demand is again for the commitment, the seriousness which makes the difference between the aesthetic and ethical, and imposes on one the kind of limitation of identity which Adam and Lord Ivywood refuse.

But secondly, when he comes to consider despair, Chesterton recognizes that mere commitment is not enough: that human personality must pass into very strange regions indeed before it can continue its commitment to ethics or even to living. There is after all something of the idea of the Superman which is common to Chesterton's two ultimate men, Michael and King Alfred, and to his picture of St Francis as well. Like Lord Ivywood they are alone, and find something beyond tears and laughter. Their difference is that after having made the movements of infinity, they make those of finiteness. The phrases are Kierkegaard's, from his description of the knight of faith. It is probable that Kierkegaard is the thinker nearest to Chesterton: the most Chestertonian passage in literature is this same description, of the man who delights in watching the new omnibuses on his Sunday afternoon walk, is interested in everything that goes on, in a rat which slips under the curb, in the children's play, who looks like, indeed is, a bourgeois Philistine or the grocer over the way smoking in the twilight—yet who makes at every instant the movements of infinity. 'He knows the bliss of the infinite, he senses the pain of renouncing everything . . . and yet finiteness tastes to him just as good as to one who never knew anything higher.'[126]

Parabolically, when Innocent Smith throws away his house and marriage and walks round the world to find them again— to find a house with a green lamp post and a red pillar-box— he is acting out the secret Kierkegaard agonized to know—the secret by which he could marry Regine Olsen while still doing justice to his own frightful vocation and solitary temperament. He reconciles flinging the world away with taking it up again, and challenges besides the classical and Enlightenment incredulity that an infinite God could be interested in particular individuals and events. Smith believes both that we are all in exile, and that God has bidden us love one spot to defend us from worshipping infinity. 'Paradise is somewhere and not

anywhere, is something and not anything.'[127] Even 'God is not
infinite; He is the synthesis of infinity and boundary.'[128]
Smith's gesture is repeated by others of Chesterton's lunatic
heroes, as they sever themselves from their lives to find them
again—by Gabriel Syme, Gabriel Gale, Patrick Dalroy, Ewan
MacIan and by the Wild Knight. And he models his picture
of the mysticism of St Francis on the same experience.

> Sunder me from my bones, O sword of God,
> Till they stand stark and strange as do the trees[129]

writes Chesterton, and the quotation from *Hebrews*—'the word
of God is . . . sharper than any two edged sword, piercing even
to the dividing asunder of soul and spirit, and of the joints and
marrow'[130]—is not just a trope: the sense of pain is intended,
the pain of being separated from oneself in order to wonder at,
know and save oneself—'I know there's a fellow called Smith,
living in one of the tall houses in this terrace', says Innocent
Smith. 'I know he is really happy, and yet I can never catch
him at it.'[131]

The outcome of this is always wonder, and the end is the
peculiar simplicity—'costing not less than everything'[132]—of
Alfred, Michael and St Francis. They have believed, have
despaired, and have picked up the world again through something infinite which lies on the other side of despair. Grounded
in infinity, loving the finite, Man's whole happiness consists in
being a creature, in receiving the world as a child receives a
present, as 'a surprise'. 'But surprise implies that a thing came
from outside ourselves; and gratitude that it comes from
someone other than ourselves. . . . Those limits are the lines
of the very plan of human pleasure.'[133] This is the answer, and
the right answer, which Gabriel Gale gives to the terror of
solipsism in the story with which we began.

Kierkegaard has at the end of *Fear and Trembling* another
Chestertonian passage, in which he compares the discontent of
his generation, who have not reached faith, yet 'assume the
place which belongs by right only to the Spirit which governs
the world and has patience enough not to grow weary', to
children who always want a new game because they lack 'the
lovable seriousness which belongs essentially to play.'[134]

Chesterton likewise says that in considering the perpetual
repetition of the universe it is possible to feel that 'we have
sinned and grown old, and our Father is younger than we.'[135]
Alfred is compared to a child playing and a child playing to
God. A healthy man, again, is known from a lunatic because
his minor acts are 'careless and causeless'[136]: the final secret of
God, Christ and Christianity is joy.[137]

Perhaps the most convincing proof of Chesterton's own
wisdom and even sanctity is his capacity for sheer humour.
One must list among his triumphs *The Club of Queer Trades*, the
conversation of Humphrey Pump in *The Flying Inn*, 'The Rolling
English Road', and even such a remark as Misysra Ammon's
that 'the Arabic article "Al" as in Alhambra, as in Algebra
[has many appearances in connection with English] festive
institutions, as in your Alsop's beer, your Ally Sloper, and your
partly joyous institution of the Albert Memorial.'[138]

Kafka said apropos of *Orthodoxy* and *The Man Who Was
Thursday*, 'He is so gay, that one might almost believe he had
found God.'[139] In spite of darkness, what one primarily
remembers of Chesterton is that he was a happy man: and that
he looked forward to the end of the world, when God's *delight*
shall be with the sons of men.[140]

The Man

G. K. Chesterton—Journalist

G. C. HESELTINE

George Bernard Shaw's 'colossal genius' (as he called G.K.C.) always called himself a journalist, a mere journalist, even a roaring journalist. If a journalist may be defined as one whose business is writing for or editing journals, that, and his opening to a dedicatory poem 'Words, for alas my trade is Words' will suffice.

It was not the superficial or silly or jolly part of me that made me a journalist. . . . I like to see ideas or notions wrestling naked, as it were, and not dressed up in a masquerade as men and women. . . . I could be a journalist because I could not help being a controversialist. . . . I have always been and presumably will always be a journalist.

He began late. He was nearly five years old before he could talk clearly. But from then on he seems to have become a compulsive debater—at home with his younger brother, Cecil, at school in the Junior Debating Club, and for the rest of his life with anyone, whether G.B.S. or Binney, the office boy of *G.K.'s Weekly*, when given a chance. His poetry and essays started with the school magazine and continued ever after whenever editors had the luck to print them.

He tells us that his 'first regular job in support of a regular cause' was made possible by J. L. Hammond and his friends in the new *Speaker*. These included Oldershaw, a schoolfellow at St Paul's and journalist, F. Y. Eccles and E. C. Bentley. Through this group he met Hilaire Belloc. Soon after, when G.K.C. married in 1901 and lived in Battersea, near Belloc in Cheyne Walk, their famous friendship matured. But they were very different both in range and style. Where Belloc wielded a broadsword, Chesterton flashed a swordstick, with more effect. 'It was there that I wrote along with many pugnacious political articles a series of casual essays afterwards republished as "The Defendant".' He had in fact, when at school, contributed a poem 'The Song of Labour' to the old *Speaker*, and art reviews to the *Academy* and the *Bookman*, but not by way of his 'trade of words'. It was when he began to work for Hammond that he was 'let loose on the world'. The *Speaker* paid him (as he wrote to his mother) £150 a year and he was soon to make it more. He was about to write his famous column for the *Daily News* and on the way to reaching the target of £500 a year which his mother regarded as the minimum for marriage, which seems, only seems, to confirm his hero Dr Johnson's dictum that 'no man but a blockhead ever wrote except for money.' I say *only seems* because G.K.C. later wrote for many causes for nothing, never for 'just the money.'

The Defendant was the first Chesterton I read, as a schoolboy. I was at once fascinated by the wit, the commonsense and the irresistible compulsion to go on reading—the provocation to argument—hallmarks of good polemical journalism. The first essay in the book was 'A Defence of Penny Dreadfuls'. I was not addicted to Sexton Blake and Deadshot Dick and the rest of the heroes so 'quick on the draw'. Apparently G.K.C. always was. He could be seen in Fleet Street with bundles of them bulging out of the capacious pockets of his enormous flapping cloak. That defence of Penny Dreadfuls of seventy years ago is typical of the topicality which permeated all his work to the very end. Naughty boys were already beginning to be excused, and only the 'penny dreadfuls' were to blame!

The Defendant includes defences of Rash Vows, Skeletons, Publicity, Nonsense, Planets, China Shepherdesses, Useful Information, Heraldry, Ugly Things, Farce, Humility, Slang, Baby Worship, Detective Stories, Patriotism. They all show an incredible range of reading, by references galore to the classics and the moderns. The poetry of the artist emerges in the Defence of Skeletons.

The tops of two or three high trees when they are leafless are so soft that they seem like the gigantic brooms of that fabulous lady who was sweeping the cobwebs off the sky . . . so dim and delicate is the heart of the winter woods . . . that a figure stepping towards us in the chequered twilight seems as if he were stepping through unfathomable depths of spider's webs. . . . Surely the idea that its leaves are the chief grace of a tree is a vulgar one, on a par with the idea that his hair is the chief grace of a pianist. . . . A strange idea

has infected humanity that the skeleton is typical of death. The truth
is that man's horror of the skeleton is not horror of death at all. . . .
The fundamental matter which troubles him is the reminder that
the ground plan of his appearance is shamelessly grotesque . . .
however much my face clouds with sombre vanity or vulgar
vengeance, or contemptible contempt, the bones of my skull
beneath it are laughing forever.

Defending Nonsense, he says:

While Lewis Carroll's Wonderland is purely intellectual . . . a
country populated by insane mathematicians . . . Lear introduces
quite another element, of the poetical and even emotional. Carroll
works by the pure reason . . . mankind in the main has always
regarded reason as a bit of a joke . . . to draw out the soul of things
with a syllogism is as impossible as to draw out Leviathan with a
hook.

It has been the habit of most critics of G.K.C. to sneer at his
excess of paradox and puns, most marked in his journalism. He
would not think it at all excessive if he succeeded in shocking
the reader into shaking out the full meaning from the words
which he clearly chose to this end. It is true that to the hyper-
critical literary mind this may not all be good 'literature'. But
I suggest that the best literature is that which succeeds best in
communicating to the reader exactly what the writer wishes
to say in the most effective way. If the mode is sometimes
irritating—and I confess that at times (though rarely) it
irritated me—no one can question or rival the success. Certainly
not if judged by the demand from editors. He said he never
made a joke for the sake of being funny—'though some may
have thought it funny because I said it'—and the same applied
to puns and paradox. He may have got all the fun he could
out of them, but for good reason. On any showing he had no
trace of the Humpty-Dumpty 'impenetrability' style of journalism now current, in which a word 'means just what I choose it
to mean neither more nor less.'
    I do not think G.K.C. ever saw a rejection slip or indeed
ever had to hawk his wares around. From the earliest days of
the *Speaker* articles he had an accelerating demand. He writes
to his mother in 1901: 'It is at least a remarkable fact that

every one of the papers I wrote for (he lists them) came to me and asked me to write for them from the *Daily News* down to the *Manchester Sunday Chronicle*.' Within a few years he had contributed to some thirty other periodicals here and overseas.

It was in the *Speaker* days that G.K.C. became a real Fleet Street man, joining his colleagues on that paper. Fleet Street was a city within a city, with a teeming population of men (very few women) who had enormous enthusiasm for the craft of journalism. From editors through subs, reporters, crime and Lobby men, columnists, freelancers, cartoonists, compositors, printers, engineers, oilers and loaders, there was a common bond of the craft hard to find in any other industry. This flourished until the creeping dutch-elm disease of take-over and monopoly began to spread throughout the Street in the 'Twenties when dog was driven to eating dog and the axes fell suddenly, leaving fine professionals jobless and freelancers forced out to sell themselves in an alien market.

The regular journalists 'whose trade is words' kept their wits whetted and ideas fruitful by foregathering in the best places— the pubs. Not, as wives and dons supposed, to drink themselves drunk (though some did that). They were to be found at all hours in the Cheshire Cheese, the George, El Vinos, Peele's, the Bodega, the Devereux—and a dozen more, drifting on to the Pharos Club in Henrietta Street, full of Socialists, Fabians and Radicals. There G.K.C., with his brother Cecil, met, and of course argued with incessantly, all the lively gaggle of scribblers who provided the news, fed the spring of public interest and discussion for the Press which in those days led the world of ideas—T. W. H. Crosland (author of the 'Unspeakable Scot' and the very best book on the English Sonnet), Will Dyson, master cartoonist of the *Daily Herald*, Strube and Low, Thomas Derrick, Philip Gibbs, Arthur Machen, W. R. Titterton and, later, D. B. Wyndham Lewis ('Beachcomber' of the *Daily Express* and 'Timothy Shy' of the *News Chronicle*), his successor as Beachcomber, J. B. Morton, J. K. Prothero (Ada Jones, who later married Cecil, G.K's brother), a few amongst those I remember. With these men, G.K.C., a larger journalist than any, gained a stimulus which he found nowhere else. The Press Lords who later felt the sting of G.K.'s rapier were driven to referring to him and Belloc as a couple of drunken buffoons. In all the twenty years between the first world war and the second I never found either the worse for good drink, and they were no doubt as much the better for it as many of their fellows.

Putting in 'A Word for a Mere Journalist' in the *Darlington North Star*, G.K.C. said:

The poet . . . may or may not have an intellectual right to despise the journalist: but I greatly doubt whether he would not be morally better if he saw the great lights burning on through darkness into dawn, and heard the roar of the printing wheels weaving the destinies of another day. Here at least is a school of labour and of some rough humility, the largest work ever published anonymously since the great Christian Cathedrals.

Here we have the Good Journalist using his licence to the full. But that was before seventy years of the Big Business and Efficiency Tycoons had spread their blight over the Street of Adventure.

G.K.C. wrote in the Street, in the pubs and in the clubs— they saw him chortling (as he lawfully might) over what he wrote. One could not be with him for long before realizing that he was always in live earnest. He meant what he wrote.

Since he burst into Fleet Street like a bomb and soared like a rocket, here is his secret. In his autobiography (mostly about other people) he tells us:

On the whole I think I owe my success (as millionaires say) to having listened respectfully to the very best advice given by all the best journalists; and then going away and doing the exact opposite. For what they all told me was that the secret of success in journalism was to study the particular journal and write what was suitable to it. . . . I have a notion that the real advice I could give to a young journalist is to write an article for the *Sporting Times* and another for the *Church Times* and put them into the wrong envelopes. . . . This is perhaps a little faint and fantastic as a theory; but it is the only theory upon which I can explain my own undeserved survival in the journalistic squabble in the old Fleet Street. I wrote on a non-conformist organ like the old *Daily News* and told them all about French Cafes and Catholic Cathedrals and they loved it. I wrote on a robust Labour Organ like the old *Clarion* and defended medieval theology . . . and their readers did not mind me a bit.

That advice should, of course, be treated as he treated the best advice given to him. But for himself he added 'I discovered the easiest of all professions which I have pursued ever since.'

In 1908 he moved, or was moved, from Battersea to Beaconsfield. It was always said, probably fairly, that his wife moved him. It may be true also that, as his brother Cecil is reported as saying: 'We all know that Frances can't bear Fleet Street.' No doubt his Fleet Street friends were very jealous of the loss of his company there, and not far away in Chelsea, Belloc, already with another base in Sussex, deplored it. The lady who later became Cecil's wife, 'J. K. Prothero', herself a brilliant journalist whom G.K.C. called 'The Queen of Fleet Street' (as she was), is for the same reason most unreliable on the matter of her sister-in-law and Beaconsfield. There is no doubt that his wife, by this move from Fleet Street, saved G.K.C. for us, for journalism, literature and posterity, for many years. It is most likely that G.K.C. left the stimulating comradeship and humanity of the Street with great regret but at least some relief from physical strain. It was in no sense a complete severance for he continued to visit London frequently. He was still at heart a Londoner born and bred.

The demands upon him at this time were enormous—weekly articles for the *Speaker*, *Daily News*, *Daily Herald* and after 1905 the *Illustrated London News*, plus frequent articles for other dailies, books reviews for the *Morning Post* and others. Added to this, enough for any journalist, he had written eight books including *Browning*, *The Napoleon of Notting Hill* and *Orthodoxy*. I heard him say (circa 1924) that he considered *Orthodoxy* to be 'the book I thought most needed writing'. Such output clearly involved very extensive reading as well as writing, *Orthodoxy* more than most. In London and the Street he certainly could not have dictated some thirteen to fourteen thousand words of a book a week, in addition to his weekly journalism, as he did at Beaconsfield.

Just before the first world war G.K.C.'s enthusiasm for 'Liberal' journalism, especially in the *Daily News*, began to wane. He had become disillusioned not so much with Liberalism as with the pacifists in the Party and particularly the political plutocratic Liberals and the Party's dependence on wealthy sponsors, such as the Cocoa Press. After a squib in praise of wine—despising cocoa (though this was not the cause) he gave up the *Daily News* column. He continued in the *Daily Herald* not so much because he liked Socialism as he did the sincerity and liberal-mindedness of the men who then supported it, before the infiltration of the undemocratic tyrannical version of Marxism into the original Trades Union movement. He now felt that what he called 'that hunger of humanity which is the true Liberalism' was disappearing from the rest of the Press. He also objected to the pacifism which came before patriotism. He could never be a 'peace at any price' man. The aggressive mood of Germany against small nations fired him to fight in their defence; just as he had resisted our own aggression (as he saw it) in the Boer War. He was never an imperialist but would support a true commonwealth, a patriot before a nationalist.

It was at this time that he and his brother Cecil with their friends of the now defunct *Speaker* launched the *Eye Witness* with Belloc as first editor. It was to be independent, free from any pressures of political party or big business, though a business man who was of their independent mind was a backer. It was to provide an open forum for free speech against corruption—political and financial, oppression and injustice—applied to countries as well as individuals, and to work for the liberty of the subject.

Belloc, who had recently served as a Liberal Member of Parliament, joined with Cecil Chesterton to write a vigorous book on the party system which exposed the menace to democracy in the selection of candidates and the whip system, denying a member the right to vote according to his conscience or in the proper interests of his constituency. They attacked also the patronage at the disposal of the party in power. G.K.C. wholeheartedly supported them in this and their conduct of the paper. But Belloc was no editor. With an output which rivalled G.K.C.'s, and family and other interests, he was far too busy. After twenty-six issues he handed over to Cecil, with G.K.C. as chairman. Early contributors included Maurice Baring, H. G. Wells, Algernon Blackwood, George Bernard Shaw, Arnold Bennett, Desmond McCarthy, A. C. Benson, Edward Thomas, Cunninghame-Grahame, Quiller-Couch, H. A. L. Fisher, to name a few only. The paper so full of brilliance, enthusiasm and courage soon built up an exceptional circulation for its age, all set for success on its merits.

But merit was already ceasing to be enough for success or even survival. The business side was hopeless. Even the backer failed them. Difficulty over the copyright in the title arose, so the *Eye Witness* ended. The same friends followed immediately with the *New Witness* with the same format and principles, and lack of money, as before. Edward Chesterton (father of G.K.C. and Cecil) provided for the carry-over until Odham's Press took on the printing. This paper survived for another five years.

I did not meet G.K.C. personally until 1917-18. I had read all his books, from *The Defendant*, as they appeared and his articles in the *Eye Witness*—memorably his verse (the splendid 'Lepanto'!). When I left my native Yorkshire for London in 1913, to be independent and work for my living whilst reading for a science degree at night classes at the East London College, I had the good luck to meet in my job as a hospital clerk a fellow Chester-Belloc enthusiast. We were both avid readers of everything they wrote. We found a third in the librarian of a small new public library near the hospital in Homerton. He took the *New Witness* every week and obtained G.K.C.'s and Belloc's books as they appeared. The Marconi affair was in full swing.

The *New Witness* launched a vigorous attack on ministers and others who had gambled in American Marconi shares on inside information about a contract between the GPO and the American Marconi Company, formed to develop the new communications with America. The chief attacker was Cecil, who accused Herbert Samuel, Postmaster General, Lloyd George, Rufus Isaacs, Attorney General and his brother Godfrey Isaacs, who sold the shares, and others of operating in shares which the contract (so far not made public) would soon send soaring—as it did. But Cecil bungled, attacking (as Belloc said) with vigour, not always with discretion. He had gone too far, among many justifiable accusations, in stating true but irrelevant facts about Godfrey Isaacs' career as a company promoter and Isaacs sued him for criminal libel. At the trial Cecil was unable to produce the necessary witnesses to support his allegation and was found guilty and fined a nominal sum of £100, but the publicity of the trial had served the purpose.

The subsequent report of the Government enquiry and the Hansard record of the debate on it in the House of Commons which followed make excellent reading. That record no amount of subsequent whitewash could obliterate. G.K.C. had supported his brother out of loyalty as well as detestation of the Marconi affair as a whole, though he never indulged in the reckless language of Cecil's attack.

This matter is relevant because it has brought upon Belloc and G.K.C. a thoroughly unjustified charge of anti-Semitism. This arose from Cecil's unrestrained emphasis on the Jewish element in the targets of his attack. I cannot speak for Cecil, whom I met only once, just before he went as a soldier to Flanders and his death at the end of the 1914–18 war. I have already publicly refuted the charge against Belloc and he has more ably refuted it himself.

Unhappily, distinguished writers, even amongst those who admire G.K.C., persist in accepting the false charge albeit regretfully. It is not true. Condemning American gangsters does not make me anti-American, or the Catholic murderers in Ireland make me anti-Catholic. Gilbert Chesterton, with whom I was closely associated from the days of the *New Witness* to the end of *G.K.'s Weekly* (which died with him), was quite incapable of being anti-racial in any sense. His incredibly charitable and humble mind made that impossible. The mere fact that so many of the objects of his criticism were Jews in the financial and monopoly fields was solely because there were—and I believe are—more of them in those circles open to criticism. G.K.C. attacked the conduct of the Oppenheimers, Beit and the rest in South Africa, Godfrey and Rufus Isaacs and the Samuels and others including Lloyd George involved in the Marconi scandal, Mond in the chemical industry takeovers, and equally all monopolists, Gentile or Jew. He and Belloc criticized Beaverbrook (who was neither) but that did not make them anti-Canadian. G.K.C. fully recognized that the Jews were forced into the financial world by their history of oppression, persecution and segregation which left them with only their wits to live on; that consequential inbreeding, and close family ties and culture, intensified their intelligence—by the law of genetics—hence brilliant musicians, mathematicians and scientists, that the cleverest of them of our own culture may be

the more dangerous. Many of G.K.C.'s life-long friends were
Jews. He never forgot that Our Lord Jesus Christ and His
Mother were born and died Jews.

In the early *New Witness* G.K.C. gave us 'Lepanto' and began
The Return of Don Quixote as a serial. The paper took up cases
of oppressive police action, such as that of the young man who
stole Bernard Shaw's doormat and gave himself up. Shaw did
his best to stop the prosecution. The comment, obviously
Cecil's, showed a grossly erroneous view of the law and the
conduct of the police courts and the extent of responsibility of
the Home Secretary. Another case, that of Oscar Slater, was
used with the same irresponsibility. In a strange way G.K.C.'s
love for and loyalty to his brother caused him to take a quite
unreasonably jaundiced and erroneous view of the law (particularly libel) which he carried over to *G.K.'s Weekly*. This
sometimes weakened what was in fact and law a good case
against an injustice. In a later case of a high-spirited Irish girl
who smacked a policeman's face in righteous indignation at an
insulting accusation and was sent to a home for mental defec-
tives, escaped and earned a good living for five months until
she was found and taken back into custody, G.K.C. went to
the Home Office where some senior official showed him the
simple intelligence questions which the girl had failed to answer
and he innocently gave the wrong answer himself. She was not
returned to custody.

Early in the 1914 war G.K.C. published two pamphlets. The
first, *The Barbarism of Berlin*, showed why and what we
had to fight, not merely for self-preservation but as an over-
riding moral obligation. Compact of history, logic and simple
English, it demolished the German excuses. Then followed *The
Crimes of England*—the paradox showing that the crimes we had
now to repent lay in our repeated toleration of earlier Prussian
crimes of rape on all their weaker neighbours in Europe and
our making the Germans allies and their petty princelings our
kings. Though he did not live to see the end of our later appease-
ment he did see his prophetic warning beginning to come true.
In 1914/15 he had been very ill, yet on taking over from Cecil
he was still working at full pressure and living out of London.
No doubt Mrs Cecil and Titterton did the actual day to day
editing of the paper, but the war had hit Fleet Street and the

literary journals very hard, and the lack of business acumen was gradually making it almost impossible to continue.

The League for Clean Government had been formed largely as a result of the Marconi exposure and now became the New Witness League.

Early in 1918, being 'grounded' and unfit for further flying service, I was posted near London. This enabled me to visit Fleet Street and the lively public meetings of the League for Clean Government at the Essex Hall, Cannon Street Hotel and Holborn Restaurant. The object was to attack political corruption (as exposed by the Marconi affair and the sale of honours by Lloyd George's party), to restore personal liberties abrogated by the War, to obtain the repeal of oppressive Acts, to secure the rights of small nationalities and the protection of private property. On April 11, 1918 the New Witness League was formed replacing the old League for Clean Government. I was an early member, thus meeting G.K.C., Belloc and many contributors including Cecil Chesterton, invalided home from Flanders, soon to return and die there. About this time the *New Witness* paid me three guineas for my first effort in journalism. G.K.C. as first president of the League spoke of the boycott of the *New Witness* by the more powerful organs of the press. This was followed later by a boycott by the bookstalls (which we defeated).

The ideas debated at the meetings had all along run through G.K.'s journalism and continued to do so with wide-ranging exposition of his philosophy and the religious inspiration behind it. That had long been Christian but was not typically Catholic.

The end of the war was the half-way point in time of G.K.'s journalistic work. Many of his friends, particularly J. Desmond Gleeson, held that the first was the better half and there is something to be said for that opinion. But it was not, as some think, because of the influence of Belloc on him or of his formal adoption of the Catholic Faith in 1922. He had from his schooldays (and not from family tradition) the *anima naturaliter christiana*—even *catholica*. *Orthodoxy* (1908) would have been given the *nihil obstat* and *imprimatur* without difficulty.

By 1920 the *New Witness* could only carry on by not paying contributors. Most of them continued for a while. The standard did not flag. G.K.C. was of course the major attraction,

writing all the leaders and much more. But the aftermath of
winning the war and losing the peace increased the difficulties.
Circulation (and advertisements) fell. The Business Manager
(who was elderly and deaf) had carried on faithfully, but
loyalty was his only asset. On May 4, 1923 the paper died,
forecasting its resurrection as *G.K.'s Weekly* for which a company
was formed. H. G. Wells wrote:

I love G.K.C. and hate the Catholicism of Belloc and Rome so that
I sit by your bedside, the Phoenix from which *G.K.'s Weekly* is to be
born, with very mingled feelings. Now if it was only Rothermere's
last squeak how happily we might rejoice together. If Catholicism
is still to run about the world giving tongue, it can have no better
spokesman than G.K.C. But I begrudge Catholicism G.K.C.!

The response to appeals for capital was good. But inexplicable
delays accumulated. A year later G.K.C. broke it to J.K.P.
(Mrs Cecil): 'I think one Chesterton on the paper is enough'.
No doubt his reluctance to say this earlier accounted for much
of the delay. The lady was a brilliant journalist, but a very
forceful character. By now she was veering politically left.
Perhaps it was felt by G.K.C. as well as others that if she stayed
as assistant editor it would not be *G.K.'s Weekly*.

G.K.C. always insisted that he was carrying on out of loyalty
to his brother's ideals—also his own and Belloc's and many
others'—that had inspired the New Witness League. They
included also the ideas later called Distributism, as a proper
course of social reform.

G.K.'s Weekly appeared at long last in March 1925. In spite
of the waste of original enthusiasm it received a great welcome
from the literary world including rival weeklies. Belloc rallied
round at first with instalments of 'Mrs Markham' and other
items, Sir Henry Slessor dealt with Parliament, J.K.P. reviewed
drama, and several others reviewed books. Publishers advertised. G.K.C. wrote the bulk of the paper—the leader, many
Notes of the Week, a column 'Found Wandering', 'Top' and
'Tail' and book reviews—probably rather more than all his
other weekly journalism.

The Catholic press since 1922 had plagued him more than
ever for copy. Some even sold and serialized his articles at a

profit to themselves, none to G.K.C. He visited the office frequently on press day and was never late with his copy. Once when we were about twenty lines short on a page he lit one of his strong cheroots, went out for a walk, returned in twenty minutes and dictated a sonnet.

W. R. Titterton was assistant editor, and the first two issues had page numbers hopelessly mixed and the first volume appeared equally muddled with a quite inaccurate index. W.R.T. was a good journalist who boasted he had been sacked by nearly every editor in Fleet Street; lively and friendly, he sang his own songs well but was sensitive and vain, a Bohemian poet manqué—but no better as a stand-in than G.K.C. as an editor. When he allowed a contributor to be offensive to H. G. Wells, G.K.C. wrote apologising to Wells: 'I am honestly in a very difficult position, because it is physically impossible for me really to edit it and also do enough outside work to be able to edit.' He often had to pay the printer by writing another 'Father Brown' story.

Despite the warm welcome and lively start *G.K.'s Weekly* soon began to feel the throttling effects of the hangover of inefficiency from the *New Witness*. Alderman Chivers, a distinguished bookbinder and perennial mayor of Bath, continued his generosity as Chairman of the Board. But Bath was too far away. Other patrons and younger enthusiasts were determined to save G.K.C.'s special platform. All his journalism was indeed a platform to G.K.C., but this was his very own.

By the end of the first volume G.K.C. had started serializing 'The Outline of Sanity', meaning the sanity of his social philosophy of Distributism; this was the kernel of the movement which it stimulated.

A 'Letter to the Editor' from the provinces, and a more positive move by the late H.S.D. Went (Captain of Marines) started what was ultimately the Distributist League, whose first job was to support the paper and propagate G.K.'s social theory.* Before long branches had been formed in all the major towns and universities. This greatly extended the editor's labours, at his expense. He had crowded meetings in the biggest halls everywhere. The only time I ever saw or heard

*See Brocard Sewell's and Patrick Cahill's contributions to this volume for more about Distributism.

him in any way 'cross' was at the Randolph, Oxford, when a cocky young man boasted how he had got past G.K.C.'s secretary by a trick. G.K.C.'s severe rebuke was an indignant vindication of his secretary, not mentioning his own discomfort. He then gave the meeting an uproarious and hilarious evening.

At this time I was secretary of the League. The full story of its activities for Distributism must be told elsewhere. In that capacity I was co-opted to the board of the paper. The kind old business manager was gently but firmly replaced by a far worse, selected by W.R.T. and another no better in business affairs. Within a couple of months it was necessary to accuse the new man of falsifying accounts and concealing debts to show how well he was salvaging our finances! G.K.C. was painfully distressed, as I feared he would be, but production of the books and further enquiries amongst our advertisers proved the charge true. He had to go. Drastic changes followed and dissensions arose. As an experiment, the price was reduced from sixpence to twopence—each reader to buy three copies and give away two to extend circulation. In the next year the paper actually, for the first and only time I believe, broke level. My recollection is that it showed a balance of income over expenditure of £11, nobody being paid except the printers. But that could not last. There was internecine strife by extremists who wanted to fight the menace of monopoly and big business by outlawing machinery and going the whole hog—even so far as sharing his sty—and others who would concentrate on the limitation of combines and re-direct invention towards small units instead of serving only to enrich Big Business and near-Monopoly still more. Even the many practical attempts at settling unemployed on their own small holdings were wrecked by the dissension and disloyalty (even dishonesty) of the beneficiaries. But Government officials (who read *G.K.'s Weekly*) adopted the plan of one of the schemes and successfully established the Land Settlement Association with the necessary rules and discipline. It was on the Distributist plan but could enforce the discipline.

Too many of G.K.C.'s devotees, which included drifters and failures who hung around the office, had a perverted notion of G.K.C.'s enthusiasm for freedom. He hated making any decisions which might hurt the least of his 'friends'. Some of the Catholic element strove to drive out brilliant non-Catholic contributors, though G.K.C. always insisted firmly that the paper was not a Catholic paper. Such matters as the conduct of Catholic Mussolini against Abyssinia were points of bitter dispute. I wanted to leave quietly for good personal reasons. G.K.C. urged me to stay. After 1929 I did give up the secretary-ship (to an excellent non-Catholic, Keston Clarke). At G.K.C.'s request, until his death in 1936, I continued to give my support with articles, book reviews, fund-raising activities and speeches at branch meetings in the provinces. Upon G.K.C.'s death, the Board, Richard O'Sullivan, KC, Maurice Reckitt and I at once met and agreed to ask Belloc and Mrs G.K.C. their wishes about the paper. Before the reply we met at the request of a country printer (who had never helped the paper). He abruptly asked 'What's your price?' and after being told that the paper was not for sale, was politely shown the door by the Chairman. In due course we transferred our shares to Belloc and his son-in-law with the proviso that the title *G.K.'s Weekly* should not be continued. They took over as the *Weekly Review*, and kept the now much dimmed light of Distributism flickering.

The best of G.K.C.'s periodical journalism is published in over a score of collections from *The Defendant* to the more recent posthumous *Glass Walking Stick* and *Chesterton on Shakespeare*, both edited by Miss Dorothy Collins. His journalism was always read avidly, and in places where it had effect. As I have mentioned, there was a boycott of *The New Witness* and its personnel both in Fleet Street and in W. H. Smith bookstalls—though leader writers and columnists could not resist an occasional lift with or without acknowledgment. I was present when the news leaked into G.K.'s office that Beaverbrook had sent his friend Rothermere a collection of cuttings from the *New Statesman* and *G.K.'s Weekly* saying: 'All this stuff emanates from one source. I have given an order to the *Express* newspapers that neither G. K. Chesterton nor Hilaire Belloc are to appear in the columns of those papers. They spend so much time in writing articles in abuse of me elsewhere that I feel they have not time to do good work for the newspapers with which I am connected. In the *Evening Standard Diary* there was a perfect passion for mentioning the names of Chesterton and Belloc. I have cut down the space allotted to advertising them. Now their names seldom appear. Besides their journalism is so dull and their statements are utterly unreliable.'

Beaverbrook's biographer, A. J. P. Taylor, who quotes this in his hero's favour and does not scruple to defame the dead, adding his own comment, after an unsupportable innuendo about litigation and libel actions, 'Chesterton and Belloc were not aggrieved at lack of mention. They were aggrieved at lack of pay. Neither scrupled to take Beaverbrook's money even when they were abusing him.' When challenged, he failed to produce any evidence of this.

Apart from his unscholarly inability to distinguish between criticism and abuse Mr Taylor should now be told that in fact far from being aggrieved Gilbert Chesterton roared spontaneously with laughter when told of Beaverbrook's pathetic squeal. As for lack of pay he did not, and would not, take Beaverbrook's money. At that very time he had, as always, far more world-wide demand for his journalism than he could supply. He had produced more than fifty books, many still selling. Everyone in Fleet Street who knew him knew that nobody ever cared less about money. His disregard of it was notorious and his generosity, charity and humility unbounded.

It may properly be said that G.K.C. wrote all his life 'Words that never lie, or brag, or flatter or malign' (however dull!) to expound and propagate his *philosophia perennis*, for the defence of the common man and his freedom against the tyranny of plutocracy and Capitalism and the Communism that these evils spawn. He did this not for riches nor political power nor peerage, but in the unselfish service of his Maker and Mankind.

Devereux Nights

A Distributist Memoir

BROCARD SEWELL

In September 1928, fresh from my minor public school at the age of sixteen, I entered on my first job: that of personal assistant to the Secretary of the Distributist League, a post which I combined with that of office-boy and general factotum to *G.K.'s Weekly*.

A few weeks earlier Chesterton's assistant editor, W. R. Titterton, the man actually responsible for the production of the paper each week, had resigned under stormy circumstances. (These have been recounted, very magnanimously by Titterton himself in his *G. K. Chesterton: A Portrait*, and by Desmond Gleeson in Maisie Ward's *Return to Chesterton*.) An editorial board, consisting of able and devoted men, most of them professional journalists, had taken over the running of the paper, with Edward Macdonald as the Assistant Editor in charge.

In 1928 the *Weekly* was struggling along in an uphill fight against insufficient capital, insufficient circulation, and a lack of advertisement revenue. The paper existed to propagate Distributism, the social and political ideology offered by Hilaire Belloc and by Cecil Chesterton and G.K.C. as an alternative to the twin evils of Capitalism and Socialism. In 1926 the Distributist League had been founded to support the *Weekly* in this task, and partly, also, to gain support and an extended readership for the paper. In 1928, whereas the paper was not doing well, the League had reached its apogee.

I had arrived on the scene just too late to be able to attend the first really large-scale Distributist public meeting, the Shaw-Chesterton debate at Kingsway Hall, which was broadcast by the B.B.C. and gave Distributism publicity on a national scale for the first, and only, time. In 1928 the League had over two thousand members; not a large number for a national movement, but the largest it ever had. There were branches all over the country, and in Scotland also. The Secretary of the

League, George Heseltine, had no staff apart from myself. Heseltine was a forceful public speaker, and an able journalist. Previously he had been a successful smallholder, so that he could speak with authority on agricultural matters. A new national agricultural policy was one of the main planks in the Distributist platform.

With an energetic and extremely competent Secretary in charge, and with a weekly paper bearing G.K.C.'s name as its organ, and after the huge publicity of the Shaw-Chesterton debate, Distributism ought by 1929 to have begun to 'catch on'. It never did. Why not? Partly, perhaps, because by then the idea of a society based on widespread small ownership was too alien to the general trend of the times, which was towards bigger and bigger business, and larger and larger industrial units, and more and more industrialization: whether under 'Capitalist' or 'Socialist' control made no fundamental difference.

But there were more immediate reasons. When Heseltine resigned the secretaryship there was not enough money for the League to continue to pay a whole-time organizer, and the lack of such an official soon made itself felt, in spite of the hard work put in by a series of devoted Honorary Secretaries. The lack of funds was chronic. Looking back, one wonders how it could ever have been imagined that a national movement of this kind could be run on a basic revenue of £100 per annum. (The annual subscription was fixed, unbelievably, at One Shilling.)

It was also a mistake, I think, not to have organized the League as a political party, with the intention of presenting candidates for election to Parliament. But Chesterton had no wish to enter politics, and most Distributists were inclined to share Belloc's view that nothing could be accomplished through the House of Commons. But there was no lack of Distributists who would have made good parliamentary candidates, and if only one of them had been returned to Westminster the movement would have benefited. About this time there was a solitary Communist MP, Mr Saklatvala, and if he did nothing else he certainly gained a national hearing for Communism.

The Communist Party of Great Britain has never attracted a wide following or accomplished very much; but at least it managed to found and to maintain a daily newspaper. The Distributist League published some well thought out and attractive programmes of social reform, but had no means of presenting them effectively to the public. The League's various branches, with the exception of the Birmingham branch, which possessed two men of first-rate mind in K. L. Kenrick and Harold Robbins, were really little more than a collection of affiliated debating societies.

In London there were two branches: the North London Branch, which met at The Spaniards, on Hampstead Heath, and the Central Branch, which met at The Devereux Inn, just outside The Temple, in Devereux Court, a minute's walk from Little Essex Street. It had originally been The Grecian Coffee House; Dr Johnson may well have taken a dish of tea or coffee there from time to time. In spite of damage caused by the blitz, The Devereux looks today just as it did in the Nineteen Twenties and Thirties, and as it must have done in the Eighteen Nineties and even earlier. Inside, there has been some modernization on the ground floor.

Before the second world war, when you entered The Devereux you found to the left of the ground-floor passage the spacious bar; to the right the dining room, which was fitted up with high-backed settles, so that each of the tables, covered with its white cloth, was in a cosy nook by itself. The food was good, and you could choose your own mutton chop or beef steak, and the chef would cook it for you on the open range. The clientèle was in part old-fashioned: quaint old lawyers of a bygone generation, with clothes and hats of antique style and cut. In spite of the presence of their younger confrères, formally dressed in more modern fashion, the atmosphere could be described as Dickensian. Distributists, however, being mostly poor, seldom ate there, preferring a glass of beer and a sandwich at The Cheshire Cheese in Little Essex Street, or, against all their principles, a light refection in one of the ABC or Lyons' teashops in the Strand.

The Central Branch of the Distributist League met at The Devereux on Friday evenings at 7 p.m. throughout the year, except in the month of August. Various other societies met there too. On the notice board in the passage on the ground floor we were always listed as 'G.K.'s League'; perhaps the landlord,

Mr Sammon, was unable to master the awkward word Distributist. We met in a large room on the first floor. An adjoining room was fitted up as a Masonic Temple. Sometimes —the Craft did not meet on Fridays—the door of the Lodge would be accidentally left ajar, and through it one could glimpse the twin symbolic pillars known, I believe, as Jachin and Boaz.

The room in which the Distributists met was long, and relatively narrow. A long table was placed lengthwise down the middle of the room, and against its top end—to your right as you came in—a smaller table was placed crosswise. At this top table, facing down the room, sat the speaker for the evening, the Secretary of the Central Branch, and one or two other members. The audience, if that is the right word, sat on either side of the long table, and also on the chairs placed on a low platform running down the side of the room through which you entered. Other chairs could be placed about the room according to need. An average attendance at the meetings would have been about fifty; in the summer the number might fall as low as thirty or twenty; but on nights when a celebrity was announced to speak the room would be packed with a hundred or a hundred and fifty people, many of whom had to stand.

For the session of 1930–31 I was myself the Honorary Secretary of the Central Branch. There was a Committee to whom the Secretary was responsible; but in effect he had a free hand in arranging the speakers for the meetings. We had plenty of talent of our own to call on. For instance: George Heseltine, Gregory Macdonald, Desmond Gleeson (civil servant and author of *The Tragedy of the Stewarts*), C. E. Baines (civil servant and detective story writer), C. T. B. Donkin (an engineer, who also wrote detective stories, under the pseudonym Thomas Kindon), E. H. Haywood (of the Workers' Travel Association), Bill Titterton (one of Fleet Street's best known and best loved figures), John Cargill ('Honest John', engineer and Scotsman, faithful to the creed of Calvin and Knox), Archie Currie (the author of the satirical articles 'by Agag' in *G.K.'s Weekly*), Francis Cowper and James Colclough (witty and trenchant young barristers), F. Keston Clarke (schools attendance officer and contributor of short stories to the *Evening News* and the

Argosy magazine), George Coldwell (bookseller and pioneer of 'Catholic Evidence' meetings in the London parks): these and many other names come to mind.

I have mentioned no women. Distributism was always essentially a man's movement; this was another of its limitations and weaknesses. The only lady who was ever prominent in the League's affairs was Miss Agnes Mott, who lived in Bournemouth and was very active in the civic life of that town. She was a JP, I think, and subsequently received the OBE. The League's Bournemouth Branch was her creation. The only women whom I can remember seeing regularly at The Devereux were Mollie Titterton and Betty Currie, whose husbands have just been named, and Jim Colclough's two sisters. None of them held any official position in the League.

During my year as secretary of the Central Branch I invited some well known guest speakers, among them Eric Gill, who offered for our discussion the first chapter of his forthcoming book *Typography*, which he read from the galley proofs. Gill was one of the few Distributists who saw clearly that to produce a satisfactory programme of social reform they would have to tackle the difficult question of monetary reform; that is, how to free the banking system from the domination of 'international' finance and organize it on a new basis. But very few members seemed to see the point, in spite of Ezra Pound's contributions to the subject in *G.K.'s Weekly* during 1935.

Gill did not mention the monetary problem on this occasion; but a little later we were addressed by the then Duke of Bedford, one of the leading advocates of the Social Credit system of finance propounded by Professor Soddy and Major Douglas. The Duke, a most unassuming man, was already a public figure of some note. A few years later he became known to a still wider public as the founder of the short-lived British People's Party: the only party, except for Sir Oswald Mosley's British Union, to oppose Britain's entry into the war in 1939.

Speakers from all sorts of interesting minority movements came to The Devereux on these Friday evenings. One whom I particularly enjoyed was the late Father St John Groser, vicar of Christ Church, Watney Street, a slum parish in the East End. He was a leading member of Conrad Noel's Catholic Crusade— later renamed the Order of the Church Militant, which propagated a colourful kind of Anglo-Catholic Communism. The revival of traditional crafts was advocated by the Thaxted movement—Conrad Noel was vicar of Thaxted in Essex; and Father Groser had a loom in his vicarage, where he wove his own vestments and altar hangings. Distributists also were interested in the revival of craftsmanship, so Groser was assured of a sympathetic hearing.

The question of the place of machinery in a Distributist society was always being discussed at The Devereux. Some Distributists held that it had no place at all, believing that machines of every kind inevitably reduced the worker to 'a subhuman condition of intellectual irresponsibility'. Others believed that in the modern world it was unrealistic to think that *all* mechanization and *all* large-scale industry could be got rid of, and that therefore the right policy to adopt in this area would be the introduction of various kinds of co-operative organization or workers' ownership, as suggested by Orage, Penty, and the other Guild Socialists. Those who took this reasonable and moderate line could claim the authority of Hilaire Belloc, especially in his book *The Restoration of Property*.

Others, however, of a more idealistic school of thought, regarded this attitude as a betrayal of Distributist principle, and held that the use of machinery was incompatible with man's responsible, creative nature, and that there could be no place for it in a Distributist state.

These discussions on machinery were apt to engender more heat than light; in fact, they were often acrimonious. Eric Gill was supposed, rightly or wrongly, to be responsible for the idea that a tool is a device that helps a craftsman in his labour, while a machine is a device that displaces or abolishes labour. (Gill himself was no doctrinaire; while he would tolerate no machinery in his own stone-carving shop, he sanctioned the use of automatic printing-machines in the Press run by himself and René Hague. Hague, one of the most accomplished printers of the present century, had earlier been a prominent frequenter of The Devereux: but that was before my time.) This dictum attributed to Gill gave rise to endless discussions of such subtle points as whether a dentist's drill, for example, was to be considered a tool or a machine. Needless to say, this problem was never satisfactorily resolved.

Whereas the 'moderates' in this controversy claimed the authority of Mr Belloc in support of their view, the 'extremists' looked to Father Vincent McNabb, the great Dominican, as the classic advocate of 'pure' Distributism. Father McNabb, however, always declined to be drawn into affirming that machinery was evil in itself; but he went as far as he could to reject its use in his own life, and urged others—especially those engaged in Distributist back-to-the-land ventures—to do the same. Living in London, he walked everywhere, and never used any form of mechanical transport if he could avoid it. One of the busiest of men, he received a large post every day. Normally he answered every letter on the day he received it, and in his own handwriting. People marvelled at the amount of work he got through; but part of the secret was that he never wasted time, as he used to put it, in taking holidays, going to the cinema, listening to the radio, or reading novels. He had long been one of the sights of London—'a piece of old London walking about', as he described himself—since he was unique among his brethren in always wearing publicly the striking black and white habit of the Friars Preachers. In the end he became a national figure; largely on account of the success of his broadcast talks and meditations. He did not enjoy broadcasting, but did this work 'under obedience'.

Father McNabb was held in great veneration by all Distributists, and no session at The Devereux was complete without a talk by him. When he entered the room everyone rose—a tribute paid to no other speaker except Mr Chesterton on his rare appearances—and it was the same at the end of the evening, when he left to walk the four miles back to his priory in Hampstead. Chesterton once said that Father McNabb was one of the few really great men that he had known, and that he was great 'mentally and morally, mystically and practically'. We all of us felt this about him. At The Devereux he always drew a packed audience, and for latecomers it would be a matter of Standing Room Only. The passage of time has vindicated many of the hard sayings that he put before us.

One of Father McNabb's most ardent disciples was a young man named John Hawkswell, now living in Alberta, Canada. After his schooling at Ampleforth, Hawkswell had been for a time a Carthusian monk, and then a pig-breeder in South

Africa. He was now expecting to make his fortune on the London Stock Exchange; but of course he never did. He was a considerable orator, and might have been a great success as a trade union leader or a Socialist cabinet minister, had his paths lain in those directions. His part in the Distributist movement went beyond his membership of the League; when the history of the movement is written his name will have an important place.

One winter evening John Hawkswell was the advertised speaker at The Devereux, and he held us all spellbound with an impassioned denunciation of our attraction to the fleshpots of Egypt and an urgent exhortation to each one of us to leave the City of Destruction and return to the land before it was too late. Sitting in the audience was a small elderly lady, whom no one remembered having seen before, with a young girl who appeared to be her daughter. At the end of the evening, as the meeting was breaking up, this lady came up to John and said: 'Mr Hawkswell, you are right. We must act. My name is Mrs Judges, and tomorrow I shall send you a cheque for £2,000.' She did; and that was the beginning of the Catholic Distributist settlements at Langenhoe in Essex and at Laxton in Northamptonshire. The latter is still in being today.

One of the strangest men ever to appear at The Devereux was Alexander Stewart Gray, a wild-looking old man with a straggly beard, who had once played a notable part in the Socialist movement in Britain, in the days of H. M. Hyndman, William Morris and Keir Hardie. Stewart Gray had his own back-to-the-land settlement near Langenhoe, Essex. He preached much the same gospel as Hawkswell and Father McNabb, but in more attractive terms. According to him, life on the land presented no great hardships or difficulties. As he put it: 'It's a most enjoyable life. I spend my time reading and writing and printing my own poems, and let the women get on with the work.' Some account of the wayward life of Alexander Stewart Gray will be found in Roy Campbell's autobiography, *Light on a Dark Horse*.

It was E. H. Haywood who had persuaded Stewart Gray to come up from Essex to talk to the Distributists. Haywood seemed to know everyone in the Labour Party, and was on terms of friendship with most of the leading Labour politicians.

He could have gone far in the Party himself had he wanted to;
but he preferred to stay with the Workers' Travel Association,
where he had risen to a high position. Haywood was as Cockney
as Sam Weller and had come from a poor home. He began life,
after leaving school, as a postman, but had been 'discovered'
by Douglas (later known as Hilary) Pepler,[1] who helped him
to get into Ruskin College, Oxford, where he did well. Haywood, who claimed to be both a Socialist *and* a Distributist, was
one of the most popular members of the League's Central
Branch, where his good nature and generosity, as well as his
Cockney humour, were much appreciated. Some of his
contributions to *G.K.'s Weekly* and its successor *The Weekly
Review* would be worth reprinting, especially his obituary
article, written in 1943, on Father Vincent McNabb.

Then there was Commander Herbert Shove,[1] who was
for a short time the League's Honorary Secretary. Shove, a
burly, bearded man who looked almost exactly like William
Morris, was a brother of Gerald Shove, the Cambridge
economist, and brother-in-law of the poet Fredegond Shove.
Invalided out of the Royal Navy's submarine service, with the
DSO and a pension, at the end of the 1914–18 war, he had
settled on Ditchling Common, in Mid-Sussex, where he
acquired the small farm, Halletts, which had previously been
occupied by Eric Gill, and then by Hilary Pepler.

A man of many parts and aptitudes, with a pungent nautical
turn of phrase, Shove at first farmed a bit; then he opened a
small grocery shop, which failed for lack of customers. Next he
took up bee-keeping, and sold excellent honey; finally, after
taking lessons from Dunstan Pruden, a London Distributist and
Devereux habitué who had moved his silversmith's workshop
to Ditchling Common, he became a competent worker in
metal, and augmented his pension by making and selling
pewter mugs. He made a valuable contribution to Distributism
with his book *The Fairy Ring of Commerce*. It would be interesting
to know what his brother Gerald thought of it.

In the late Thirties Commander Shove took up the study of
the writings of St John of the Cross, the Carmelite mystic, and
Montague Summers's histories of witchcraft, and professed
himself an authority on mysticism and demonology. Presumably
all these varied activities and interests—music was another, in

spite of his being tone-deaf—were part of a long fight against
boredom. His heart had always remained with the Navy, and
he never really took to a quiet life on shore. In the end, the
second world war came to his rescue. He was recalled to active
service and put in charge of the defences of the Port of London.
Promoted Captain, he was then assigned to a special mission
on the Gold Coast. Here the climate undermined his health,
and he came home only to die, after having been awarded the
OBE.

A Sussex neighbour of Shove's who was seen quite often at
The Devereux was Captain H. S. D. Went, the actual founder
of the Distributist League, who lives in Haywards Heath.
'Toby' Went was, and has remained, a staunch Anglo-Catholic
of High Tory outlook. At The Devereux he sometimes clashed,
on points of Distributist theory, with Bill Titterton; but he had
an unfailingly effective way of bringing Titterton round to his
own point of view. Both men were great admirers of that fine
writer Arthur Machen. In discussion with Titterton, Went
would begin a defence of his own position with the words: 'As
Arthur Machen says . . .' This always had the effect of
causing Titterton to withdraw his objections and come round to
Went's point of view. Titterton would not have been an easy
man to hoodwink; but so great was his reverence for Machen,
whom he had known in Fleet Street, that he never continued
to dispute any thesis in support of which Machen's authority
was cited. Bill Titterton was outstanding among Distributist
personalities. As a young man he had worked as a sculptor's
model for Rodin in Paris; in Fleet Street he had known the
giants of former days, among them Frank Harris, T. W. H.
Crosland, Lord Alfred Douglas, and Horatio Bottomley, for
whom he had worked on *John Bull*. The brilliant duels between
Titterton and Went at The Devereux would have been worth
going a long way to hear.

Chesterton himself did not come often to The Devereux. The
meetings did not finish until 9.30, when the Distributists and
their guests descended to the bar on the ground floor for a
final social half-hour. By 9.30 it would have been too late and
too tiring for him to have to make the journey back to Beaconsfield, and he did not care to be away from his home for a night

unless it was unavoidable. When he did have to spend a night, or a few days, in town he usually stayed at Artillery Mansions, in Victoria Street, where I sometimes had to take him proofs that needed immediate attention, or collect from him an article for the *Weekly*. More often I saw him in Little Essex Street, at the *Weekly*'s office, where he would appear from time to time, wheezing heavily up the steep and narrow stairs, and sinking gratefully into the editorial swivel chair normally occupied by Edward Macdonald. During the editorial conferences he would draw at a mild cigar, and I seem to remember that he was provided with a single glass of sherry, which he sipped slowly. He would doodle on the pad of paper provided for him; but this did not interfere with his attention to the business in hand. After he had left, Edward's brother, Gregory Macdonald, always appropriated these doodles, and they now form a valuable collection.

In the course of my life I have heard some of the best speakers of our time; some of them in private conversation as well as on the public platform. (Of course, the good public speaker is not necessarily a good conversationalist; but often the two talents go together.) Among those whom I have most admired and enjoyed are Bernard Shaw, Hilaire Belloc, Sir Oswald Mosley, and Father Vincent McNabb: each one of them a remarkable man by any definition. But I can only say that for a sheer unceasing impromptu flow of wit and wisdom I have never heard anything to match the conversation of Gilbert Chesterton. He was a truly great talker; but he did not *dominate* the company he was with, and was as anxious to hear them as they were anxious to hear him. It was the blend of courtesy, wisdom, wit, and humour that made his conversation so extraordinary. I have heard nothing like it since. My impression is that the quality of Chesterton's talk was superior to Oscar Wilde's; partly because Chesterton had a humility that Wilde lacked. He never talked for effect, and in his talk there was none of the 'smartness' and 'contrivance' that sometimes marred Wilde's brilliant conversation. Wilde was an extremely kind and generous man; but he was not always charitable in what he said. Chesterton was.

The Distributist gatherings at which G.K.C. was most often seen, besides the League's annual dinners, were the big public debates in the Essex Hall. Some of his biographers have placed it on record that in his later years a lecture by Chesterton was liable to be a somewhat rambling affair. In debate it was a different matter. His expository remarks might be delivered slowly, and might occasionally stray from the strictly relevant into some fascinating byway of reminiscence and humour; but when he came to the point of exposing the fallacies and inconsistencies in the case put forward by his opponent, he did so with rapier-like sharpness and devastating wit. It is a great pity that none of these debates was recorded, as were G.K.C.'s broadcast talks, which are now preserved in the BBC's sound archives.

I remember him saying in the course of a debate—I forget with whom—on The Freedom of the Press, that to talk of the freedom of the press in modern Britain was like talking of snowballing in South Africa. This was typical of his style in debate. This particular apothegm he might have thought of *before* the debate; but he could produce others just as good on the spur of the moment, in circumstances where no previous preparation would have been possible.

I have the feeling that those who were responsible for organizing these debates, which drew big audiences, did not always choose opponents worthy of him. Perhaps such were hard to find. Maisie Ward in her *Return to Chesterton* has an account of a debate, on Total Abstinence, between Chesterton and Mr Edward Scrymgeour, a dour Scots Presbyterian MP. Scrymgeour, who was an honest man, and had supported many good causes in Parliament, could not make head or tail of Chesterton's line of argument, because he could not see the point of any of his jokes, and evidently thought that a speaker to a serious motion who kept making his audience laugh could not himself be serious.

It must have been in 1934 or '35 that Chesterton paid a visit to the Mid-Sussex Branch of the Distributist League. This was something almost unprecedented; I can recall no other occasion on which he visited any of the League's branches apart from a visit to the High Wycombe Branch some time in the mid-Thirties. But High Wycombe was only half an hour's drive from Beaconsfield. On that occasion he was supported on the platform by Eric Gill, Father Vincent McNabb, and

Montague Fordham (founder of the Rural Reconstruction Association), all of whom spoke.

Memorable though this occasion was, the Ditchling visit was, in its own way, even more so. The meeting was held in the Free Christian Church's historic meetinghouse in the Twitten ('Twitten' being a Sussex dialect word meaning a narrow alley or passage). The Free Christians, I believe, were a kind of Unitarians; so that the venue was a suitable one in view of the Chesterton family's Unitarian background. G.K.C.'s lecture was supposed to be on Distributism; but it was a very hot summer evening, and he was obviously feeling the heat; so it was perhaps not surprising that the lecture seemed to be on, to use G. I. Gurdjieff's phrase, 'All and Everything'. Perhaps it was all the more enjoyable for that.

'Fond memory brings the light/Of other days around me.' What an experience those Devereux nights were. If only one had kept a diary in those days how much more one would be able to recall. But some mention must be made of the convivial evenings which were an essential part of each year's programme. At these evenings politics and economics were put aside in favour of song and good fellowship. And then there was the great annual dinner each autumn, attended by provincial as well as London members, after the League's annual general meeting. The AGM was held at the Essex Hall, adjoining the Unitarians' headquarters in Essex Street, in the afternoon. It was followed in the evening by a dinner, usually at Carr's Restaurant in the Aldwych. G.K.C., as the League's President, presided, unless, as rarely happened, he was prevented. After the meal, and the customary toasts and speeches, the evening would be rounded off with song. Chesterton joined in all the choruses, and thoroughly enjoyed the whole affair.

Distributists sang mostly their own songs, of which the most popular was Titterton's 'King Solomon's Wives'. This began:

> King Solomon took ten thousand wives
> From Tarshish and from Tyre,
> With a Columbine from Samarkand
> Whenever he might require.

But whether he fetched 'em fat or lean,
   Or whether tall or short,
There were no flies on the shy gazelles
   King Solomon took to court.

King Solomon had ten thousand wives
   In his house of cedar wood.
There was Sheba's queen, and Helen of Troy,
   And Little Red Riding Hood.
But whether their skins were white as milk,
   Or black as a chimney-sweep,
There were no flies on the shy gazelles
   King Solomon used to keep.

Yo ho! yo ho! yo ho!
Then send the drink around
And here's to every fancy lass
In London to be found!
For Solomon wouldn't have cornered queens,
Or cuddled a Columbine
If he'd booked a passage to London Town,
A galley of Tyre to London Town,
Nor'-nor'-west to London Town
And met that gal of mine—yo ho!
That sporty old gal of mine.[2]

Desmond Gleeson always gave his 'The Stormy Nore'; Charles
Donkin's 'Alfred the Great' and 'Truth in Advertising' were
invariably called for, the former being a trenchant and witty
satire on Sir Alfred Mond (subsequently the first Lord Mel-
chett), who was regarded, perhaps not altogether fairly, as
the archetype of all that Distributists were opposed to. Jim
Cragg's 'Church and King', a High Tory song set to the tune
of 'The Vicar of Bray', always won applause, and so did
Dunstan Pruden's rendering of 'The Old Orange Flute'. One
of the most rousing choruses was that to 'A Jug of Punch' by
F. E. Yarker, an old friend of Titterton's.

Of course, most of these songs were drinking songs, and a
good deal of beer was drunk in the course of the evening. But
there was nothing resembling the 'cult of beer' of which
Chesterton and his followers have sometimes been accused.

For those of us who attended regularly those meetings at

The Devereux, they were gatherings of *friends*. A passage in the fourth chapter of Chesterton's *Charles Dickens* catches their spirit perfectly: 'To every man alive, one must hope, it has in some manner happened that he has talked with his more fascinating friends round a table on some night when all the numerous personalities unfolded themselves like great tropical flowers. All fell into their parts as in some delightful impromptu play. Every man was more himself then he had ever been in this vale of tears. Every man was a beautiful caricature of himself. The man who has known such nights will understand the exaggerations of *Pickwick*. The man who has not known such nights will not enjoy *Pickwick*, nor (I imagine) heaven.'

That is how it looks to me, across the interval of thirty and more years. I do not think it is a matter of distance lending enchantment to the view.

Marshall McLuhan has said that Gilbert Chesterton 'never failed to focus a high degree of moral wisdom on the confused issues of our age'.[3] It was this belief that brought us all together at The Devereux; those of us who survive believe it still.

Recollections

DOROTHY E. COLLINS

Wherever you go among booklovers, when they hear that you live in Beaconsfield, they at once remark, 'Isn't that where G. K. Chesterton lived?' This is understandable, as there is quite a lot about Beaconsfield in his *Autobiography* and also in the *Biography* and *Return to Chesterton*. In the *Autobiography* he says: 'I have lived in Beaconsfield from the time when it was almost a village to the time when, as the enemy profanely says, it is almost a suburb. It would be truer to say that the two things in some sense still exist side by side; and the popular instinct has recognized the division by actually talking about the Old Town and the New Town.' This is largely true today.

In the early years of Chesterton's marriage, he and his wife Frances lived in London and one week-end decided to go into the country. At the station he asked for two tickets. 'Where for?' said the booking-clerk. 'Wherever the next train goes,' was the surprising answer. This happened to be Slough, so to Slough they went, and from there walked through country lanes to Beaconsfield and stayed for the week-end in the Old Town at the White Hart. They were delighted with Beaconsfield and decided that one day the place should be their home, which happened about eight years later in 1909 when they went to live at Overroads in Grove Road. From there they moved across the road to Top Meadow in 1922, which they had built on ground they had bought owing to the threat of a laundry being built on the site. I came to know them as I used to stay with friends who lived next door to them, with adjoining gardens.

Gilbert Chesterton was a much loved boy and man, which was largely because of his intense sincerity, sense of justice and love of all men, young and old. He was always the centre of any company in which he found himself and his school friends have told me how they all competed for his friendship, and of how jealous they were of each other. At St Paul's School he

Drawing (Beaconsfield, 1909); the original is coloured

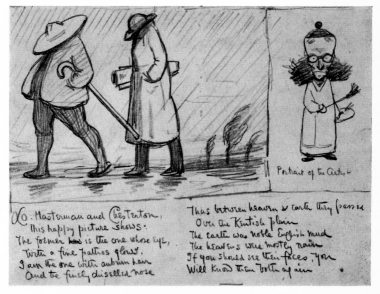

Thank-you letter to Mrs C. F. G. Masterman

Figure for toy theatre pantomime about Sidney and Beatrice Webb.

Drawing done for a child

Toy theatre figures made for the amusement of young relatives. The originals of all drawings shown on this and the opposite page are coloured.

Drawing for The Missing Masterpiece *by Hilaire Belloc (1929): 'Enthusiasm of the public of the Great Republic for the symbolic representation of the Love destroyed by the Years'*

carried off the Milton Prize for Poetry when he was very young; and when I say carried it off, this is an exaggeration, for having got onto the platform to receive it he walked off and left it behind, so confused was he at his success. Here we see his sincere humility which lasted through his life. It gave him no pleasure to excel over other people.

He was apparently oblivious to everything that passed before him, but really he was a much closer observer than most, and remembered what he had seen and what he had read. There is one story which illustrates this. He was sitting quietly listening to a discussion about what books various friends would take with them if they knew they were going to be wrecked on a desert island. Gilbert clinched this rather highbrow argument by saying, 'I think I should take Thomas's Guide to Practical Shipbuilding.'

I can only speak for the last ten years of his life because I did not know him until 1926. He was tall—six foot four, and of large proportions, with a fine head and delicate hands. As he himself said, 'I always enjoy myself more than most. There's such a lot of me having a good time.' In the give and take of conversation, Chesterton would take the smallest contribution from the youngest and the most nervous of his listeners and toss it about, add to it, embroider it and return it with a remark that that was just what he needed to illustrate his point. The smallest contributor felt enlarged by his response.

He was completely unselfconscious about his work and could work anywhere I could balance a typewriter. In the most unlikely places he would suddenly say, 'I think we will do a little work, if you're sure you don't mind.' When he was at home, he never missed a day's work. He went very late to bed and was equally late in the morning, having his breakfast at about 10 and coming into the study by 10.30 where he worked all day. On the occasions when the Catholic Church demanded attendance at Mass on a weekday, as it was a small parish there would be only an early morning Mass and he would drag himself from his bed. As he got fasting into the car, I have heard him say, 'What but religion would bring us to such a pass.' But never did I know him miss a Day of Obligation either at home or abroad. In fact the first signs of his last illness showed at a Mass on Ascension Day at Clermont Ferrand when he had

to come out before the Mass was finished and did not feel well
enough to enjoy his breakfast.

When he was at home, he worked from about 10.30 until
dinner-time, with small pauses for lunch and tea. After dinner,
he would sit at a table with his books and his cigars, either
reading a detective story or making a few notes for the next
day's work in a shorthand of his own invention which no one
else could read. He talked about his work quite often before he
started, but never when he was actually dictating, which he
did straight to the machine, reading each page as it came off the
typewriter. As he knew exactly what he wanted to say there
was only an occasional alteration. He had a prodigious memory and could quote from readings of his youth without further
reference, especially from Dickens. He would map out a book
with the headings, and would dictate chapter by chapter,
though not always in the final order.

There were many calls on his purse, as he was educating
various children in whom he and Frances were interested. To
this pressure and to large printer's bills for *G.K.'s Weekly*, we
owe some of the Father Brown stories. I would say, 'We have
only got £100 in the bank.' 'Oh, well. We must write another
Father Brown story', and this would be done at lightning speed
a day or two later from a few notes on the back of an envelope.
Or, in more serious mood, after clearing the weekly articles, he
would suddenly say, 'Shall we do a bit of Tommy?' and that
is how his *St Thomas Aquinas*, which delighted the Dominicans
and which Gilson judged to be the finest book on Aquinas ever
written, was completed; without fuss and as a result of many
hours of forethought, but with very little reading. He had read
the *Summa* in his youth. I obtained a list of books on Aquinas,
to which G.K. referred but had to make no alteration to the
already half-finished book.

Chesterton was in constant demand as chairman of this and
that and for after-dinner speeches, lectures and debates.
Latterly, he was to find a new and congenial medium in broadcasting and was much sought after by the BBC for series of
fortnightly book talks. Much of the non-fiction sent to the BBC
came to him for review. At the beginning of a series of six talks
he would give me headings to which he would talk, such as
History, English Letters, Social Affairs, Biography, Travel, etc.

As the books came in, I would sort them and mark the passages which I knew would interest him, and quickly before each talk he would take a pile and make a talk which introduced and briefly reviewed a few, and mentioned some of the others. These were published as full-page articles in the *Listener*. I always thought the literary world showed the greatest integrity, for never did he receive a request from an author, many of whom he knew, asking for a review of his book. In spite of his success he was always very nervous beforehand and he would not undertake the series each year without a promise that his wife or I or both of us should sit in the studio with him. He liked it best that way and talked direct to us, which gave his talks the intimate character which the public so much enjoyed. He had Stuart Hibberd as his introducer who was always arrayed in a dinner-jacket, a custom of the BBC of those days for the evening talks, even though the announcer could not be seen. He would watch the green light turn to red and with an agonised glance at us, he would begin, and immediately be oblivious of his surroundings as he read and improvised his script as he went along. On Christmas Day 1931 he broadcast a Christmas message to America, which was in those days looked upon as a minor miracle. I have letters in the file from the Director of Talks and others, begging for more. 'The building rings with your praises,' 'You are a born broadcaster and we must have much more of it,' wrote the Director. There was still a certain amount of resistance in those days among diehards who would not have a wireless set in the house, but news was reaching us at Beaconsfield of those who had bought sets just to listen to Chesterton.

Less than three months before his death he was broadcasting in a series called 'The Spice of Life'. At the end of a character-istic talk, he said, 'I will defend the spiritual appetite of my own age, I will even be so indecently frivolous as to burst into song and say to the young pessimists:

> Some sneer, some snigger, some simper,
> In the youth where we laughed and sang;
> And *they* may end with a whimper
> But *we* will end with a bang.'

Although full of fun, he was not a back-slapping hearty person, but rather the embodiment of old-world courtesy and reserve. He was himself a paradox. He had a mystical regard for women. I have even seen him rise from his chair when a young girl came into the room. He always remembered what he had seen and those with whom he had talked, not so much by their faces as by their minds—for that is how he saw people.

His wife Frances, who was a very great friend of mine, gave him the security he needed. She was a profound character with depths of understanding and sympathy, and he was entirely dependent on her for his happiness. 'Where is Frances?' he would say, 'I don't want her now but I might want her any minute.' Their domestic life was tied up with children. The disappointment of having none of their own saddened but did not embitter them, and the house was constantly filled with other people's children. If a treat was to be given, it was the child who chose what it should be. One of the small boys, allowed up for tea for the first time after a spell of illness, and asked what he would like to do, said, 'I should like Auntie Frances to sit on one side of the fire mending stockings, and I should like Uncle Gilbert to sit on the other side, and I will sit in front of him and we will talk about fireworks.' There is a story of Gilbert with a slipper in his hand saying, 'Frances, the children must stay up late,' and slapping the table, much to the children's delight, 'You see, I am putting my foot down.' One's thoughts go back to those happy days at Top Meadow and of G.K.'s spontaneous humility. He always wanted to be one of a very normal household. I remember an anxious remark one day about rather a stupid little dog we had. 'I think Dolfuss quite likes me, don't you, Frances?'; and another time, 'I know we always have liver once a week because Dolfuss likes it.' I may add that Dolfuss had it most days and we occasionally. The cats also entered into his domestic life. Gilbert was fond of kippers for breakfast and so was Perky, who one day got onto the table and started on his master's breakfast; he remarked, intent on the preservation of the remains, '*I* don't mind eating after Perky.'

He enjoyed his food and certain drinks, chiefly red or white wines from France. He abominated spirits and never drank them. He was a small eater. His wife would say, 'Will you have some more, Gilbert?' and he would either pass his plate to her in an absent-minded way or would say, 'I will if you like,' to which she would reply. 'Well, make up your mind.'

He had a great many friends among the men of his time. As Hilaire Belloc remarked, 'It was a benediction to know him', and H. G. Wells once said, 'When he is there I notice that the whole gathering is by a sort of radiation convivial.' He preferred his friends to come to Beaconsfield rather than to go to them, and they all came with their suggestions and their requests. Bernard Shaw came imploring him not to waste his time on journalism, but to take up play-writing, and he once brought an elaborate scenario from which he implored G.K. to write a play, but nothing came of it. Gilbert went his own way. He wrote three plays but they were not inspired by Shaw, *Magic*, *The Judgment of Dr Johnson* and *The Surprise*.

Frances and I thought he spent too much time on journalism and on his paper, *G.K.'s Weekly*. Many did not agree with us, but this certainly put much pressure on him and time and energy were spent on extra work, which was necessary to finance his paper and keep it going. Even so, he never satisfied all the requests for books, and from the newspaper and magazine editors. Father John O'Connor, who inspired the Father Brown stories, very often came to stay and did his utmost to wean Chesterton from journalism, but Frances warned him, 'You will not change Gilbert; you will only fidget him. He is bent on being a jolly journalist.' I think Hilaire Belloc had more understanding of this point of view. There were so many controversies and injustices to be dealt with in the press, that they could not refrain from dealing with them. Belloc needed Chesterton, and would come like a whirlwind with the plot of one of his satirical novels, saying that he could not possibly write the story until Gilbert had drawn the pictures. They would go into the study after lunch and for the length of a hilarious afternoon they would be closeted together. At tea-time they would emerge, Belloc triumphant with twenty-five illustrations for his book. The characters had come to life through the medium of the drawings. Chesterton was a considerable artist and could have earned a living by his pencil and brush, if his pen had not taken precedence. When he left school, he went to the Slade School of Art, but very soon after, Professor Tonks, the Head of the School, told his parents that he had such a mature style of his own that they could not teach him anything without spoiling his originality, which he thought amounted to genius.

In 1914–15, owing to worry about the War and overwork for the Ministry of Information, he became seriously ill and was unconscious for a week or more. When he momentarily recovered consciousness, his wife, hoping he knew her, said, 'Who is looking after you?' 'God,' said Gilbert, and lapsed into unconsciousness again. After many weeks, he made a slow recovery.

We had many expeditions to foreign countries. He had written a great deal of propaganda for Poland which managed to regain her freedom in 1917 from the occupying powers of Russia, Germany and Austria which had dominated the country for 150 years. The government of the reconstructed country invited Chesterton to come and see what had been done in the ten years of freedom from alien rule. This was in May 1927. He was fêted and lavishly entertained throughout the country. On arrival at Warsaw we were met at the station by an escort of Cavalry Officers and representatives of the PEN Club which had been made responsible by the Government for arranging the visit. This was during the time of Marshal Pilsudski, so everything in Warsaw was very dashing and military. A romantic speech in French was made by one of those gorgeously clad cavalry men, and we were driven with cavalry escort to the Europyski Hotel. The welcoming speech on the station extolled the callings of poet and cavalry officer as being the finest in the world for a layman, which amused G.K. and appealed to the romantic side of his nature. This officer said, 'I will not say you are the chief friend of Poland, for God is our chief friend,' in those words summing up the spirit of the country.

We stayed in Poland for about five weeks and were much entertained at numerous banquets both at the British Embassy and the Polish universities. While we were in Warsaw the entrance of the hotel suddenly became full of beggars of every nationality, with a result that the manager came to see Chesterton to ask him not to give money in the street, as he was acting as a magnet and they found it quite impossible to get rid of the army of beggars who were finding the foreigner such a splendid source of income. This sort of thing happened everywhere he went and, I need not say, in England as well, with this most generous of men, who could never keep ten shillings in his pocket.

At Lwow we stayed at the Hotel George, where we were served by peasant women in their national costume and with bare feet—national costume as was worn daily and not put on for tourists. There were no air services in those days and we travelled all over the country in Wagon-Lits by night. From Warsaw to Vilna on the Russian border, I had to share with a Russian woman and in advising me as to whether to take the upper or lower berth, Gilbert remarked, 'What you have to consider is whether you prefer to be stabbed through the front or the back.' I decided for the back and took the upper berth. My companion turned out to be charming! At Vilna where there were still many signs of the oppressive Russian domination, we saw a procession in the Catholic Cathedral and I have never seen such a collection of down and outs, led by an old priest with St Vitus's dance. It was a truly tragic sight.

In 1929 we had three months in Rome in the Hotel Hassler overlooking the Spanish Steps, and here in a first floor room Chesterton wrote *The Resurrection of Rome* while below the windows a stream of every nationality passed to and fro on those lovely steps, at the foot of which stands the house where Keats lived and died. We had seats for memorable occasions in St Peter's and an audience with Pope Pius XI, who talked to G.K. of his book on St Francis of Assisi among other things. Chesterton also had an audience with Mussolini, who in those days had not spoilt his record by colonial expansion and lust for power. He asked, 'Explain the Church of England to me,' which Chesterton found it difficult to do. Their conversation was in French. A friend of mine in Rome had been teaching him English for some months and told me that he was so intelligent that he was reading and appreciating Bernard Shaw's play *The Apple Cart* within a few months of instruction.

On our way home we had a pleasant visit to Max Beerbohm and his wife, who lived in a villa overlooking the Bay of Rapallo. He had gone to that coast for his honeymoon and had lived there ever since. In his inner sanctum he had many treasures which he enjoyed showing to his friends. When we were there the favourite was a small white bear, sitting up with a little drum round its neck which had come from a Parisian sweet shop. Max Beerbohm would wind him up and he banged away on his drum to everybody's intense satisfaction. Max had drawn an amusing fresco on the wall over the dining-room door, depicting many of his friends going in to a meal, and leading them was Chesterton.

We also met Ezra Pound and his wife who were living at Rapallo. At that time he was foreseeing the salvation of the world by means of the Douglas Credit Scheme, a financial experiment which was being tried out in Canada, and he told me that Max Beerbohm was an active supporter. Next time we met Max, I said, 'I hear you are in favour of the Douglas Credit Scheme.' 'Am I?' he replied. 'One only has to smile, look pleasant and avoid an argument, to be accused of supporting something one knows nothing about.'

Our next big campaign was in 1931–32 when we went to Canada and the United States for about nine months. We went on one of the smaller P. & O. boats which was able to sail up the St Lawrence to Quebec and Montreal. There was a very jolly party on board of all ages and Chesterton thoroughly enjoyed the fun. On one occasion a treasure hunt was suggested and he was provided with reams of brown paper and coloured chalks and was asked to make the clues. He spent a whole day writing verses and drawing pictures to be hidden around the decks. The whole thing was an uproarious success and when I went round afterwards to collect up the clues there was not one left. Others had been before me, and they are now most probably collectors' pieces.

The object of our visit was an invitation from Notre Dame University, South Bend, Indiana to give two courses of lectures on English History and Literature of the Victorian Age, running concurrently. There were 5,000 students and those taking these subjects attended. After six weeks at the University, where we lodged in the house of a Middle West estate agent with his wife, two children and the old grandfather—the sunny side of Main Street, as Gilbert called it—'Uncle Gilbert and Auntie Frances', as they were to the four-year-old, reluctantly left for a lecture tour which took us all over the country by train. Gilbert talked to enormous audiences and everywhere we went we were entertained and he was interviewed by the press. With all this travelling the strain was intense, and Mrs Chesterton broke down from exhaustion and had to be left in a nursing home in Tennessee with two nurses, while G.K. and I trekked up and down the country, worried about her, but unable to cancel the engagements. Added to all this lecturing and travelling G.K. was working on his regular weekly articles all the time. It was a great experience and I have many memories of the kindness and hospitality we all received. One of many charming little episodes happened when Gilbert in his usual absent-minded way was sitting in the Pullman car of a cross-country train. Just before we were due to arrive, along came the fatherly old negro car-attendant to clean his shoes and brush his coat, as was the custom. G.K. waved him away, to be met with the remark, 'Ho, Ho, young man, you'se getting old afore yer time. You must keep yerself nice for the gals.' His day was made, but anything more out of character could not have been conceived. With all this constant travelling it was difficult to keep him clean and tidy, brushed and pressed, especially when Mrs Chesterton was ill, as that was her department.

America was in the throes of Prohibition, which Chesterton observed meticulously, saying that a visitor should always observe the laws of the country in which he found himself. The thuggery which resulted from Prohibition was at its height. At Portland there was a hold-up and a killing outside our hotel which, much to the distress of the taxi-driver, we just missed by minutes. We then went into Canada, with the banks of the St Lawrence ablaze with the autumn hues of the shumack, landing at Quebec and then Ottawa and going on to Montreal and Toronto. At the end of the trip, we entered Canada again from America by the West coast, visiting Vancouver and British Columbia where we stayed at Victoria. Lectures were given at all these places, as well as in the Middle West and East and West coasts of the USA.

The next year we went to Rome, Sicily and Malta by train and boat, and in 1935 I drove them both to Spain and through the South of France to Italy in my own car. In Florence Chesterton gave a lecture on English Literature and the Latin Tradition as the English contribution to an International Festival. We came home through Switzerland and Belgium.

This trip was a great success as they were wonderful passengers. Gilbert did once remark rather plaintively, 'Frances, I wish you wouldn't keep telling Dorothy to admire the view when we are hanging over precipices', but on the whole they had no fears.

I remember at one time arriving in the centre of Barcelona at midday on a Saturday with heavy traffic. There were coloured lights which at that time were unknown in England and the workings of which I did not understand, added to which, characteristically and in accord with Gilbert's idea of a holiday, we did not know where we wanted to go. With traffic to the right and to left of us, police whistles blowing, lights flashing, G.K. sat in the back of the car, quite oblivious, reading a detective story. Having driven into a back street, I got out and went on foot to find Cook's office, our letters and an hotel. As we sat over a very late lunch, I said, 'You weren't much help to me in my hour of need!' 'Ah, my dear Dorothy,' he said, 'You don't realize how much more helpful I was than I should have been if I had been shouting directions from the back seat.' However, over lunch, we decided to go to Sitges, a small town on the sea coast near Barcelona, where we spent several happy weeks and did a great deal of work.

At the age of 62, Chesterton died of heart failure after only about ten days' illness, three weeks after we got back from another foreign tour, this time to France, which he had much enjoyed. He had sung songs from Gilbert and Sullivan with much gusto and less tune on our long drive home from the coast, and had shown no signs of illness. Frances was devastated and unable to attend to anything. Two days before he died, his old school friend E. C. Bentley, author of *Trent's Last Case*, came down and was not able to see Gilbert, so he sat in the study with me. We had kept his illness from the press, but during the afternoon, the *Daily Mail* rang up to say they had heard the news: was it true? 'Yes', I said, 'it is true, but Mr Chesterton has to be kept very quiet and we must not have telephones and doorbells.' I extracted a promise that they would not publicize his illness. E. C. Bentley looked at me as if I were a newborn baby and said, 'You don't expect them to keep that promise, do you?' 'I do,' I said, 'but yon know the press better than I do. I still hope they will.' And they did. I wrote

to the Editor after G.K.'s death to thank him for his great
courtesy. We had two male nurses and I had to fetch one of them
out of the morning Mass on Sunday, June 14th, as Gilbert was
dying. There must have been a local press agent in the con-
gregation, for before lunch, the press from London were at the
door.

I was left as literary executor and have been busy ever since
keeping in touch with enquiries, interviews, etc and have chosen
and edited material for several posthumous books of essays, the
last two of which were *The Spice of Life* and in February 1972,
Chesterton on Shakespeare. *The Spice of Life* contains the last
broadcast.

Towards the end of his life G.K. seemed disappointed at the
way the world was going and foretold the future which was
coming to Europe. There was unrest everywhere, and he
used to say, 'The issue is clear. It is between light and darkness
and everyone must choose his side.' He had chosen his and
became more withdrawn from a saddening world. In spite of
these external worries, he seemed spiritually happy and serene
in his faith in God, to the glory of Whom his daily work was
always dedicated—by a cross on the top of the page, and even
on the line below his signature, and by a sign of the cross made
as he entered his study. In the words of his friend Walter
de la Mare, with whom there was great understanding:

> Knight of the Holy Ghost, he goes his way,
> Wisdom his motley, truth his loving jest,
> The mills of Satan keep his lance in play,
> Pity and Innocence his heart at rest.

The Relevance

A Liberal Education

JOHN SULLIVAN

The White Hart, Beaconsfield, stands at the roundabout where the A40 goes through to London. Some years ago, when the roundabout was a crossroads, I was driving by when I recalled that this was Chesterton's first port of call when he and his wife walked from Slough one day in 1909 and decided to leave Battersea for Beaconsfield. I had never been inside and thought I would now repair the omission. It was a busy Saturday night; the small bars were crowded. In one of them, I was delighted to find, in a corner case, a bust of Chesterton. The wooden frame of the glass door obscured the base of the bust and there was no indication of the name of the original. As I bought my drink, I asked the busy barman.

'Chap called Chesterton,' he said, Jingle-wise, 'Writer. Used to live down the road. This was his local. Carried home dead drunk every night, he was.'

'That's not true, you know,' I said.

'Oh! Isn't it? Well, I wouldn't know but that's what the guv'nor told me to say if anyone asked.'

Over my drink, I pondered this legend. There are so many stories about Chesterton, many authentic and many, like this one, pure fictions. But all, true and false, convey something of the image of this remarkable man which lives on in the memory of many people and in the pages of many books.

Quite recently I was reminded of this experience of years ago when I was examining a new book on Dickens. It was one of those numerous handbooks now to be had, compiled by academics for consumption by undergraduates and other inmates of the enclosed and stifling room of Eng.Lit. So thorough and exhaustive of the life and times and works of their subjects are they that one wonders when the earnest student finds time to read the originals. Maybe he doesn't. Chesterton knew all about this kind of production: 'I rather doubt whether Browning is re-read or whether Mrs Browning is read at all. There seem to be more details remembered out of the story of the Brontës than there are details remembered of the Brontë stories.'

Anyway, this recent work on Dickens carried a prefatory note by the general editor of the series: 'Dickens, popular in his own lifetime, has never lost his appeal to ordinary readers during the century that has passed since he died . . .' How true, I thought. Then followed these golden words: 'But it is not until fairly recent years that he has gained the approval of academic critics. . . .'

Thus prepared, it was with no surprise at all that I found the bibliography at the back studded with OK names such as Leavis, Edmund Wilson, Orwell, but innocent of any reference to the book that T. S. Eliot called simply 'the best essay on that author that has ever been written'—Chesterton's *Charles Dickens* (1906). This was wholly in keeping. If the academics have taken a century to get around to recognizing the towering genius of Dickens, it is not to be wondered at that Chesterton, dead a mere 37 years, even had he Dickens's genius, should be ignored by the schoolmen.

> 'Remote and ineffectual don
> That dared attack my Chesterton'

wrote Belloc, but with a few distinguished exceptions (William Empson in a revealing footnote in *Seven Types of Ambiguity*; C. S. Lewis in *Surprised by Joy*), Chesterton was not so much attacked by the dons, or even neglected by them, as not even recognized to exist. Jorge-Louis Borges may lecture on him in Buenos Aires, books galore and theses may be compiled on him and his works in England, Australia, Canada, France, Japan and the USA but he remains outside the academic establishment of Eng.Lit. It follows that the students of that establishment, who in due course teach Eng.Lit. in our schools and colleges, hardly know him either.

It was by a most fortunate chance that my own introduction to Chesterton came in my schooldays. Not from my English master, I need hardly say. He added to what may be called the hundred-year rule, his own peculiar requirement for the seal of approval that the Great Author must also be a Good Man. Thus, Milton was a GA but Byron not. (He had some trouble, I recall, over Wordsworth when that Good Man's relationship with Annette Vallon was revealed.) Chesterton would certainly have satisfied him on the Good Man score but the question did not arise, since Chesterton did not exist.

No, it happened in history when we were studying the Tudor enclosures. Of all that I then learned on that topic, I now remember only one thing—perhaps the one thing worth remembering: Thomas More looked out and saw the sheep eating the men. Memory tells me that I read it in a book I found in the library, *A Short History of England*. This, I believe, was my first acquaintance with Chesterton and the beginning of a lifelong attachment.

The epigram was not, of course, Chesterton's but More's own, in *Utopia* and Chesterton made due acknowledgment of the original:

When, therefore, we look at the world with the eyes of More, we are looking from the widest windows of that time; looking over an English landscape seen for the first time very equally, in the level light of the sun at morning. For what he saw was the England of the Renascence; England passing from the medieval to the modern. Thus he looked forth, and saw many things and said many things; they were all worthy and many witty; but he noted one thing which is at once a horrible fancy and a homely and practical fact. He who looked over the landscape said: 'Sheep are eating men'.

This brilliant spotlighting of a central idea enchanted me and I wolfed the *Short History* and moved on to other Chestertons that I found available though which, and in what order, I do not now recall. It was in this accidental way that, at an early age, I was fortunate enough to become hooked on Chesterton though, as C. S. Lewis observed of his own experience, I did not know what I was letting myself in for. Nor did I know at that time that Chesterton was alive and living in Beaconsfield, for in my school, as in many others, all authors worth talking about were, by definition, dead.

From that start, I embarked upon a reading of Chesterton in all his delightful variety: the poetry, the essays, *The Ball and the Cross*, *The Man Who Was Thursday*, *The Napoleon of Notting Hill*, the Father Brown stories, the literary criticism, the travel books, all stamped with the mark of an original. Who could resist a novel whose first sentence starts: 'The human race, to

which so many of my readers belong . . .'? I came across
Chesterton's version of the second wave of enclosures, this time
in verse:

> The people they left the land, the land,
> But they went on working hard;
> And the village green that had got mislaid
> Turned up in the squire's back-yard:
> But twenty men of us all got work
> On a bit of his motor car;
> And we all became, with the world's acclaim,
> The marvellous mugs we are.

So, as a kind of undercurrent to my formal education, I
entered upon a genuine, if by me then unrecognized, course of
liberal education. I remember an occasion at this time during
the school holidays when I arrived in Cork city on my way
home some hours before the boat was due to leave. It was a
dreary, wet day and I sheltered in the doorway of a bookshop.
Presently, through the deserted, sodden street there came a
man leading a wretched donkey bearing a placard: 'Everyone
in Cork has gone to the Shamrock Cinema to see "Lorna
Doone" except me, and I'm an Ass.' I was thinking of spending
my last half-crown and my last hours in Cork at the Shamrock
when, in the bookshop window, I saw *The Club of Queer Trades*
by G. K. Chesterton at two and sixpence, and the Shamrock
was forgotten. Later, the sun came out and I sat on deck,
fellow to the Ass, reading that strange book.

A few years later, I was editing my college magazine and,
by now aware that G.K.C. was very much alive, I wrote to
him asking for a contribution. A polite reply from his secretary
brought me news better than any contribution. Mr Chesterton
regretted that he was so busy preparing his new paper, *G.K.'s
Weekly*, that he was unable to meet my request. Glorious news!
When it appeared, there he was, week after week, in prose
and verse and story and drawings, and I revelled. When an
announcement appeared of a meeting at which Chesterton
would speak, I was there to see him for the first time; and when
the League for the Restoration of Liberty through the Distribution of Property was formed and the Friday night meetings at
the Devereux began, I became a faithful attender. I would not,

however, join the League, for from the first, Distributism seemed to me a non-starter. The meetings were fun, for in addition to keen believers, the Distributists attracted all manner of people from flat-earthers to Esperantists. From time to time one also saw and heard G.K.C. himself, Belloc, Eric Gill, and even Shaw. Indeed, the great debate, *Do We Agree?* between Chesterton and Shaw, with Belloc in the chair, held in the Kingsway Hall was, to my mind, the final nail in the coffin of the League.

The meeting was organized by the League and was to be broadcast. Arrived early, I sat in a packed hall awaiting the arrival of the gladiators. When they came, and the proceedings began, little could be heard of the opening rounds because latecomers with tickets, finding themselves shut out, forced the doors and invaded the aisles with much shouting and clamour, all of which was duly broadcast. The organizers had apparently muddled the seating and oversold the hall. No, I had little time for Distributism but suffered it for the sake of G.K.C.

There he stood on the platform: enormous, out of condition, beaming and benign: on the other side of Belloc stood Shaw, non-smoker, teetotaller, vegetarian and eighteen years Chesterton's senior, slender, upright and sparkling. The physical contrast could hardly be more striking. Yet when the row had subsided and we could hear what was being said, it became apparent that intellectually, they were in the same league. It seemed to me that Chesterton gave as good as he got and conjured a slender case into a redoubtable one against Shaw's experienced, confident Fabian banter.

It was soon after this that I took the fateful step of beginning to collect Chesterton. In Charing Cross Road I picked up for two shillings a second-hand copy of an attractive little scarlet book letttered in gold: *Poems*. It had been issued in 1915 and, as I learned much later, was designed by Francis Meynell. The collection was made up of poems from a variety of books and periodicals ranging from the famous 'Chuck it Smith!' to a hymn, 'O God of earth and altar', together with a group of love poems which appeared for the first time. This book, with my Cork acquisition, *The Club of Queer Trades* and one or two others that I bought about the same time, formed the nucleus of my collection. I was fascinated by Chesterton's range and variety; every book seemed different, yet all were delightfully the same. Before long, I found myself fired with the desire to have all his books. Inevitably this meant that for many items I had to move into the field of first editions, and the hunt was on.

Chesterton was himself by nature the very opposite of a book collector, and I sometimes think that he went out of his way to make things as hard as possible for anyone who should try to collect *him*. His first known work was never published. It is called *The History of Kids* and was dictated to an aunt at the age of three, the transcript signed by his father. His first published book was *Greybeards at Play* (1900) and his latest (but possibly not his last) *Chesterton on Shakespeare* (1972), thirty-six years after his death. The *Collected Poems* (1927) characteristically omits two volumes of verse (*Greybeards* and *The Queen of Seven Swords*) and is arranged chronologically backwards. The *Autobiography* and several other books appeared from two different publishers simultaneously. The *Autobiography* itself was published posthumously: it was followed in succeeding years by no fewer than eleven other books using material available. Most authors used to find one publisher and stick to him: Chesterton had about thirty. He produced over one hundred books and contributed to two hundred others. He designed the title-page of some of his own books and illustrated them, and illustrated the satirical novels of Belloc and several books by other authors. For most of his working life of thirty-six years, he wrote a weekly essay in *The Illustrated London News*, contributed to a weekly called successively *The Eye Witness*, *The New Witness* and *G.K.'s Weekly* and for much of the time edited and financed it to boot. His output was prodigious and in the first quarter of the century, the more he wrote, the more he was in demand. Newspapers, periodicals and popular magazines all carried his work. The fountain overflowed.

Had I been aware of this when I set out seriously to collect Chesterton, I might well have been daunted by the prospect. There was no bibliography to guide me, and in my ignorance, I decided to attempt the task myself. This is not the place to discuss the delightful and exasperating business of compiling the bibliography, which ultimately appeared in 1958. Rather would I write of what lay behind the collection and reading of Chesterton during the years before and after that date.

As I acquired and read more of his books I realized that however much I had enjoyed my sight of the living Chesterton, it had been during his autumn period. To read, for instance, an uncommon book like the record of the *Trial of John Jasper for the Murder of Edwin Drood* before Mr Justice Chesterton, which lasted nearly five hours on January 7, 1914, with many notables in court and Bernard Shaw as foreman of the jury is to recapture something of the intellectual high spirits of vanished, leisurely days. At the other extreme, *The Coloured Lands*, produced after Chesterton's death, includes nursery stories, poems, drawings and paintings done by him for various godchildren and friends and never intended for publication. Most copies of this lovely book were destroyed in Paternoster Row during the blitz: some enterprising publisher should re-issue it for, like *Greybeards at Play*, it is in the best tradition of Lewis Carroll and Edward Lear.

One of the most rewarding features of my long attachment to Chesterton has been that, in addition to the actual reading, it has led to adventures and encounters that can only be described as truly Chestertonian. There was the summer's day when I spotted in Potters Bar a cafe called 'The Flying Inn'. The burly man who served me with a cup of powerful tea had never heard of the book. 'The place had to be called summink.' I forebore telling him that this was the ultimate paradox: The Flying Inn, the last and only place in England to sell ale, was now, under his sign, offering nothing but tea and Coca Cola. Or quoting to him that

> Tea is like the East he grows in,
> A great yellow Mandarin
> With urbanity of manner
> And unconsciousness of sin;
> All the women, like a harem,
> At his pig-tail troop along;
> And, like all the East he grows in,
> He is Poison when he's strong.
>
> Tea, although an Oriental,
> Is a gentleman at least;
> Cocoa is a cad and coward,

Cocoa is a vulgar beast,
Cocoa is a dull, disloyal,
Lying, crawling cad and clown,
And may very well be grateful
To the fool that takes him down.

As for all the windy waters,
That were rained like tempests down
When good drink had been dishonoured
By the tipplers of the town;
When red wine had brought red ruin
And the death-dance of our times,
Heaven sent us Soda Water
As a torment for our crimes.

At a dinner for Sir Edmund Hillary, my neighbour, a total stranger, quoted Chesterton at some length. It turned out that he was a member of Hillary's team and on three climbs in the Himalayas and the 1957–58 expedition to the South Pole had always taken one book with him: it was *Wine, Water and Song*. No, he hadn't read anything else of Chesterton but that one he knew by heart.

Delightful days were spent in Beaconsfield following the Chesterton trail. It begins with The White Hart, which now has a Chesterton Room with the bust displayed in a lighted niche and a small collection of books, drawings and MSS. Thence one proceeds 'down the road', as the barman said, to 'Overroads' where the Chestertons first lived in Beaconsfield, and opposite is Top Meadow, the modest house they built and lived in until their death. It was here that Chesterton wrote most of his works from 1922 till 1936 with a truly ferocious energy. And across the garden is Top Meadow Cottage in which Miss Dorothy Collins, who worked with him in those years, keeps her treasure house of Chestertoniana. Lower down the road is a large pub which used to be called the Railway Hotel, one bar of which incorporates the small hut that was formerly used by the Catholics until their new church was built. It was here that Chesterton was received into the Catholic Church by Monsignor O'Connor, the original of Father Brown. (One wonders, in passing, if there is any other instance of a book written about an author by the original of one of his fictional characters, like Monsignor O'Connor's *Father Brown on Chesterton*.) The church of St Teresa and the English Martyrs was completed as a memorial to Gilbert Keith Chesterton 'through the generosity of his friends and admirers throughout the world' as a tablet at the entrance records. The little tour ends with a visit to the cemetery where Gilbert and Frances Chesterton lie beneath a headstone carved by Eric Gill, and perhaps a return to The White Hart to drink their health.

After one such visit recently, I sat in The White Hart and thought: 'Chesterton, popular in his own lifetime, has never lost his appeal to ordinary readers during the thirty-seven years that have passed since he died.' Would this do? Hardly. On the evidence, one must say, for 'ordinary' read 'some'. Clearly his popularity has diminished since the days when the initials G.K.C., like those of G.B.S., were familiar to the man on the Clapham bus. For a time after a writer's death, there is inevitably a falling-off in public interest since no new work appears to keep him in mind. In Chesterton's case, both his enormous literary output and the vigorous impact of his personality were lost. Then, for reasons already mentioned, the younger generation is not introduced to him as an author worthy of study: in the age of Beckett and Genet, Chesterton, glibly labelled 'optimist', has no place. Finally, his very versatility has told against him.

He was a specimen of that now extinct species, the Man of Letters, like Dr Johnson with whom he has so often been compared. He could, and did, turn his pen to almost anything and even within each branch of letters displayed variety. A close examination of the *Collected Poems*, for instance, reveals that he exploited most poetic forms, from the epigram to the epic, and invented new ones, such as Answers to the Poets. His parodies and his translations from the French, though few, have won high commendation whilst his satirical poetry is remembered in days when the subjects of them are half forgotten. This fecundity and versatility would not be notable were it not for the fact that, among a great deal of run-of-the-mill stuff, there is so much and in so many literary forms, that is first-class of its kind. Moreover, some of his observations of the way the world was going we can now recognize as having been profoundly true. Reference has often been made to his

anticipation of a colossal war that might come, a war that he
did not live to see. No reader of *Private Eye* who also knows his
Chesterton can fail to note, in its temper and its choice of
subjects for attack, the *G.K.'s Weekly de nos jours*. The Marconi
Case, which Chesterton held to be so important in its revelation
of corruption in high places but which was successfully played
down by most publicists and historians, is now replaced by the
Poulson Case, bigger and better than ever. Chesterton foretold
a time when our newspapers would be few in number and would
be advertising sheets on the back of which would be printed
such of the news as their handful of millionaire owners deemed
it suitable for their readers to know. Lord Beaverbrook banned
the names of Chesterton and Belloc from his *Express* newspapers, thus testifying in a comparatively small way to Chesterton's views on the power of newspaper proprietors to manipulate
the 'news'.

Reading his books and his contributions to the books of
others, his articles, letters and controversies conducted in
almost every journal of note in his day, one catches something
of Chesterton's zest for living, his truly democratic temper, and
his essential goodness. After all his literary and platform battles
he left no enemies: even H. G. Wells could not quarrel with
him. 'Dear old G.K.C.' wrote Wells in 1933. 'If all my
Atheology turns out wrong and your Theology right, I feel I
shall always be able to pass into Heaven (if I want to) as a
friend of G.K.C.'s. Bless you. . . ." In fact, the only really
vicious attack upon Chesterton by anyone of worth came some
years after Chesterton's death from one with whom he had never
crossed swords, Sean O'Casey. In *Sunset and Evening Star* (1954),
O'Casey relates that he and his wife, taking a flat at forty-nine
Overstrand Mansions, Battersea, learned that the Chestertons
had once lived for some years in forty-eight—'next door,
be God!' At this point, O'Casey's observations on Chesterton,
and later in the book contrasting Chesterton with his hero
Shaw, were so violent and wrong-headed that I wrote to him
in protest. My reward was two further pages of objurgations
which might have come straight from *Juno and the Paycock* but
which carried no word of reply to my arguments.

Signs of a true recognition of Chesterton's worth in our own
day have appeared in very recent years. In 1969, John Gross,

in *The Rise and Fall of the Man of Letters*, devotes a separate
section of eight pages to Chesterton. Whilst rating him as a
journalist (which is no more than Chesterton ever claimed for
himself) who wrote too much, Gross says: 'He was a man of
remarkable gifts, far more remarkable than his present over-
clouded reputation would suggest. At his finest, for instance,
he was a wittier writer than Oscar Wilde or Max Beerbohm (as
Beerbohm himself readily acknowledged): wittier because he
had a deeper understanding of life.' In 1970, W. H. Auden
made a selection of Chesterton's non-fictional prose and in
1972, Volume 4 of the *New Cambridge Bibliography of English
Literature 1900-1950* filled four pages closely printed in double
column with the Chesterton record. In the same year, Kingsley
Amis edited a selection of Chesterton's short stories with a
critical introduction. The review of this book in the *Times
Literary Supplement* ends: 'It seems likely that we can all accept
at last that Chesterton belongs to the great writers, and it may
be possible for him soon to be taken seriously by scholars.'

Not that Chesterton would have cared. No writer ever had
less concern for the fate of his books or for his chances of
literary immortality. But it is good to see these tributes at this
time and I hope that those who, like me, have derived a liberal
education from encounters with Chesterton, will grow in
numbers,

'For there is good news yet to hear and fine things to be seen,
Before we go to Paradise by way of Kensal Green.'

Chesterton and the Future of Democracy

PATRICK CAHILL

To an essay on the importance of Chesterton's social philosphy
and its relevance to our times, T. S. Eliot's obituary tribute for
The Tablet (June 20, 1936) makes a most pertinent introduction.
From this I quote:

The notices that I have seen in the general Press seem to me to have
exaggerated Chesterton's achievements in some obvious respects,
and to have ignored his achievements in much more important ones.
His poetry was first rate journalistic balladry, and I do not suppose
that he took it more seriously than it deserved. He reached a high
imaginative level with *The Napoleon of Notting Hill*, and higher with
The Man Who Was Thursday, romances in which he turned the
Stevensonian fantasy to more serious purpose. His book on Dickens
seems to me the best essay on that author that has ever been
written. Some of his essays can be read again and again; though of
his essay-writing as a whole, one can only say that it is remarkable
to have maintained such a high average with so large an output.
But it is not, I think, for any piece of writing in particular that
Chesterton is of importance, but for the place that he occupied, the
position that he represented, during the better part of a generation.
And when I say 'place' or 'position' I attach significance also to his
development, to his beginnings as well as to his ends, and to the
movement from one to the other.

To judge Chesterton on his 'contributions to literature', then,
would be to apply the wrong standards of measurement. It is in
other matters that he was importantly and consistently on the side
of the angels. Behind the Johnsonian fancy-dress, so reassuring to
the British public, he concealed the most serious and revolutionary
designs—concealing them by exposure, as his anarchist conspirators chose to hold their meetings on a balcony in Leicester
Square. (The real Johnson, indeed, with his theology, politics and
morals, would be quite as alien to the modern world of public
opinion as Chesterton himself.) Even if Chesterton's social and
economic ideas appear to be totally without effect, even if they should
be demonstrated to be wrong—which would perhaps only mean that
men have not the goodwill to carry them out—they were the ideas
for his time that were fundamentally Christian and Catholic. He did

more, I think, than any man of his time—and was able to do more than anyone else, because of his particular background, development and abilities as a public performer—to maintain the existence of the important minority in the modern world. He leaves behind a permanent claim upon our loyalty, to see that the work that he did in his time is continued in ours.

Many Chestertonians deplore the master's preoccupation with social, political and economic ideas and regret that so much of his writing was devoted to public affairs instead of to literature. To them one must say that he himself would have deeply appreciated Eliot's assessment; for Chesterton deliberately dedicated his genius to speaking out for justice, freedom and common sense in a society devoted to the pursuit of money and the things it bought. Gently but much in the tradition of the ancient Jewish prophets, he called the people back to the truth and away from the idols of ruthless greed and mechanical power.

However, there is no necessary conflict between Chesterton's literary achievement and his social teaching. In the kind of society he wanted—with art not separated from the people but integrated in the crafts and uses of town and countryside—there should be a permanent demand for fine story-telling and first-rate ballads, informed by wisdom and humanity and blessed with a bounty of humour and wit.

That society, the 'Distributive state', was the centre of Chesterton's 'most serious and revolutionary designs'. It is my concern in this essay to show that Chesterton's Distributist ideas, and his attitudes to certain fundamental social and political questions, are as relevant and right today as they were half a century ago. It will therefore often be necessary to analyse the situation of today in order to suggest how it relates to Chesterton's reactions of yesterday. I shall briefly re-state the principles of Distributism here in terms which will be readily understandable in the context of a modern industrialized society. My statement, I hope, will be seen to be consonant with Chesterton's own writings, and to reflect his distinctive belief in, and optimism about, ordinary human beings.

Distributism bases democracy on the widest distribution of

economic power amongst the people. Its two principles are:
(1) that a secure and sufficient economic independence is
normally necessary for individual freedom;
(2) that, consequently, workers should own or control the
means of production, whether as self-employed or co-operative
producers, or in such other ways as best express the principle
in particular cases.

The aim is a general social character of ownership and
democracy—in a dynamic equilibrium which encourages
initiative and multiplicity without danger to the common good.

Distributism has very much in common with the industrial
democracy emerging today as a people-centred reaction to the
work, institutions and government of our anomic and alienated
society. Even the slogan and concept of 'participation'—so
popular today—were written by Chesterton into a founding
document of the League as long ago as 1926:

> The commercial and industrial progress which began by professing
> individualism has ended with the complete swamping of the indi-
> vidual. The concentration of capital in large heaps controlled by
> little groups has now become equally obvious to those who defend
> and those who deplore it. But even those who deplore it seldom
> really try to reverse it. The problems of centralised wealth has pro-
> duced proposals that what is centralised should be centralised even
> more, by State ownership or nationalisation, but it has not produced
> the perfectly simple proposal that what is centralised should be
> decentralised by the voluntary co-operation of small owners. . . .
>
> *Distributism* advocates and will work to secure the break-up of
> plutocratic concentration in agriculture, industry, and finance not
> only by the distribution of tangible assets (Land and Tools) but by
> obtaining for all a *participation* in the natural and accumulated
> wealth of the community.[1][Emphasis—P.C.]

The nature of work

Most work in a capitalist economy is proletarian: work
without satisfaction—often in stupidity, discord or servility—
ranging from the dull triviality of the less burdensome tasks to
the harsh boredom of oppressive toil. In other words workers
are alienated from their work and the community. The
situation is no different in the nationalized industries of the
mixed economy as everyone in Britain knows to his cost. Nor

has the nationalization of the means of production by communist states in any way overcome the workers' alienation from the factories; indeed it has deepened it because of the increased bureaucratization of management.

Chesterton much more positively than Marx thought that it is not only human servitude but human dignity and freedom which are involved in the relation of the worker to production. Furthermore the only workers who massively demonstrate their integrity are peasants. There is no alienation to be found between the peasant and his labour and produce, which directly support him and his family; nor between each peasant and his neighbours in the local community. And the peasant's artistic activities integrate him into the national culture, so variously and delightfully expressed in different parts of the world. Yet the peasant has always been criticized as a creature of convention, stupid and stick-in-the-mud and bound to a dull and dreary existence. 'I know', says Chesterton,

it is said that a man must find it monotonous to do the twenty things that are done on a farm, whereas, of course, he always finds it uproariously funny and festive to do one thing hour after hour and day after day in a factory. I know that the same people also make exactly the contrary comment; and say it is selfish and avaricious for the peasant to be so intensely interested in his own farm, instead of showing, like the proletarians of modern industrialism, a selfish and romantic loyalty to somebody else's factory, and an ascetic self-sacrifice in making profits for somebody else.[2]

The truth about the peasant is that he persists despite the hostile environment of urbanized big business and government. He (and other small independents) have never been subsidized in the way society has subsidized and suffered from industry and its proletariat. Had comparable funds been spent in rural areas the problem of urbanization would not now be ubiquitous, nor the peasants and their supporters be accused of medievalism and conservatism. The Polish peasantry, for example, still owns three-quarters of the land, feeds the nation, and provides one-third of the national exports; yet until recently it was excluded from the health service and subject to constant threats and inequalities.

The massive persistence and resilience of peasantries everywhere derives from the nature of their work, the integrity of their communities and the natural wisdom engendered by closeness to the soil. Even at the level of bare subsistence and unjust conditions of land tenure, 'It All Depends on the Peasant'. This headline, with the message 'small is beautiful', is the gist of a report from the UN Economic Commission for Asia—even in the knowledge that there will be 500 million more to be fed in Asia before 1980. Whether in commune or co-operative, 'the real point of following a policy that gives priority to the peasant is that only in this way do any of these countries have even a hope of laying the foundations for self-reliance in the future'.[3]

Another aspect of the nature of work is particularly recalled by the craftsman, the second Distributist type. It is expressed in a saying of Eric Gill, the sculptor and engraver, a friend and supporter of Chesterton: 'the artist is not a special kind of man, but every man is a special kind of artist.' The implication is that all workers have the need of human work and productive responsibility, so that in full variety they may express their birthright of creativity and contribute to the construction of the world. Indeed the sophists of torture in Auschwitz recognized this truth by depriving craftsmen of their crafts when the normal organization of work would have called for the use of their skills.

The third exemplar whom Chesterton favoured is not, at first glance, so obviously a Distributist model as the peasant and the craftsman. Yet if one reflects on one's local shopping centre it is clear that much shopkeeping involves skills, such as those of the butcher, the barber, the shoe-repairer, the cook and so on—all in addition to the service of providing goods with a certain grace that is absent from hired work. Certainly the small man still provides a widespread service which big business cannot render profitably, and he would do this with more security if the public (whose general interest he so definitely serves) could persuade its individual members that always to 'shop cheap' may not be in their long-term interest.

Fortunately, in the affluent society there is at last some recognition that people seek work from which they can obtain satisfaction. The assembly line, with its monotonous, repetitive cycle swiftly recurring throughout each day, has in some cases been advantageously superseded by workers assembling the whole product themselves. There have even been experiments in restructuring industry on the basis of autonomous work groups —as well as in encouraging production through humanizing industrial relations.

The industrial psychologists are satisfied that the experiments show improved quantitative results, fewer stoppages and lower labour turnover. People, they assure us, work best when they enjoy their jobs, and the better integrated they are with their work the more they will exercise their creativity. If the trend towards responsibility and involvement develops into a Chestertonian conception of work, it may yet be discovered that the extent to which work benefits society varies directly with the degree to which the worker makes it his own. Ownership is the reverse of alienation.

Bigness and bureaucracy

Many of Chesterton's readers thought his championship of the small against the big simply the chivalric and romantic expression of a quixotic mind—a defence of old traditions against the inevitable march of progress. Without doubt his natural inclination was to favour the small, the poor and the weak. He was also fully aware that all the institutions of capitalist society are unfairly biased in favour of the big.

Twice in my life has an editor told me in so many words that he dared not print what I had written, because it would offend the advertisers in his paper. . . . On both these occasions he denied me liberty of expression because I said that the widely advertised stores and large shops were really worse than little shops. That, it may be interesting to note, is one of the things that a man is now forbidden to say; perhaps the only thing he is really forbidden to say. If it had been an attack on Government, it would have been tolerated. If it had been an attack on God, it would have been respectfully and tactfully applauded. If I had been abusing marriage or patriotism or public decency, I should have been heralded in headlines and allowed to sprawl across Sunday newspapers. But the big newspaper is not likely to attack the big shop; being itself a big shop in its way and more and more a monument of monopoly. But it will be well if I repeat here in a book what I found it impossible to repeat in an article. I think the big shop is a bad shop. I think it bad not only in a moral but a mercantile sense; that is, I think shopping there is not only a bad action but a bad bargain. I think the monster emporium is not only vulgar and insolent but incompetent and uncomfortable.[4]

Chesterton's ideas about the nature of work led him to support small businesses in general since their workers tend to have direct and human relations with the owner-managers and have a better chance of being well integrated, happy and independent at work. Such firms are flexible and adaptable and take a greater interest in the requirements and needs of workers and customers. The Bolton Committee on Small Firms which reported to the Government in 1971 evidenced revived interest in this field and provided information and measures designed to remove discrimination from a sector engaging a quarter of the national work force. The findings show that there is no evidence that these firms are less efficient than the big, and, further, that they are the principal source of new ideas and inventions for industry. Chesterton, however, is more positive:

Large organisation is loose organisation. Nay, it would be almost as true to say that organisation is always disorganisation. The only thing perfectly organic is an organism; like that grotesque and obscure organism called a man. He alone can be quite certain of doing what he wants; beyond him, every extra man may be an extra mistake.[5]

To enlarge on this simple logic, it is true that the bigger an organization the greater will be its human tendency to inefficiency and disintegration. The various steps in the decision and action cycle are carried out by many persons instead of by few; and their widely varying experience, perceptions and goals require to be controlled and united by costly and time-absorbing mechanisms of internal communication which in transmission inevitably involve errors and distortions. Evaluation is necessarily fragmented because no one ever knows the whole story; and few understand it better after the specialists have done with it.

In order to counteract this natural tendency to disintegration, organization has adopted the mechanism of a formal structure of authority. This comprises the offices, institutions and procedures within and through which the powers and functions of the organization are exercised, particularly those of unitive discipline and of decision-making in accordance with the laws laid down. Authority is expressed through the superior-subordinate relationship, and apart from the top and lowest grades of the hierarchy every office-holder has the double role of superior to some people and subordinate to others. Each role is accountable for performing certain tasks and using resources in performing them, with appropriate discretion and within the limits established. The ideal type of such a formal structure is an hierarchical organization centrally directed to the service of its lawful authority.

Almost inevitably, however, powers and discretion allocated or appropriated by the organization are in varying degrees exercised, not for its lawful purposes but for the benefit of members or of the organization itself, whether it be for power, for prestige or for private gain. In such cases the organization is in the strictest definition a bureaucracy, for it is under the autonomous rule of office-holders.

One of the characteristic defence mechanisms developed by the bureaucrat is issuing regulations to protect himself in case anything goes wrong. From apex to base the burden of regulation multiplies step by step until work by the masses is almost impossible. Consequently the regulations are substantially ignored by the workers unless observance can be utilized during a dispute in support of their claims. Then, instead of striking, they impede or halt the organization simply by working to rule without forfeiture of pay. Such bureaucrats are well described by Robert Michels:

Bureaucracy is the sworn enemy of individual liberty and of all bold initiative in matters of internal policy. . . . The bureaucratic spirit corrupts character and engenders moral poverty. In every bureaucracy we may observe place-hunting, a mania for promotion and obsequiousness towards those on whom promotion depends; there is arrogance towards inferiors and servility towards superiors.[6]

The irresponsibility built into the very structure of bureaucracy is reflected in its incompetence and vulnerability. The organization has to act through a complex and expensive system of forecasting and planning, but out-of-date figures, errors and omissions are so multiplied by projection that the effort degenerates into futility. As regards business failures, the big get proportionately much more financial credit than the small; so the bigger the losses the more helpless are the shareholders and employees, unless the failure and incompetence be of such a size as to embarrass the government. The solution then is to pour taxpayers' money down the open drain in the hope that the smell will go away.

The litany of lame ducks adds up to millions of pounds, but these figures are nothing compared with the expenditure and waste of big governments. Any Briton can savour this for himself in almost any report from either the Public Accounts and Expenditure Committees of the House of Commons or the Comptroller and Auditor General.

In general the cost of government activities, and the secrecy, anti-social nature and irresponsibility of many of them, make one shudder for the future of democracy. We ordinary citizens, incapable of thinking in terms of the tens, hundreds, even thousands of millions of pounds which big business and big government spend and waste, think it doesn't matter much anyhow. But the figures always reflect the production and labour of the people: it is the commonwealth that is always diminished, and it is a privileged élite that always benefits, whatever happens to the rest.

According to a report issued by Ralph Nader,[7] political pressures and inefficiency in the enforcement of United States anti-monopoly laws cost consumers between £20,000 million and £25,000 million a year in excess charges. 'Like sex in Victorian England', the report says, 'the reality of big business is our big dirty secret.' To stress the enormity of but one example, the figures quoted are equivalent to half Britain's gross national product and far exceed the national products of most countries in the world. The work which Mr Nader is doing in the United States for his fellow citizens has proved that bigness, corruption, waste and inefficiency go together.

The following principle may be derived from Chesterton's utterance on the subject: An organization should be no bigger than it has to be for the performance of its functions and services.

And, if the principle is circumvented, one might then add: The people who perform those functions and services should be directly responsible for them; that is, they should be owners.

The technocrats

The sin is not that engines are mechanical, but that men are mechanical. Inventions have destroyed invention ... instead of the machine being a giant to which man is a pygmy, we must at least reverse the proportion until man is a giant to whom the machine is a toy.[8]

Unfortunately (but perhaps inevitably) the industrial revolution developed in a country where great wealth was already concentrated in the hands of a few and where capitalists were already exploiting workers in the heavy industries. Thus, in Britain, inventions and the new technology were directed to support large enterprise instead of small, and science and economics were speedily perverted to the pursuit of larger and larger profits for the privileged owners.

There was an obvious affinity between the mechanical organization of big business and the applications of science and economics to heavy industry and manufacturing. The dominant factor in the union of technology and bureaucracy varied according to circumstances. In so far as the pursuit of techniques became the 'sweet' and supreme good, the resulting technology developed more complex machines and more intense division of labour until the machine-minder's sub-human tasks were assumed by the electronics of automation.

Paradoxically, although the technological mastery of nature opens the way to higher levels of human existence, technology which should be the servant of humanity can itself become a principal obstacle to advance if it strives to dominate man. The right name for it then is *technocracy*. As the following statements indicate, we are quite incapable of forecasting the full effects and the future abuses of modern technology, or the restrictions on freedom and other counter-measures which may consequently be necessary.

(1) 'The Bomb' inevitably symbolizes the technology of warfare, and to some the mere availability of nuclear power, whatever its application.

(2) The multiform pollution of the environment notoriously threatens the future of our species. It is relevant that the reaction of the doomsters recalls the Distributist land colonization movements of the 1930s.

(3) The centralization of industrialized economies has made them vulnerable not only to warfare but to nearly all human vices, deficiencies—and virtues! For instance, a few people can hold a country to ransom either by halting large sections of industry for whatever reason, or by merely threatening to do so.

(4) In a world of massive unemployment and underemployment technocracy devotes itself to designing labour-saving machinery which provides economic benefits mainly for a minority. So our planet has both to bear the huge additional cost of the capital investment and continue to provide subsistence for the labour recklessly and unnecessarily displaced. The human costs of unemployment are not to be compared with sectional or local gains.

(5) President Tito's deputy has warned his party against a technocracy which neglects the real needs of man and creates anti-human relationships under the slogan of progress or modernization. (Yugoslavia's unique experiment in self-management by the workers is substantial and, despite economic difficulties, resembles the proposals of Chesterton's Braintree quoted at the end of this essay.)

(6) The psychological harm that mass production techniques have done to workers has resulted in open and secret sabotage and a high percentage of rejections, labour turnover and absenteeism—not to mention the notorious deficiencies discovered only after the product is bought.

(7) There is no sound economic evidence which confirms that production-line techniques generally are the most efficient and profitable methods of production.[9]

(8) A principal vice of the technocrats is their impetuosity and immaturity. They are like those children who prefer experimenting with the real thing to playing with toys. Let us hope it is an exaggeration to suggest that technocratic irresponsibility in general is on such a scale as to merit comparison with the special case of the Bomb. Yet there are indications. One case is the central generation of electricity which entails

the waste of 60 per cent of the heat generated. This thermal pollution and waste could be avoided by total energy systems in which electricity is generated near where it can be used for water- and space-heating and similar purposes.

(9) Professor Zuckerman tells us that it is not technology but we ourselves who are to blame for its failure to provide us with justice and peace. What often happens is that those who rule us rely on the econometrists and such specialists to keep the technocrats under control, and that in many cases is like putting a lively and undisciplined child in the charge of someone who is blind, lame and deaf. Neither the economist nor the technocrat knows where he is going. But a demonic activism presses on regardless, with huge capital expenditure based on inaccurate projections of commercial trends and figures no longer relevant. According to a saying of Chesterton, progress is finding a good place to stop—if only to reflect on his question, 'If everything changes, including the mind of man, how can we tell whether any change is an improvement or no?'[10]

Technology is fully capable of serving the growth of economic democracy; it could do so if technologists resisted the temptation to become tear-away technocrats and learned what services society needs of them. Evidence already exists that semi-autonomous work teams achieve greater job satisfaction and thereby produce more and better goods in less time, at less cost and with lower labour turnover.[11] Further experiments in restructuring industry in a people-centred way need to be matched by a new industrial revolution. No longer can the degradation of human beings and the extreme division of labour be tolerated. What is wanted is the reduction and devolution of the machine in a technology appropriate to self-managing groups. In this connection the notion of decreasing the size of machines has not been explored intensively. Yet present technical data and experience could well develop new methods capable of humanizing work and producing new kinds of commodities. Such production could well move nearer the tradition of the craftsman and away from the commerce of mass-produced and mediocre uniformity—the sort that fits the foot to the shoe and the man to the beer instead of the other way around.

This new technology would be in natural alliance with

labour-intensive Intermediate Technology[12] which is designed
for the needs of the vast majority of workers who inhabit the
rural areas of developing countries—a very substantial part of
the world's workers whose basic needs must concern us all. It
is essential, therefore, that the requisite development technology
be accompanied by such just socio-economic structures as will
bring peace, prosperity and goodwill to the masses whose need
is greatest.

Were it not for one extraordinary thing, these ideas might
well seem utopian in a society where big business and central
government unite in an all-powerful technocracy. The thing
that happened was that in April 1973 the European Commission recommended the abolition throughout the Community of
assembly-line operations—the type of all collectivist production,
in which the worker, doing one small task repeatedly, can do it
well only by becoming a mechanical slave. A mere recom-
mendation, socio-economic and dull-sounding, but to one
Chestertonian a trumpet-blast of revolt against the tyranny of
the machine!

Consolidarity

If we proceed as at present in a proper orderly fashion, the very
idea of property will vanish. It is not revolutionary violence that
will destroy it. It is rather the desperate and reckless habit of not
having a revolution. The world will be occupied, or rather is already
occupied, by two powers which are now one power. . . . One of
these powers is State Socialism and the other is Big Business. They
are already one spirit; they will soon be one body. For, disbelieving
in division, they cannot remain divided; believing only in combination, they will themselves combine. At present one of them calls
it Solidarity and the other calls it Consolidation. It would seem that
we have only to wait while both monsters are taught to say Consolidarity.[13]

The tendency to consolidarity between the industrialized
countries of East and West is a natural consequence of their
bureaucratic structures of control. Technocrats and managers
everywhere have much in common—especially a proclivity to
establish a meritocracy. Nor is it surprising to learn that the
Soviet Union with its centrally controlled and planned economy

has borrowed heavily from American corporate practice in its latest reform of industrial management.

On the international scene the alliance between Russian state capitalism and cosmopolitan plutocracy was long foreseen, with a division of the world into two spheres of influence nominally opposed but each exploiting the many for the benefit of the few. This capitalist-socialist concensus of remote autocrats and faceless bureaucrats is characterized by the same hypocrisy and injustice and the same irresponsible technology, racial oppression, violence, militarism and secret-police power. When we compare Russia in Czechoslovakia with America in Vietnam, the corruption of the United States appears worse because democratic protest and exposure still survive there.

Clear evidence of consolidarity is to be found in the British economy. In a plutocracy it is, of course, the practice that the failures of private enterprise become the burdens of the taxpayer, and that its lame ducks receive infusions of public money when there is a chance of future profits for the privileged. It will not be a matter of great surprise that public expenditure is well over half the gross national product and that the taxation burden is 42½ per cent of GNP.[14]

In the remainder of the economy big business accounts for more production than do the unorganized small firms (20 per cent of GNP) and independents. The Confederation of British Industries (CBI) is deemed to represent the whole of this side of industry. Similarly, the other side of industry—the employees—is represented by the Trades Union Congress. Membership of unions affiliated to the TUC is about 40 per cent of the total work force of 25 million. But half of the members are in the nine largest unions which have a monopoly power in those industries essential to running the economy.[15]

As a consequence the higher civil servants have seen the need and the convenience of a new bureaucratic structure for economic control. Accordingly, the Government has already offered management (the CBI) and unions (the TUC) an unprecedented share in the running of the country, and the new arrangement should entail legal recognition of the somewhat sketchy representative quality of the new organ of consolidarity. Doubtless it will follow the well-tried procedure of government orders flexibly modified when necessary by nudge and nod.

Generally speaking once an organizational structure is
securely established—that is, when it is fully bureaucratic—
the machine controls the methodology and the information
available to the office-holder. Then, if everything functions
perfectly, the consequent decisions of a Tory are barely
distinguishable from those of a Socialist. So bureaucracy like
technocracy is a powerful agent of consolidarity.

When Shadow Minister Wedgwood Benn was last in office
he spent his time and our money in encouraging the amalgama-
tion of large companies in the private sector. Now, in welcoming
and listing 17 new areas of Government control, he con-
gratulates the Conservative Government on their reciprocal
spadework for Socialism in the following words:

These Bills and Acts together with the Prices and Pay Code,
constitute the most comprehensive armoury of Government control
that has ever been assembled for use over private industry, far
exceeding all the powers thought to be necessary by the last Labour
government. [1964–1970][16]

To show that both parties are openly agreed I quote the
comments of the conservative *Daily Mail* on two gifts of the
same Government—a mere £6½ million—designed to encourage lame ducks to swim together:

Monopoly is the name of the game. We are all size-worshippers
nowadays. Call it rationalization or nationalization, but both
Labour and Tory now agree 'bigness is best'. . .
    Free enterprise as we have known it is dead. The competition is
now between nations. And there can be no going back.
    But the hard truth is that size in itself is no recipe for financial
success. It's management that matters.
    Rolls-Royce didn't go bust because it was too small.[17]

Apropos of ultimate consolidarity, Chesterton was once
reported as saying he had no sympathy with Communism—no
more than he had with cannibalism. They both represented
the doctrine of the complete unification of man in man.[18] But
as we go on to consider Parliament, the interesting question
arises: Who swallows whom?

The Party System

One of the most obvious arguments of the Socialist is that the system of this country is already a hierarchy, with people controlling departments, landlords and commercial magnates. He says: 'It is idle to talk of whether property shall be concentrated. It is already concentrated; only it is not concentrated for the public good.'

But these big owners are, by a universal chorus of modern magazines and newspapers, saluted as the strongest and most sagacious figures of their time. This millionaire, we are told, gained his power by sheer pluck, that one by sheer grit, the other (one often hears) by sheer Christianity. In the same way one duke is called the best of landlords, another the most quiet and capable of politicians. There, then, are the holes in the new machine gaping for lords and masters; and there are a set of men perpetually praised to the populace for their lordship and mastery. I will bet any ordinary pair of boots that when the revolution comes these men step out of their shoes in order to step into them again, or do not step out of them at all. . . . I seriously believe that the storm of socialism will pass, and leave our whole oligarchy standing.[19]

Bureaucratic consolidarity has long been a particular feature of the British Party System. Hilaire Belloc and Cecil Chesterton published their book on front-bench collusion, *The Party System*, in 1911, the same year as Robert Michels published his profound study of the oligarchic tendencies of modern democracy in general (*Political Parties*). The special feature of the British system is not merely the illustration of Michels' Iron Law of Oligarchy—'the power of the leaders is directly proportional with the extension of the organization'—but the unified and unique way in which the system acts as a cover for a privileged establishment, apparently amorphous but possessed of undefined, anonymous power. Most of the other structures, institutions and systems of our society also operate to maintain the status quo; but the primary function of these is not deception. In politics, however, it is otherwise, as Chesterton long ago pointed out: 'The party system itself implies a habit of stating something other than the actual truth. A Leader of the House means a Misleader of the House.'[20]

Chesterton's conception of the British Party System remains as valid as ever. His view of party politics profoundly affected him

as a human being and as a citizen, as a public figure and as a
man of letters. It was central also to the propagation of his
social ideas in this country and may have affected his life at
deeper levels.

Let me first briefly outline the British parliamentary system,
before relating it to Chesterton's views:

(1) Members of Parliament are elected by universal suffrage
at elections held on the average once every $3\frac{1}{2}$ years.

(2) The majority of Members so elected normally provides the
Prime Minister and his Government.

(3) The Government submits legislation and policies to
Parliament for debate and decision, and the opponents may
submit alternatives.

(4) The House of Commons effectively has sovereign power.

(1) Although in theory it is possible for 630 independents to
be elected to Parliament, in practice there is no real choice
because with rare exceptions a candidate has to be a nominee of
one of the parties in order to ensure the money and publicity
necessary for election. The range of choice between Tweedle-
dum and Tweedledee discloses a very limited part of the
political spectrum. Indeed the programmes presented sometimes appear to reflect an agreement to keep important questions from public consideration. This, however, is not a matter
of great moment because programmes can be changed,
reversed or interchanged at any time without reference to or
protest from the citizens. One would thus expect those voting
to be a low percentage of the electorate; but as Chesterton
says, 'The question is not so much whether only a minority of
the electorate votes. The point is that only a minority
of the voter votes.'[21]

(2) The Prime Minister is not selected by Parliament. The
party organization has already made him and probably the
Government he nominates. 'Who says organization says
oligarchy. Every party organization represents an oligarchical
power grounded upon a democratic basis. We find everywhere
electors and elected. Also we find everywhere that the power
of the elected leaders over the electing masses is almost un-
limited. The oligarchical structure of the building suffocates
the basic democratic principle'.[22]

(3) The principal function of Parliament is simply to pass the Government's programme of legislation by each supporter voting as he is told. The irrelevant charade of speech-making and debate is futile, for (as a recently elected Member[23] says) they play no part in influencing the voting which is on rigid party lines. 'The present rotten system' (as he calls it) could not exist without its rewards and privileges. Nor, it might be added, without the collusion of the parties which control the time-table and the machinery of the House.

(4) Although the House of Commons has the capacity to legalize the most revolutionary proposals, Members normally vote on rigid party lines at the behest of the Whips. The House of Lords, which has certain minor powers of delay, appears to be maintained by the party-consensus chiefly in order to avoid any possibility of reality stealing in with a new second chamber.

The Lords as a non-institution is at least harmless and obvious. But the negative and principal function of the Commons is more sinister than the rubber-stamp approval of legislation at the behest of the parliamentary executive (regardless of the play-acting and what is said in the debates). There is more to it than Chesterton's reasons why we have lost democracy: '(a) The omnipotence of an unelected body, the Cabinet; (b) the Party system, which turns all politics into a game like the Boat Race'.

Many intelligent people would agree with that early diagnosis without feeling the need to hate the Party System or even to decline participation in it. But Chesterton also knew and deeply felt that the System was bound up with the distribution of property in the modern world. This injustice he called, in his great debate of 1927 with Shaw, 'a monstrosity and a blasphemy'. Before and since spokesmen of the left have said likewise. Yet, today, a few of them frankly admit how remarkably little change there has been in that area.

Both major parties lack completely any credibility in these fields. Cynicism and apathy toward politicians and Government are gnawing at the vitals of our democracy. On such foundations are dictatorships built. The prospect is horrendous![25]

Chesterton hated the Party System because it was 'an

enormous and most efficient machine for preventing political conflicts.'

The real evil of our Party System is commonly stated wrong. It was stated wrong by Ld. Rosebery when he said that it prevented the best men from devoting themselves to politics, and that it encouraged a fanatical conflict. I doubt whether the best men ever would devote themselves to politics. The best men devote themselves to pigs and babies and things like that. And as for the fanatical conflict in party politics, I wish there was more of it. The real danger of the two parties with their two policies is that they unduly limit the outlook of the ordinary citizen. They make him barren instead of creative, because he is never allowed to do anything except prefer one existing policy to another. We have not got real Democracy when the decision depends upon the people. We shall have real Democracy when the problem depends upon the people. The ordinary man will decide not only how he will vote, but what he is going to vote about.[26]

The Party System ensures that the foundations of inequality are organized out of politics into the process of non-decision. Throughout this century the Party System has succeeded in preserving the establishment substantially unchanged in its pristine inequality of wealth, power and privilege. This incredible success has been achieved despite the rise and fall of parties and—on the surface—great changes in Parliament, in the personnel concerned and in taxation. How it has been done is hidden within the secrecy and anonymity which conceal most of those who rule us.

Since we are told that question-time is vital to House of Commons democracy, here are a few pertinent questions. How far does the educational system still cherish the Whig tradition of history and clothe the Party System in the ancient robes of Parliament? Do English people cling to their aristocratic roots and still prefer to be ruled and deceived by their betters? How widespread is the wish for a quiet life at any cost? Why should not professional politicians be abolished? Is the system worth preserving for fear of something worse? Is beer really best?[27]

The reader may derive further questions from the objective assessment of the System by a contemporary Conservative statesman: 'Our system of government in effect has interpreted democracy as the temporary dictatorship of the party enjoying a parliamentary majority at any one time. . . . But it is a system which is tolerable only where there are definite prospects of a change being brought about by democratic means at not too infrequent elections.'[28]

Just 65 years ago Chesterton contrasted Irish politics with British, and preferred the unpleasant reality of Belfast to the lumbering hypocrisies of the prosperous Parliamentarian.[29] (Are they right—'The people of England, that never have spoken yet'—are they right in being slow to acquire a taste for such democracy?) It does seem, however, that the faint possibility of a change in the Party System has arisen as a response to violence and deep division in Ulster. For in connection with the creation of the Northern Ireland Assembly in 1973, there were introduced into British legislation the use of the referendum for popular consultation, proportional representation of minorities and the opportunity of power-sharing through participation government. However these measures may fare across the Irish Sea, the movement for political devolution may reasonably claim at least equal democracy for Scotland and Wales. If the regions of England did likewise, it would indeed be a joyful outcome of Chesterton's reaction to the Imperialism and Socialism of his youth. 'Both believed in unification and centralization on a large scale. Neither could have seen anything in my own fancy for having things on a smaller and smaller scale.' Strangely enough, this fancy coincides with the considered observation of Max Weber: 'Bureaucracy inevitably accompanies modern *mass democracy* in contrast to democratic self-government of small homogeneous units.'

It would be ironic if the return of these units of democratic self-government were assisted by expanding into Europe, particularly when that decision resulted fron the Party System's managing to keep the question of United Kingdom sovereignty out of the General Election of 1970. This important illustration and confirmation of the process of non-decision holds force despite Labour's post-election reservations. The decision on entry appears to have been made by the oligarchs above party politics; and, although it would be mere coincidence if the interests of the establishment were also those of the people, entry may yet prove to have brought Britain nearer to economic democracy—that movement to which the citizen must turn when disgust with the System imposes de facto disfranchisement.

Economic democracy

'Self-Government: that is, the power of the citizen in some degree to direct his own life and construct his own environment.' Chesterton clearly intended this principle to be applied to the workplace, for he always believed that work and democracy belonged together. Why, after all, should people not be democrats at work, an activity which involves the greater part of their lives and most of their contribution to the commonwealth? If we were not all utterly conditioned to the maintenance of the establishment, it would be clear that it is at work, if nowhere else, that we need to enjoy freedom, equality and fraternity.

Economic democracy is founded on security, sufficiency and the maximum dispersal of economic power amongst the people. Half a century ago Distributists tended to locate freedom mainly in the widely distributed ownership of the means of production, in families and small firms. Even now this sector of our economy is substantial (20 per cent according to the Bolton Report). There are still over 400,000 small shops; the majority of farmers own their own land (but would not like to be called peasants); and the professions and independent craftsmen generally are actual (though unconscious) Distributists. The rich seldom patronize the big when they seek the best products, and their custom may be among the reasons why the independents have not developed a collective consciousness— so necessary if the appetite for freedom is to grow amongst their fellow citizens. Are doctors and dentists, for instance, in a position where they do not need the people for the fight against bureaucracy in the Health Service?

Numerous and potentially powerful as the independents may be, it is right and just that the main concern should be with the vast majority who are employees. In recent years there has been a great growth in interest concerning proposals and ideas which go under the narrower general description of 'industrial democracy'. This movement aims to match the freedom of independence with the freedom of interdependence.

Already there are many systems in operation and numerous schemes proposed; and none of them need be rejected out of hand (except, of course, that sort of democracy which is fulfilled by a rare vote about nominal or irrelevant choices). Every such scheme should help to humanize the existing situation in the industrialized society and encourage progress towards the participation of the workpeople in their work.

In Chesterton's words, 'Democracy is easiest under plain and primary conditions, where all the citizens can shout in the market place, or all the fathers of the tribe talk under a tree. You can always give the power to the masses if they are not too many.'[30] The modern equivalents are the primary groups of industry which should be encouraged to develop as semi-autonomous small cells rather than as sections for the receipt of orders.

'Participation' is a vogue word which like so many others is in danger of losing its meaning. By itself it may mean, in our context, taking part in anything from job enlargement to self-management, from profit-sharing to co-partnership; from joint consultation to industrial co-operatives, and from share-owning to board representation. Long ago Chesterton used the word 'participation' in connection with distributed property, but the vague modern use does have a significance as evidence of a change of mood and as a harbinger of further changes to come.

Participation in management and decision-making is the vital object of industrial democracy. At present managers in industry regard themselves as a class apart because of their function and because, historically, they were once the higher servants of the rich and thus responsible solely to them. Nowadays they often have become quite independent both of the few and the many—indeed, if they are technocrats they attempt to control the technological society, without acknowledging responsibility for it to anyone. They find themselves in this position of self-perpetuating power usually because their masters have yielded up their directorships, or are incapable of exercising effective control over anything but dividends.

There is no good reason why managers should not be prepared to share their power with the workers in various fields, and numerous examples of this are available within the EEC.[31]

Nor is there any reason (except perhaps snobbery) why managers should not feel themselves to be colleagues of their workpeople, as they formerly were servants of the rich. If they are not fools, they will have the sense to recognize that the monopoly power of labour together with its capacity to hinder production and manipulate pay, must be diverted from industrial conflict to bringing out the full potential of the people. 'The real hidden resources in this country are not under the North Sea but right there on the shopfloor.... The management challenge is to release it constructively.'[32] When this is done through participation, the manager who surrenders the barren power of social class will harvest the fruits of freedom and creativity for the benefit of the community.

Participation is a stronger growth in the European Community than amongst British leaders of labour and industry.[33] It was, therefore, particularly pleasing to hear a British trade union president note recently that the demand for participation is gathering strength.[34] He also deplored the deliberately created image of trade unions and their members as 'greedy, grasping, selfish brutes, concerned only with satisfying their own outrageous demands irrespective of their effect on others.' This is the sort of accusation always produced against the workers. It was so nearly fifty years ago when, in *The Return of Don Quixote*, a novel planned and partly written prior to the first world war, Chesterton raised the thunderous voice of a trade unionist to put forward what soon became the Distributist League's policy for democratizing large-scale industry.[35]

Listen, then, across the years, to Braintree dramatically demanding workers' control, in a speech which Chesterton wrote for the secret people 'who have not spoken yet'.

'Your masters tell you,' he said, 'that you are greedy materialists grown accustomed to clamour for more wages. They are right. Your masters tell you that you lack ideals and do not understand ambition and the instinct to govern. They are right. They imply that you are slaves and beasts of burden, in so far as you would only eat up stores and escape responsibility. They are right. They are right so long as you are content to ask only for wages, only for food, only for well-paid service. But let us show our masters that we have profited by the moral lessons they are so good as to give us. Let us return to them penitent; let us tell them we mean to amend our faults of petty stipulation and merely materialistic demand. Let us tell them that we have an ambition; and it is to rule. That we have a hunger and a high thirst for responsibility; for the glorious and joyous responsibility of ruling what they misrule, of managing what they have mismanaged, of sharing among ourselves as workers and comrades that direct and democratic government of our own industry, which has hitherto served to keep a few parasites in luxury in their palaces and parks.'

Chesterton in France
CHRISTIANE d'HAUSSY

The reader must not be misled by the slightly ambiguous title of this essay and prepare to follow Chesterton on the roads of France, a country he often visited because he loved it. In fact, the question we are going to ask is whether his was a requited love and to do so we shall have to turn our backs on him and look at his reflection in the eyes of those who saw him from across the Channel.

If in London he was recognized by every cabby, the bewildered French cabman from Besançon to whom he said: 'Take, oh, take me to see a London policeman'[1], as a remedy to a bout of homesickness, must have seen in him just another eccentric Englishman. So, the man-in-the-street did not know him and this is hardly surprising. In the French literary world on the other hand he knew certain writers and critics, who were as eager to meet him as his English friends but who had fewer opportunities to do so. This is probably why Frédéric Lefèvre who went to Beaconsfield to interview him in 1924 was conscious of his privilege in actually seeing him. Those who knew him well and loved him, like Claudel or Maritain for instance, have not left any memento of their conversations with him, except perhaps in their diaries. Therefore his reputation in France is that of Chesterton the writer and not of Chesterton the man, a blessing in disguise if it saved the French critical approach from the sentimentality that has marred too many assessments of his work by some of his English contemporaries. A good illustration of the difference in approach between French and English critics is provided by Father Martindale who translated into English Professor Las Vergnas's brilliant essays on Chesterton, Belloc and Baring: he decided on the rather unusual course of adding an appendix of his own to the translation which brought out this difference.

We asked ourselves whether really these were the Chesterton the Belloc and the Baring whom we thought we had known. We decided that the author was not meaning to give an account of the complete men—the men as they live, or alas, in the case of one of them, had lived, but an account of their literary work, its style and content.[2]

No doubt such too was the intention of most of those who wrote about Chesterton on the other side of the Channel, with the possible exception of Charles Sarolea who wrote in his introduction to the translation of *The Crimes of England* that Chesterton was 'much greater than his work'.

But before examining French criticism on Chesterton and the influence of his work on French writers, we must see how Chesterton was made available to the French reading public who had no knowledge of English. The Italian phrase 'traduttore, traditore' is particularly relevant when we are dealing with the work of such a brilliant stylist—though this opinion is not universally shared. Maximilien Vox, one of his best translators, wrote: 'It is because his writing follows his thinking so closely that his style so easily passes the barrier of translation.'[3] But as we shall see, the barrier was too high for some to negotiate.

Besides the obstacle was not only linguistic: Chesterton was not only a stylist, he was also a journalist, or rather what we call *un chroniqueur*, often *un chroniqueur parisien*, and he was very much *un chroniqueur londonien*. It was because the *Autobiography* is dense with allusions to names and events unfamiliar to continental ears that Maurice Beerblock found it necessary to provide the reader with ninety-one pages of notes when he translated the book. We may wonder whether any other work by Chesterton was honoured with such heavy critical apparatus. In addition to the obstacles of style and topical matter confronting the French reader, we may mention a third. In the words of Agnès de la Gorce, he was 'the most English of Englishmen, that is someone who is not like us'.[4] Chesterton himself would certainly not have quibbled with such a statement:

It will generally be found, I think, that the more a man really appreciates and admires the soul of another people the less he will attempt to imitate it, he will be conscious that there is something

in it too deep and too unmanageable to imitate. . . . The Englishman who has a fancy for France will try to be French; the Englishman who admires France will remain obstinately English.[5]

Yet, identity and understanding being two different things, this
obstacle was not formidable enough to be shied at by determined and enthusiastic readers as we shall see presently; many
in fact were ready to face him in his French garb.

By 1909 Chesterton's fame was firmly established in Britain
but he was completely unknown in France. In that year his
name was first mentioned in France by André Chevrillon, a
critic with a particular interest in English literature, who
managed to write a fifty-seven page review of *Orthodoxy*
without once referring to the title of the book. It was discovered
by Paul Claudel about the same period and his admiration
was such that he immediately translated one chapter of it,
'The Paradoxes of Christianity', for the *Nouvelle Revue Française*
(July 1910). The story goes[6] that he wrote to the author
suggesting that he might translate the whole book but Chesterton did not receive the project favourably. If the story is true
one can only regret that these two writers who were so similar
in many ways did not give us the fruit of their joint efforts.
However, Claudel did not bear any grudge against Chesterton
since he later became his friend.

But French readers generally did not become acquainted
with Chesterton through *Orthodoxy* since the book was not
translated until 1920. The first translation to be published in
book form was that of *Dickens*, in 1909, an important year for
Chesterton in France. Before we mention the quality of French
translations of Chesterton, we must stress the fact that complete
anarchy reigned over the choice of works to be translated.
According to Henri Massis (author of *The Defence of the West*)
and other critics, the first translation of *Heretics*, for example,
was Jenny Bradley's, published in 1930, ten years after *Orthodoxy*.
(This fact is, however, questioned by Mr John Sullivan who, in
his excellent *Bibliography*, lists a translation of *Heretics* by T. J.
Serruys, published by G. Crès in 1919. Unfortunately this
elusive translation cannot be traced anywhere and another
Father Brown would be required to recover it.) Why was
Dickens translated first? Perhaps because, Chesterton being

completely unknown in France, it was thought that if he was
not read for his own sake he would be read at least for the sake
of his subject-matter. At any rate, the book does not seem to
have attracted much attention in spite of a favourable review
by Lucien Maury in *Figures Littéraires* in 1911.

The next books to be translated were novels: *Le Nommé
Jeudi* (*The Man Who Was Thursday*) in 1911 and *Le Napoléon de
Notting Hill* in 1912. The former, together with the Father
Brown stories (the first collection of which was translated in
1919), has been the most successful of Chesterton's books in
France with the general reading public, and it has been reprinted several times. Recently it was still one of the rare
translations available on the French market. Practically all
Chesterton's novels and stories attracted the translators, even
the Distributist novel *The Return of Don Quixote* and the very
slight productions *The Club of Queer Trades* and *The Tales of
the Long Bow*. Henri Massis wondered what the French reader
who had read neither *Heretics* nor *Orthodoxy* and was consequently
unaware of the underlying philosophy of their author could
make of such fictions as *The Man Who Was Thursday* or *The
Napoleon of Notting Hill*. He was probably slightly bewildered—
though was his position really so very different from that of the
casual English reader buying a Father Brown volume to read
on the train?

Most of the major works were eventually translated. *The
Everlasting Man*, strangely enough, was translated in two stages.
Maximilien Vox was responsible for the first, which appeared
in 1927 under the title *L'Homme Eternel*. In 1947, after an interval of twenty years, L. M. Gautier translated the second part
entitled *L'homme qu'on Appelle le Christ*. Some readers, and even
some critics, consequently assumed that those two books were
written separately by Chesterton. Maximilien Vox again
translated *Saint Thomas Aquinas*. The *Autobiography* was translated as *L'Homme à la Clé d'Or*. Even *What's Wrong With the
World* was translated in 1948, probably because it was considered a good document by those who were interested in the
social doctrine of the Church. Only one major title is missing:
The Victorian Age in Literature. This is the more surprising as
other literary essays such as *Dickens*, *Browning* (1930) and
Chaucer (1937) were not overlooked. Some privileged French

readers who read the *Revue Bleue* knew about the existence of the *Victorian Age* after Jacques Lux had analysed one of its chapters in an issue of 1914.[7]

The works mentioned so far are those that anyone acquainted with Chesterton's output would expect to find translated because of their philosphical interest or entertainment value. As could be expected, few collections of essays—either general or social and political—crossed the Channel, probably because many of them were too topical and because the essay is a less popular *genre* than the novel, especially when the link between various essays in a book is not obvious. There are however two exceptions: *What's Wrong with the World* and *The Defendant*, translated in 1946, but already made popular by Charles Grolleau when he translated 'A Defence of Farce' in 1936.[8] In a different field one can understand the interest J. Fournier-Pargoire found in *The New Jerusalem*, a remarkable book in many respects, and H. Thiès in *Sidelights on New London and Newer York*, but the necessity of translating *A Short History of England* seems much more dubious. And some publications did not add to the fame of Chesterton as a writer, but they served some purpose at the time they were translated: *The Barbarism of Berlin* (1914), *Letters to an Old Garibaldian* (1915) and *The Crimes of England* (1914) were pure war propaganda, equally effective on both sides of the Channel, particularly since they were favourable to France. 'Ce qu'un grand Ecrivain catholique anglais pense de la guerre anglo-irlandaise', translated in 1921 from an article in the *Manchester Guardian*, must have afforded some readers malicious pleasure on account of the ways in which John Bull was treated by the author. *Divorce* (1931) and *l'Eglise Catholique et la Conversion* (1952) were religious pamphlets. In all these cases Chesterton was made use of rather than served.

We have left to the last a brave attempt, though doomed to failure from the start: in 1938 E. M. Denis-Graterolle translated twenty-three poems, but the deceptive simplicity of Chesterton's poetry relies so much on rhythm, particularly in the ballad, that a merely accurate translation is unable to convey its magic to the French ear.

Thirty-six out of the hundred odd books that make up Chesterton's collected works have been translated into French, the great bulk of them, hardly surprisingly, during his life-time. One may say that, in the past, French readers were provided with a good selection of texts that reflected pretty well Chesterton's many-faceted talent. Yet there may be less reason to rejoice than seems legitimate. Gallimard kindly gave us such figures as they had: we know that 7,800 copies of *Le Nommé Jeudi* were sold, 3,300 of *Chaucer* and 4,400 of the collected Father Brown stories. Gallimard being one of the best known of Chesterton's publishers in France, we can hardly be impressed by those figures. Obviously none of these books ever reached best-seller status. They are all out of print now, with the exception of *The Innocence of Father Brown*, or rather *La Clairvoyance du Père Brown*, which was rejuvenated when it was chosen by Julliard in 1971 to feature in a new detective story series devoted to masterpieces of the *genre*. So Chesterton's French readers were a happy few at all times and they are even more so nowadays.

Some of the translations are very good, those of Maximilien Vox or Jean Florence among them, some are adequate, others simply overcome difficulties by ignoring them, whilst others leave the reader who knows the English original completely bewildered. This is particularly true of the early translations, that of *Dickens* for instance. The ideal of beauty of the two translators must have been a very conventional one; they were so shocked by the gargoyle that confronted them that they set out to turn a *jardin à l'anglaise* into a *jardin à la française*, ruthlessly pruning, trimming what they considered unallowable growth, suppressing whole paragraphs, dropping one word here, one word there, systematically cutting down repetitions. It needed all the literary acumen of Lucien Maury (unless he had read the English text) to discover Chesterton's talent in such a garbled version.

Readers who had no direct access to Chesterton's works were able to become familiar with his ideas by reading reviews and commentaries in literary periodicals. The bulk of French criticism on Chesterton is however very modest and, with a few exceptions, it dates back to the Twenties and the Thirties. Not only are these critical works few in number, but they are usually very short, though one cannot deny that some of them make up in density for what they lack in length. The only book exclusively devoted to Chesterton is Father Joseph de Tonquedec's *G. K. Chesterton, ses Idées et son Caractère* (1920). Then come two substantial essays on his work as a whole, those of André Maurois in *Magicians and Logicians* (1935) and of Professor Las Vergnas in *Chesterton, Belloc, Baring* (1936), André Chevrillon[9] has already been mentioned, as have Lucien Maury[10] and Frédéric Lefèvre.[11] Their essays were also published in book form, but most other critical studies were published in periodicals or as introductions and prefaces to Chesterton's translated works. Amusingly enough, we discovered in our quest that an anonymous study in one literary paper and a signed one in another were one and the same essay.[12]

General reviews like *La Nouvelle Revue Française, La Revue Universelle* or *Le Mois* mentioned Chesterton's name and were interested in him as one of the important figures of the English literary scene, but, as can be expected, he was particularly popular with editors of Catholic periodicals: two of them, *La Vie Intellectuelle* in 1937 and *Témoignages*, edited by the monks of La Pierre Qui Vire, in 1952, devoted a special issue to various aspects of his thought. As in the case of the translations, the Thirties show a peak in popularity with a crop of obituaries in 1936 and then a steady decrease in interest, dropping to almost complete silence—sometimes broken by an odd article here and there[13]—after the early Fifties. Nowadays Chesterton is rarely granted more than a casual mention in the middle of an article devoted to something else, usually in Catholic periodicals.[14] So he is not completely forgotten but he lives today only in the memory of a few devoted admirers.

An interesting evolution can be traced in French critical attitudes to Chesterton's work. A 'discoverer', like Lucien Maury in 1911, seems to have been dazzled and to have found it difficult to make his way through the lush growth of Chesterton's style and thought.

Chesterton's one and only method consists in sustaining an erratic course: he strays, so that you are warned not to take him seriously. . . . He is extravagant with his ideas . . . and though he loves them, he does not respect them; like a careless 'nouveau riche', he is unaware of the price of his gold and he squanders it, throwing it into the face of the first comer.[15]

Yet if Maury was bewildered by the absence of structure in Chesterton's work, he warmly praised his power as 'an occasional but prodigious augur'.

In subsequent critical studies one sometimes detects a faintly patronizing tone. This is the case with Father de Tonquedec for instance, who, unlike Maury, was ready to take his ideas seriously, yet wrote that Chesterton's 'philosophy is literary and humoristic'. In spite of André Chevrillon's obvious interest in an exotic writer, the same unconsciously 'superior' attitude sometimes comes to the surface.

In the Thirties and the Forties, Chesterton's fame was more firmly established and unqualified admiration is expressed by such philosophers and theologians as Gabriel Marcel, Etienne Gilson and Father Gillet who all consider Chesterton as a fine Thomist and a theoretician of the philosophy of being. In a review of the *Father Brown Stories*,[16] Charles Albert Cingria speaks of the 'thomistic common sense of the small priest' and would not dream of speaking of 'the capricious flight of the butterfly'.[17]

So on the whole, Chesterton has not been taken lightly in France as has sometimes been the case in England. Professor Las Vergnas, who said that he was 'one of the most sumptuously gifted writers of his time', was struck by the following paradox: Chesterton, who always rushed to the rescue of French people when they were charged with frivolity by his countrymen, saw the weapon he fended off from his French friends used against him by critics in his own country.

Yet even when French critics try to understand and appreciate Chesterton for the intrinsic value of his work, they rarely fail to react in a French way. They almost unanimously mention his child-like quality, from the 'laughing outburst of a playful child' to a more elaborate comparison with Peter Pan, though Chesterton himself disagreed with what he called Peter Pantheism:

I have always held that Peter Pan was wrong. . . . He admitted it would be a great adventure to die; but it did not seem to occur to him that it would be a great adventure to live. . . . Now the mistake of Peter Pan is the mistake of the new theory of life. . . . It is the notion that there is *no* advantage in striking roots. . . . There is an advantage in root; and the name of it is fruit.[18]

In fact, if the French find it necessary to point out the child in Chesterton, it is only because they would like to believe they are more adult than him. 'There is certainly something younger in the English mind than in ours',[19] says André Chevrillon, echoed by Wladimir Weidlé: 'His soul [was] open, busy and childlike—such souls are born more frequently in England than anywhere else'.[20]

Another of our French pet beliefs is that the quality of our logic is faultless; this is why it is often set against Chesterton's logic—or lack of it. The point of Chevrillon's essay is not so much what it professes to be: the presentation of a new English writer to the French reading public as a parallel between the Hebraic turn of mind of the English that produces concrete mysticism and the Hellenic turn of mind of the French that is more favourable to abstract rationalism. Father de Tonquedec is ready to credit Chesterton with some logic, but cannot go all the way with him and draws the line at an apple-tree growing golden candlesticks. It is true that the French are very reluctant to accept nonsense: they never go beyond the looking-glass and *Alice in Wonderland* has always been a failure with children and adults alike in France: to be accepted, magic must have some kind of scientific or at least logical explanation. This does not mean that they are not fascinated by this alien universe: its prestige increases perhaps because they cannot be initiated into its mysteries.

Anyway, even if Chesterton's French readers have been fascinated they have not always been convinced, and this may be the reason why he is not an excellent export item and why Wells and even Shaw have fared better across the Channel, Wells being granted more ingenuity and Shaw more genius.[21]

This may be too pessimistic a view and must be qualified: Chesterton has been accepted whole-heartedly by a number of critics, especially Catholic critics, but even with them an evolution can be detected and we may ask ourselves whether what Samuel Hynes says of Chesterton in England would be justified in France. He violently disagrees with Belloc who wrote that his friend would be understood in his own country only if Englishmen became converted to Catholicism.

This absurd proposition assumes, as every other catholic writing about Chesterton has assumed, that he was a 'Catholic Author' and that posterity would read him, if at all, for the same reason that it would read the *Spiritual Exercises*. . . . This parochial regard has given Chesterton's reputation a kind of parish newspaper security, but it has not helped him with the larger literary audience. It is time that Chesterton was removed from the loving disservice of his co-religionists; above all, he needs secular attention.[22]

Catholic criticism is less monolithic in France. Though the essays in *Témoignages* (1952) are full of praises, one of them expresses doubts on the permanent value of some of Chesterton's attitudes:

Can we imagine Father Brown facing the ordeals Graham Greene's priest had to meet in *The Power and the Glory*? Father Brown and G. K. Chesterton believe that man is evil because he is silly, but *we* know that he is silly because he is evil. . . . We know as well as G. Greene that evil is endowed with thickness, with a structure of its own, that it is not only a lack—a deficiency.[23]

And then the author speaks of Father Brown's anachronism. Greene's name is often found at the top of best-seller lists in France, and there is no doubt that his tragic vision of life seems more congenial today than Chesterton's optimism even if this optimism is far more complex than some readers assume.

We asked at the beginning of this essay whether Chesterton's love for France was—and is—reciprocated. The answer has so far turned out to be that his books either in English or in translation have aroused a good deal of interest and admiration, but that both have been limited to a comparatively narrow circle of initiates whose deep devotion has made up in some measure for the lack of public acknowledgement his works have suffered. He received many tokens of admiration and affection from his peers, his French fellow writers, in the shape of dedicated copies of their works. Thanks to Miss Dorothy Collins's kindness, we have had access to a full book-case of them, more than one hundred. They outnumber dedicated copies from other countries: Germany, Spain, Italy, or Poland where he was appreciated too. It may be interesting to give a few names at random: Georges Bernanos, Stanislas Fumet, François Porché, Isabelle Rivière, Francis Jammes, Julien Green, Julien Benda, Nicholas Berdiaeff and René Schowb who sent *Moi, Juif* with 'his deepest admiration' (proving that *he* did not consider Chesterton a champion of anti-semitism). But the warmest and most enthusiastic tributes come from Henri Ghéon, Jacques Maritain, one of his best French friends, and Henri Massis, his most devoted disciple: *Jugement* is dedicated 'to the author of *Heretics* who has been my model and my master, who will find his name and thoughts on many a page of this book', and *Défense de l'Occident* to 'my dear master Chesterton to whom I am so much indebted for this book'. We can but agree with him, for statements such as:

European unity which has been spiritually undone since the Reformation;[24]

or:

Personality, unity, stability, authority, continuity—these are the root ideas of the West. We are asked to break these to pieces for the sake of a doubtful Asiaticism in which all the forces of the human personality dissolve and return to nothingness.[25]

—such statements read just like Chesterton. In fact, the model is not wholly absent from the English translation since he wrote its preface. He prefaced Henri Ghéon's *Secret of the Curé d'Ars* too, and his choice of words in both essays is interestingly similar: he considers that French Catholicism is a challenge and that Henri Ghéon is 'typical in that he is militant, propagandist, provocative'; then in his preface to *Defence of the West* Chesterton is very critical of the English for their

incapacity to understand the French intellect when it is militant, which is exactly when it is most French . . . these new intellectual fighters in France do not fit in with our conventions of controversy.[26]

But Chesterton's own fiery method was that of a fighter too, so if he was something of a phenomenon in Britain because of his theories and because of the way in which he put them forward, in France he was one among many and he found his spiritual home there among his friends, one of whom said when he died. 'Dear Chesterton, how we'll miss you to defend the West.'[27]

He shared his ideas and his methods with a group of French writers but even his style, though it is highly individual, is not unlike the styles of Claudel, Péguy, Bloy or Bernanos. They all believed in a direct approach to the reader, in a sublime homeliness and in rhetorical flourishes, in outbursts of verbal violence, in the flamboyant and the baroque. In fact, Albert Laffay in a subtle analysis of the baroque mentions both Chesterton and Claudel and finds a link between them in style and in religion, for be believes that the baroque is usually connected with Roman Catholicism, and therefore rare in English literature:

The baroque writer would like to show that the whole world is eccentric, it can find its centre nowhere, not even in itself. Heaven is the only justification of the baroque, heaven, a constant *elsewhere*, this kind of recurring unsatisfaction that many will call God.[28]

So Chesterton and Claudel share a common patriotism (Chesterton would probably have preferred this term to 'nationality'): they are both 'citizens of Christianity'.

Yet Chesterton's influence has not been limited to Catholic writers. André Billy 'in the enthusiasm of youth' as he put it[29] was moved to write a novel, *Barabour ou l'Harmonie universelle*, and what he described as 'a long short story', *La Malabée*, in imitation of *The Napoleon of Notting Hill*. Even when there was no real influence, a community of inspiration between Chesterton and a French writer could exist: in 'The Architect of Spears' the Englishman had imagined a Gothic cathedral coming to life; the Frenchman, Alexandre Arnoux, realized this dream in a novel *Abishag*, and Chesterton prefaced its English translation, published in 1925. And a French writer can still answer the call of his enthusiasm: Louis Pauwels, attracted by his powerful optimism, quoted him abundantly in his *Lettre Ouverte aux Gens Heureux . . .*, published in 1971. He wrote: 'For me Chesterton means understanding and a vision of everlasting man opposed to the permanent plot of materialistic scientism'.

So Chesterton's influence in France still lives and we, the small band of his devotees, believe that he has a message for our time. This message transcends the barriers of nationality and we can discover it if we read his books as he looked at the world: with a sense of wonder.

Chesterton in Japan*
PETER MILWARD, S. J.

It is, I hope, no offence to a great man to suggest that he has human limitations—least of all, to so great a man as G. K. Chesterton. And not the last of his limitations was his failure to appreciate the character of the Japanese. This was, no doubt, because he lived his life so far from Japan in the little corner of the globe that is England; no doubt, too, because he was himself so different in character and stature from the Japanese.

On the other hand, the Japanese, too, have their human limitations. And not the least of their limitations is their failure hitherto to appreciate Chesterton's character, whether as a man or as an author. In their case, however, one cannot offer the excuse that England is so far from Japan. For the Japanese in general have an intense interest in England and the English, which continues to flourish despite the continued lack of reciprocation. Hardly an author comes to the fore in the English world of letters, but the fact is immediately noticed in Japan and recorded in the innumerable books and magazines devoted to things English.

So, too, the reputation of Chesterton at least during his lifetime did not pass unnoticed in Japan; and it would be a gross exaggeration—which will, I hope, be sufficiently disproved in this essay—to assert that Japanese readers were entirely ignorant of his name. But his impact can hardly compare with that of Shaw or Wells, Hardy or Yeats, Somerset Maugham or E. M. Forster, Eliot or Greene, Joyce or Lawrence—to mention but a few of his contemporaries. And

---

*I have to express my deep indebtedness to Nakano Kii for most of the material used in this essay, which he had previously gathered for his own article 'G. K. Chesterton Juyoshi'; also to the Saint Miki Library in Sophia, which has a fine collection of Chestertoniana—founded by Father Leo Ward, it is now under the care of Father Peter Krumbach.

With regard to Japanese names, it is usual in Japan to put the family name first—and this order I have observed in the present piece. Occasionally, the second name is an author's pen name, and then he is known by this name rather than by his family name.

however well known he may have been during his lifetime, his post-war fame in Japan depends almost entirely on his Father Brown stories which are for some reason not regarded as meriting a place in 'literature'.

Today, therefore, the general impression one receives from the current state of English literary studies in Japan is that Chesterton is, if not unknown, at least ignored by the Japanese. Only when one looks back over the past sixty years or so since his first introduction into this country, does one realize the deep impact of his personality and his writings. His followers may have been few, but they have been enthusiastic; and their enthusiasm in turn has exercised no small influence on their fellow-countrymen. They have, moreover, numbered some of the most eminent scholars and writers in the nation. This consideration entitles one to hope that their enthusiasm is not entirely a thing of the past, and that it may be revived on a larger scale in the future.

The earliest recorded mention of Chesterton in Japan—so far as is known to me—is an honourable one. The great Japanese novelist, Natsume Soseki, on returning from England in 1903, spent the next four years teaching English Literature at Tokyo Imperial University. Subsequently, in 1907 he published his lectures under the title of *Bungakuron* (Studies in Literature); and in the fifth part, while comparing Browning with Tennyson, he took occasion to quote Chesterton's opinion that, though Browning may not have been so popular as Tennyson, popularity is not a necessary sign of greatness. This opinion he quotes from Chesterton's *Browning*, which had been published shortly after Soseki's departure from England. It was, however, the only mention he ever made of Chesterton; and his copy of *Browning* was apparently the only book by Chesterton he had in his library.

Nevertheless, this was by no means an isolated mention of Chesterton, but the real beginning of a growing interest among Japanese readers. One of Soseki's pupils at Tokyo University in his short period as lecturer there was Kuriyagawa Hakuson, who later became a famous writer and scholar. His association with Soseki is described by Kaneko Kenji in *Ningen Soseki* (Soseki the Man, 1957). It was Hakuson who first introduced

Japanese readers to the writings of Chesterton through his subsequent position as teacher at the Third High School, Kyoto (now College of Liberal Arts, Kyoto University). In an article entitled 'Gendai Eikoku Bundan no Kisai' (Men of Genius in the Modern English World of Letters), which he first published in the magazine *Teikoku Bungaku* in 1909, he recalled his original acquaintance with Chesterton. While a student at Tokyo University, he had been shown a copy of *Browning* by his teacher, whom he does not name—but it can only have been Soseki. This was the book which had first introduced him to the literary world in England, and which also convinced him of the important position of Chesterton himself in that world.

Apart from this personal reminiscence, Hakuson devoted the main part of his article to the prose of Chesterton—though he also finds space to speak of *The Wild Knight*. He dwells particularly on *Twelve Types*, *The Defendant*, *Orthodoxy* (which he mentions as Chesterton's most recent work) and *Heretics*, with evident preference for the last-mentioned book. What particularly fascinates him is Chesterton's skilful use of paradox and his courage in opposing the accepted thinkers of his day. His fondness for *Heretics* reappears in his subsequent book, *Kindai Bungaku Jikko* (Ten Lectures on Contemporary Literature, 1912), which was highly regarded in its time. Here he quotes approvingly from Chesterton's introduction to bring out the contrast between the light of faith and idealism in the Middle Ages and the darkness of doubt in the modern age.

It is not surprising, therefore, that Chesterton has a place in two anthologies of contemporary English Literature edited by Hakuson. In *English Essays* (1910) he included two by Chesterton, 'On Running After One's Hat' and 'Woman'; and he also translated the former essay into Japanese with general comments, and included it with his article on Chesterton's prose in a collection of essays entitled *Koizumi Sensei Sono Hoka* (Professor Koizumi—i.e. Lafcadio Hearn, who taught at Tokyo University before Soseki—and Other Essays, 1919). Later, in his *Gendai Jojoshisen* (Anthology of Modern Lyrical Poems, 1924) he presented three of Chesterton's poems, 'The Mariner', 'Du Bellay's Sonnet' and 'The Donkey', with an introduction and detailed notes for each poem. His general

opinion of Chesterton's genius is given in his autobiographical
Zoge no To wo Dete (Leaving My Ivory Tower, 1920): 'Chesterton is a great man who is always astonishing us by his oracles
that seem to have fallen from heaven. Just by his sentences he
really moves heaven and earth.'

Also in Kyoto about this time another eminent admirer of
Chesterton was Harada Tasuku, a Protestant pastor, who
became President of Doshisha University there in 1906. In his
book *Shinko to Riso* (Faith and Ideals, 1909) he singled out
Chesterton for high praise in the course of a discussion on the
use of paradox: 'In the English world of letters today Mr
Chesterton is outstanding for the way he ridicules the modern
trends of scientism and materialism and argues with vigour in
defence of faith. In this attitude he recalls Carlyle from the
previous age, only his attacks are sharper.'

Hakuson was no solitary admirer, but did much to spread
interest in Chesterton among his pupils at Kyoto, many of
whom became eminent as writers and scholars in later years.
One of the most famous of them was Kikuchi Kan, who found
special delight in Chesterton's essays in literary criticism. In an
essay of his own entitled 'Bangai Fudocho' (Points of View),
which was later published in his Collected Works in 1930, he
declared: 'I wish there were brilliant critics in Japan to compare with Chesterton, France and Shaw. I wish there was more
enjoyable criticism like theirs. I wish I could read more
criticism of this kind that scatters fireworks of wit and wisdom
and profound thought.'

In the academic world of Kyoto one may discern a line of
scholars who owe their interest in Chesterton to Hakuson's
teaching. Kurihara Motoi, who followed him as a teacher at
the Third High School, was the first to edit *Tremendous Trifles*
as a school textbook with Japanese notes in 1929. Ishida Kenji,
who taught at Kyoto University, makes favourable mention of
Chesterton in his books *Christokyoteki Bungakukan* (1932) and
Newman (1936). Originally interested in Carlyle, he was
deeply impressed by Chesterton's criticism of the Scots thinker
in *The Victorian Age in Literature*. Another eminent professor of
Kyoto University, Fukase Motohiro, better known for his studies
and translations of T. S. Eliot and Christopher Dawson,
developed the comparison between Eliot's idea of tradition

and Chesterton's idea of orthodoxy in his *Eliot no Shigaku* (Poetics of Eliot, 1949). The critic and scholar Jugaku Bunsho mentions Chesterton with approval in his *Eibungaku no Fudo* (Climate of English Literature, 1961), and refers to a passage from Chesterton's essay, 'The Wind and the Trees', in a feature called 'Favourite Words' in a recent issue of the student magazine *Koko Eigo Kenkyu* (1969).

Another scholar, who was a pupil of Ishida at Kyoto, Sudo Nobuo, speaks highly of Chesterton in his *Eibungaku to Shukyo, Rinri* (English Literature and Religion, Ethics, 1966). He has also written at greater length on 'G. K. Chesterton no Chie' (Chesterton's Wisdom) for the periodical of his university in Tokyo, *Meiji Gakuin Daigaku Ronso* (1957), where he deals chiefly with *Heretics* and *Orthodoxy* and presents Chesterton as an average man, a man of belief, a master of paradox and a humorous optimist.

Returning now to Tokyo, the first centre for the introduction of Chesterton to the literary and academic world of Japan was not Tokyo University, but the well-known private university of Keio. Here the great introducer of things and thoughts Western was Baba Kocho. He was fond of Chesterton's essays and Father Brown stories; and while he taught his pupils to appreciate the former, he was largely responsible for the translations of the latter that came to appear in the student magazine *Shin Seinen* during the Twenties, when he was on the advisory board of this magazine.

Another professor at Keio, Togawa Shukotsu, who had been a freelance writer and critic in the previous Meiji period, now became the leading Chestertonian in Japan. In his book *Eibungaku Seiko* (Detailed Studies of English Literature, 1915), a highly valued introduction to its subject, he devoted his opening chapter to 'Okashimi no Bungaku' (Comic Literature) and dealt first with Chesterton before going on to treat of Jerome K. Jerome, Leigh Hunt and Charles Lamb. He expressed his delight in such essays as 'On Lying in Bed', and went on to make the general observation: 'In each of these essays we find a paradox leading from an eccentric viewpoint to a serious conclusion, so that we spontaneously burst into laughter.' In his bibliography he mentioned *Twelve Types, Heretics, Orthodoxy, All Things Considered* and *The Napoleon of*

Notting Hill, but strangely enough he omitted both *Browning* and *Dickens* which were highly appreciated by other Japanese scholars at this time.

In his own essays, which were widely enjoyed during the Taisho period (1911–26), on account of their witty and paradoxical style, Shukotsu betrays the deep influence of Chesterton. In his thought, too, he upheld the ideal of the common man in his *Bonjin Suhai* (Worship of the Common Man, 1926) against the opposite ideal of the superman which the popularity of Carlyle and Shaw, not to mention Nietzsche, had done much to promote among the Japanese of his generation.

Another teacher at Keio, Noguchi Yonejiro, introduced Chesterton's 'nonsense literature' about this time in an article, 'Saikin Bungei Shicho' (Recent Trends in Literary Thought), for the university magazine, *Mita Bungaku* (1916). After speaking generally about Chesterton, he went on to give his translation of 'A Defence of Nonsense'. As a matter of fact, this essay had already been translated the year before by a professor of the rival university of Waseda, Masuda Tonosuke, for the magazine *Eigo Sekai* (1915); and it evidently appealed to the minds of its Japanese readers. It was subsequently included in an edition of *Modern English Essays* (1928) by Takagaki Matsuo, professor at the Anglican university of Rikkyo; while other essays from *The Defendant* were presented in an edition of this work published by Hokuseido in 1926. More recently, the essay has again been translated by a teacher at Tokyo University, Takahashi Yasunari, for a special Lewis Carroll issue of *Gendaishi Techo* (1972).

In another work of his, *Kaigai no Koyu* (Friends Overseas, 1926), Noguchi Yonejiro recalled his personal friendship with the photographer, Alvin Coburn. On one occasion Coburn showed him his remarkable photograph of Chesterton, to the author's great admiration.

The Twenties were, as has been mentioned, the period when Chesterton leapt to fame in Japan as a detective-story writer. Baba Kocho had led the way; and other writers connected with Keio contributed to the vogue. The first English edition of Father Brown stories, *The Innocence of Father Brown*, was prepared by an Englishman teaching at Keio, W. S. Vines, with the collaboration of Hori Eishiro, in 1925. General discussions

of these stories were presented by a graduate of Keio, Matsumoto Tai, in a pamphlet entitled *Gendai Eikoku Taishu
Bungaku* (Popular Literature in England Today, 1927) and
in his more widely known book *Tantei Shosetsu-tsu* (Conspectus
of Detective Stories).

Among the future writers influenced by Kocho and Shukotsu
in their student days at Keio was Kojima Masajiro, a close
friend of the more famous novelist, Akutagawa Ryunosuke (a
graduate of Tokyo University). In his declining years Kojima
has frequently recalled his connection with Akutagawa in the
Twenties, when as students they both came to acquire an
interest in Chesterton. In *Ganchu no Hito* (Men I Respect, 1956)
he tells how he felt a curiosity to read Chesterton and bought
several of his books at Maruzen, a large bookshop in Tokyo.
While he was engaged in the task of reading them with the help
of a dictionary, Akutagawa came on a visit and noticing what
he was reading asked for the loan of some of the books. He
soon returned, having perused them all, and declared—much
to the wonder of Kojima, who was a slow reader of English—
that he had found *Dickens* the most interesting. A similar story
is told by Kojima in an article he wrote for *Gakuto*, the Maruzen
magazine, on 'Akutagawa and Maruzen' in 1969. Here the
remark he ascribes to his friend is the more general one that
'Chesterton is a fine critic, but Belloc is merely a journalist'.
Again, in his biographical sketch of 'Kume Masao', contributed to the magazine *Chuo Koron* in 1966, he describes a
meeting of Akutagawa, Kikuchi, Kume and himself in the
early Twenties. To show the individual differences of these
authors, he presents their different reactions to the reading of
Chesterton. Akutagawa, as usual, makes brilliant but superficial comments, based on his rapid reading; Kume is interesting
and considered in his opinions, but can only read slowly with
the aid of a dictionary (like Kojima himself); while Kikuchi,
being a man from the country, remains silent and keeps his
opinions to himself.

In an article entitled 'Omoshiroi Hyoron, Hyoden Ideyo'
(Let There Be More Interesting Literary Criticism and
Biography), contributed to the magazine *Bungei* (1935),
Kojima repeats his friend's opinion of *Dickens* and expresses the
wish that there were more literary biographies of this kind in

Japan. Later, he tried to carry out this wish himself in his biography of the novelist, Tanizaki Junichiro, *Seitai Haiju* (Holy Communion, 1969). In this work he also quotes Chesterton's remark in *The Victorian Age* on the place of women in nineteenth-century literature, and compares it with their similar status in old Japanese literature. Another Chestertonian fragment of his is a translation of the essay 'On Lying in Bed', mentioned by Shukotsu in his *Eibungaku Seiko*.

As for Akutagawa, he carried his interest in Chesterton so far as to include the essay on 'Christmas' in an edition of *Modern Essays* published in 1924—but apparently no farther.

The other famous private university of this period, Waseda, also had its share of Chesterton admirers during the Taisho and early Showa periods. Mention has already been made of Masuda Tonosuke and his translation of 'A Defence of Nonsense'. Another professor of English at this time was Shimamura Hogetsu, whose book *Shizuku* (Drops, 1913) contains a passage on Chesterton and Shaw under the general title of 'Daigen' (Random Thoughts). A more famous professor, who subsequently became a politician and member of the Diet, Uchigasaki Sakusaburo, likewise mentions Chesterton in his book *Kindaijin no Shinko* (The Faith of Modern Man), published in the same year, in a chapter entitled 'Gendai Eibungaku no Shukyoteki Jocho' (Religious Trends in Modern English Literature).

After the first world war it was mainly Waseda that led the way in the vogue for the Father Brown stories mentioned above. This was fostered by the magazine *Shin Seinen*, whose editor, Hasegawa Tenkei, was a Waseda graduate. The stories which appeared in successive issues were for the most part translated by another Waseda graduate, Asano Genpu. His first translation was of 'The Blue Cross', literally rendered into Japanese as 'Aoi Jujika' (1922). He later collected the stories and published them under the title of *Chesterton-shu* (Chesterton Collection) in 1930, a book that soon became a best-seller in its day. Another Waseda graduate, Naoki Sanjugo, was also involved in the vogue, and he published his translations in the same year under the title of *Brown Kidan* (Brown's Adventures, 1930).

On a more academic level, a professor of English at Waseda,

Hagiwara Kyohei, edited *Essays by G. K. Chesterton* with Japanese notes in 1931. He also introduced *The Ballad of the White Horse* to the readers of another magazine, *Eigo Kenkyu*, in 1933. On Chesterton's death in 1936, he contributed a further article on two of his poems, 'A Christmas Carol' and 'A Ballade of Suicide', to a special issue of the magazine *Eigo Seinen*. In the following issue he gave a general survey of Chesterton's varied genius, while expressing the sorrow of readers throughout the world at an event he could only compare to Shakespeare's rejection of Falstaff.

Another university which played an important role in introducing Chesterton to Japan was the Tokyo University of Education—or, as it was then, the Higher Normal School, or *Koto Shihan Gakko*. A famous professor of this school, and a former associate of Shukotsu, Hirata Tokuboku, had the distinction of bringing *The Victorian Age* to the first notice of Japanese readers through the pages of *Eigo Seinen*. In his article, which appeared in 1914, he drew special attention to Chesterton's remarks about Oscar Wilde, who had then a considerable following among Japanese writers. This issue of the magazine proved very popular, mainly on account of Tokuboku's contribution, and the editor was particularly proud of it. From that time onwards, *The Victorian Age* came to be widely read by Japanese students—together with Lytton Strachey's *Queen Victoria*—though it has never been translated or edited with notes in Japanese.

About this time, an elderly professor at the same school, Ishikawa Rinshiro, happened to meet a brilliant student of his in the corridor and suggested in a chance exchange of words that he might do well to translate one of the Father Brown stories. The student's name was Fukuhara Rintaro, and the story he accordingly translated was 'The Blue Cross', to which he gave the Japanese title of 'Takaramono' (Treasure). It was duly published in *Eigo Seinen* in 1916, the first of the Father Brown stories to be translated into Japanese, and the first of a long series of publications by Fukuhara. The details of this story of his first acquaintance with Chesterton he recalled in an essay, 'Chesterton ni tsuite' (About Chesterton), published in 1918.

Subsequently, Fukuhara expressed his indebtedness to Chesterton on more than one occasion; and his students at the Higher Normal School have recalled how enthusiastically he would recommend them to read Chesterton, especially *The Victorian Age* and *Dickens*. The influence of the former book may be seen in his own *Kindai no Eibungaku* (Contemporary English Literature, 1926), where he seems to follow its general structure and quotes Chesterton in support of his opinion. On the occasion of Chesterton's death, he made two contributions to *Eigo Seinen*, one in which he seems to lament that his reputation in Japan comes more from his detective stories than from his essays or criticism, and another, entitled 'Hikoku Chesterton' (Chesterton the Defendant), recalling the time he heard Chesterton speaking at a mock trial in 1931. Finally, many years later, in his autobiographical *Dokusho to Aru Jinsei* (Reading and My Life, 1967), he describes how he was first attracted to the study of literature by two notable books in the Home University Library, W. P. Ker's *English Medieval Literature* and G. K. Chesterton's *Victorian Age in Literature*.

A younger colleague of his at the Higher Normal School, and one of the few Catholic professors of those days, Teranishi Takeo, edited *Charles Dickens* with annotations in 1932. A few years later, on the occasion of Chesterton's death, he also contributed an essay more particularly on the subject of 'Chesterton and Dickens'. He recalled a conversation with Ishikawa and Fukuhara, during which he was asked point-blank, 'Do you like Chesterton?' and he replied with some hesitation, 'Well, yes, but I don't appreciate his paradox very much.'

More recently, a former pupil of Fukuhara, who is now professor of English at the University of Education, Saito Bishu, has continued the tradition by translating Chesterton's essay on Thackeray, together with his translation of the latter's *Book of Snobs*, for the series of *Sekai Bungaku Taikei* (Outline of World Literature, 1961).

Strangely enough, the Catholic world in Japan has been rather slow in responding to Chesterton; or perhaps it is that the Catholic voice is less clearly heard in literary or academic circles in Japan. Anyhow, it was only during the Showa period (from 1926) that Catholic authors as such came to express their admiration of Chesterton, and then only after Chesterton had died. Several important essays on him appeared in an issue of *Catholic* two years later, in 1938; and of them all by far the most interesting is that of a leading Catholic priest and intellectual, Iwashita Soichi, who subsequently became editor of the magazine. Under the title 'Chesterton Kanken' (Chesterton Seen Through a Pipe), he describes his long attachment to Chesterton's writings in a humorous manner of his own:

Chesterton is not a book on my library shelf, but a book I have kept by my bedside these ten years. For me the best way of finding rest to a head and heart tired after the day's toil is to get into bed and read my bedside Chesterton. There I find a world that is most enjoyable to me. All the complexes that bother me are dissipated by his lucid arguments and his humour. If a burglar were to intrude into my bedroom on such a night, he would surely think he had come into the house of a madman. While reading him, I cannot help breaking the deep silence of the night with outbursts of laughter. Such is the enjoyment he brings me. But his is not the laughter produced by a scene in some comic play. Chesterton's humour is exceedingly intellectual. What makes me laugh is not so much his intellectual jesting . . . as his unusual way of expressing truth in its various aspects, and of exposing the intellectual limitations of men in the world. While he induces loud laughter, he is always serious. This is why I am so fond of Chesterton.

Iwashita was himself the leader of a group of young Catholic intellectuals about this time, several of whom contributed articles to this issue devoted to Chesterton. Two were foreign priests; Leo Ward, an Englishman and brother of Maisie Ward (of Sheed & Ward), who wrote of the various occasions when he met Chesterton in person; and Nicholas Roggen, a German with a degree in English from Cambridge, who presented Chesterton as a 'warrior for the Catholic faith'. Among the other Japanese, Sakai Yoshitaka, a teacher at the First High School, Tokyo (later to become College of Liberal Arts, Tokyo University), wrote on Chesterton as a poet; and Yamanouchi Ichiro, a graduate of Keio, translated Chesterton's 'The Hat and the Halo'.

Several years later, it was Iwashita who encouraged Yamanouchi to undertake the difficult task of translating *Orthodoxy* for the first time; and, in spite of the hardships of the war, it was published in 1943 under the title of *Seito Shiso* (Orthodox Thought). This title was apparently a coinage of the translator's, as the word was then non-existent in Japanese. Only a year before, however, Kobayashi Yoshio, a professor of the Catholic university of Sophia and a prominent member of the above-mentioned group of intellectuals, had translated Karl Pfleger's *Wrestlers With Christ*, with its impressive chapter on Chesterton as 'The Adventurer of Orthodoxy' rendered into Japanese as 'Seito Shinko no Bokenka' (Adventurer of Orthodox Faith).

The subsequent influence of Yamanouchi's translation on Japanese thought may be seen in the book of a well-known critic, Kawakami Tetsutaro, entitled *Nihon no Outsider* (1961). The author follows Fukase Motohiro in comparing Chesterton's *Orthodoxy* with Eliot's *After Strange Gods*, and goes on to emphasize the need for the Japanese to reconsider the problem of orthodoxy. Taking the example of the Protestant thinker, Uchimura Kanzo, in a chapter entitled 'Seito Shiso ni tsuite' (On Orthodox Thought), he points out that, while Uchimura may seem an outsider in view of the main current of contemporary Japanese thought, he is really an insider in view of his essentially Japanese way of thinking. He also adds, in what seems a Chestertonian paradox, that 'the orthodox thought of modern Japan is Christian'.

A more recent book by another critic, Hori Hidehiko, entitled *Kono Hon wo Miyo* (Behold This Book, 1970), devotes a chapter to 'G. K. Chesterton no *Seito Shiso* ni tsuite' (About Chesterton's *Orthodoxy*). It is interesting to note the other books which the author places alongside that of Chesterton: Homer's *Odyssey*, Plato's Dialogues, Plutarch's *Lives*, Boethius' *Consolation of Philosophy*, Chaucer's *Canterbury Tales*, A Kempis' *Imitation of Christ*, Montaignes' *Essays*, Rousseau's *Emile* and so on. Chesterton himself would have been astonished to find himself in such a distinguished and varied company! The author further relates how he was first captivated by Chesterton on reading the Japanese translation of *Orthodoxy*. He was filled with admiration at his wit and paradoxical humour, and particularly at his way of viewing everything in the world as if for the first time.

On the other hand, while Japanese readers have from the beginning responded with deep admiration to *Orthodoxy*, they are less than responsive to the greater masterpiece *The Everlasting Man*. It hardly even received a bibliographical mention, until Father Roggen came to speak of it in his article for *Catholic* as the culmination of Chesterton's philosophy and his first literary masterpiece after his conversion to the Catholic Church. Even now it remains untranslated and unedited, apart from one chapter, 'Professors and Prehistoric Man', which was included by Funahashi Takeshi, a professor of Doshisha University, in his edition of *The Soul of England and Other Essays*. Here, oddly enough, Chesterton finds himself taking second place to his controversial opponent, Dean Inge, who is given the title essay of the volume.

After the end of the second world war the name of Chesterton once again became popular in Japan, and again as a writer of detective stories. This time the whole cycle of Father Brown stories was translated into Japanese, and not just once, but twice and virtually three times. The movement began with the translation of *The Innocence of Father Brown* in 1955 by Murasaki Toshiro, a graduate of Hitotsubashi University in Tokyo; and he went on to complete the series of five volumes for *Pocket Mystery*, published by Hayakawa Shobo, in the next two years. His successful competitor was Fukuda Tsuneari, a graduate of Tokyo University, soon to become famous as the modern translator of Shakespeare and director of a theatrical group called *Gendai Engeki Kyokai* (Modern Theatrical Society). Beginning with a translation of several stories published under the title of *Brown Shinpu* (Father Brown) in 1956, he proceeded to retranslate the whole cycle in collaboration with Nakamura Yasuo, another Tokyo graduate, for another book series called *Sogen Suiri Bunko*. These volumes, which were completed by 1961, rapidly became best-sellers and they are still fairly popular.

Other translators of the Father Brown stories were not slow in coming forward. For yet another series, *Shincho Bunko*, the services of two more translators were called upon, Hashimoto Fukuo, who translated *The Innocence* in 1959, and Hashimoto Minoru, who translated *The Wisdom* and *The Incredulity* the following year, followed at a distance by *The Secret* in 1964. A

selection of the stories was again translated by Tanaka Nishijiro
in 1962 under the title of *Brown Shinpu Monogatari* (Tales of
Father Brown); and yet another by Miyanishi Hoitsu in 1963
under the title of *Brown Shinpu Tanpenshu* (Collection of Father
Brown stories).

Many of Chesterton's other stories were translated about
this time. *The Man Who Was Thursday* was translated by Hashimoto Fukuo in 1954, and again two years later—with notable
success—by Yoshida Kenichi, son of the famous post-war Prime
Minister, and himself a well-known critic and author. Fukuda
Tsuneari also translated *The Poet and the Lunatics* in 1957, *The
Club of Queer Trades* in 1958 and *The Paradoxes of Mr Pond* in
1959.

With this 'Father Brown boom' Chesterton attained a wide
popularity in Japan, as never before or since. It may well have
influenced the development of Japan's best known detective
story writer, Matsumoto Seicho, who tends (like Father Brown)
to see things from the viewpoint of the criminal. The impact of
this vogue on Japanese readers may be illustrated by a reminiscence of the novelist, Hotta Yoshie, a Keio graduate. In his
book *Rekishi to Unmei* (History and Fate, 1966) he has a chapter
entitled 'Chesterton Hen'aito' (Partiality for Chesterton), in
which he has this confession to make: 'After finishing my day's
work, I get into bed with a bottle of whisky; and what then,
I begin reading Chesterton. It may be *The Man Who Was Thursday*, or the five volumes of *Father Brown*, or *The Poet and the
Lunatics*, or *The Man Who Knew Too Much*, or *The Paradoxes of
Mr Pond*, or something else.' He goes on to say that he cannot
quite explain what it is that so attracts him to these books, but
he just reads and enjoys them.

Another well-known writer from Waseda, Edogawa Ranpo
(his pen-name being a Japanese equivalent to his favourite
author, Edgar Allan Poe), expresses his enthusiasm for Chesterton in his *Kaigai Tantei Shosetsu Sakuhin* (Detective Stories and
Story-Tellers Abroad, 1957): 'At night when my feelings are
composed, and I ask myself which detective story writers are
the most outstanding, the figures of Poe and Chesterton occur
to my mind. The works of these two men, I feel, stand out
above all other writers and their works.' In this connection,
mention may be made of another translation of Chesterton's

essay, 'In Defence of Detective Stories', by Suzuki Yukio, a professor of English at Waseda, in his book *Satsujin Geijitsu* (The Art of Murder, 1959).

In contrast, however, to all this popularity of the Father Brown stories, the literary merits of Chesterton as a writer have been largely ignored by the academic world of Japan since the end of the war. No place is accorded him in the sixty-volume series of *Eibungaku Handbook* (Handbooks of English Literature), translated from the British Council series of 'Writers and their Work'; and Christopher Hollis' study of *G. K. Chesterton*, translated by Oda Teizo in 1969, had to be published privately. Nor does he feature in the twenty-four volume series of *Konnichi no Igirisu-America Bungaku* (English and American Literature Today), published—like the above-mentioned series—by Kenkyusha. Nor does his name appear among the various papers given by Japanese scholars at the annual meetings of the English Literary Society of Japan (with one exception to be mentioned later), or among the studies in its periodical *Eibungaku Kenkyu* (Studies in English Literature).

Yet there is at least one academic centre where the study of Chesterton has not been neglected, the Catholic university of Sophia in Tokyo. After the war a Catholic magazine called *Boro* (Pharos) was founded, and continued for several years under the editorship of Kobayashi Yoshio. From the outset it contained several pieces on or by Chesterton. Karita Motoshi, a teacher of the English department at Sophia, contributed translations of Chesterton's essay on 'Thomas More' and the first chapter of his *Saint Francis of Assisi*, as well as an article on 'Chesterton no Ningen Gyakusetsu' (Chesterton, the Paradoxical Man) in 1948.

Subsequently, Nakano Kii, another teacher of this department, has emerged as the leading Chesterton scholar in Japan. Shortly after the war, he recalls, he was introduced to Chesterton when his teacher at Sophia, Father Joseph Roggendorf, used *The Victorian Age* as textbook for his class on Victorian literature. In those days there were not enough copies to go round, and they had to use mimeographed excerpts from the book. Incidentally, this was still the textbook in use at Sophia when I came to Japan in 1954 and was asked to take over the course in Victorian literature. So it was through Chesterton that I myself first came to teach literature in this country.

After becoming a lecturer at Sophia, Nakano Kii decided to specialize in Chesterton. His first study, 'Kikuchi Kan to G. K. Chesterton—Optimist no Kenkyu' (Kikuchi and Chesterton—A Study of Two Optimists), appeared in *Sophia*, a periodical edited by Father Roggendorf, in 1961. Two further articles he contributed to another Catholic magazine, *Seiki*, 'G. K. Chesterton no Ai to Ninshiki' (Chesterton's Love and Understanding) in 1962, and 'Brown Shinpu no Miryoku' (Fascination of Father Brown) in 1966. Most of his Chesterton studies, however, appeared in the periodical of the English Literature department of Sophia, *Eibungaku to Eigogaku*: 'G. K. Chesterton no Toritsu no Gyakusetsu ni tsuite' (On the Paradox of Inversion in Chesterton) in 1965, 'G. K. Chesterton no Heiritsu no Gyakusetsu ni tsuite' (On the Paradox of Juxtaposition in Chesterton) in 1966, 'G. K. Chesterton no Henry James-kan' (Chesterton's View of Henry James) in 1967, 'G. K. Chesterton no Bungei Hyoden' (Chesterton's Literary Biographies) in 1968, and 'G. K. Chesterton no *1984*—The Napoleon of Notting Hill Saikento' (Chesterton's *1984*—A Reconsideration of NNH) in 1970. The last-mentioned study was also presented as a paper at the meeting of the English Literary Society of Japan that same year—the only paper on Chesterton since the war.

It was also Nakano Kii who translated *Saint Thomas Aquinas* for the series of *Universal Bunko* in 1964. Subsequently, the other medieval biography of *Saint Francis of Assisi* was translated by Ishimoto Masaaki, a graduate of Sophia, and published in the same series in 1970. About this time several editions of Chesterton's essays were also published as textbooks for students. Tagiri Hisazumi, a professor of Rikkyo, brought out an edition of *Tremendous Trifles* in 1967. Yamagata Kazumi, a teacher at Senshu University in Tokyo, edited Chesterton's *Selected Essays*, on the basis of W. Sheed's Penguin edition of *Essays and Poems*, in the same year. I myself followed with an edition of Chesterton's *Essays on Shakespeare*, gathered from a wide variety of sources, in 1968; and then an edition of *Orthodoxy* in 1969.

This is the place to mention the Chesterton Society, which I founded in 1966 in conjunction with Nakano Kii soon after my recovery from a six months' illness. If I may indulge in personal reminiscences, it was during this illness that I began to re-read Chesterton's stories, as I had been forbidden anything but the lightest reading by my doctor. They now put me into such a genial mood that all who visited me were astonished at my good humour. It was thanks to them that I could make a speedy recovery from my TB; and on my return to normal life I began to think of ways of spreading interest in Chesterton. I noticed that besides Nakano Kii there were not a few teachers at Sophia and elsewhere who were interested in Chesterton. So we formed a very informal society for the purpose of literary discussion, not only on Chesterton, but with his spirit 'on anything and everything'. From outside Sophia we invited Tagiri Hisazumi, Yamagata Kazumi and Oda Teizo, as well as a few 'honorary members', such as the old Yamanouchi Ichiro and a professor of Shizuoka University, Suzuki Minoru, who had published studies on the literary viewpoint of Chesterton (in 1964) and on *The Innocence of Father Brown* (in 1969).

At one meeting we decided on a co-operative venture, in the form of a symposium of critical essays which would be the first of its kind on Chesterton in the Japanese literary world. Each of us contributed an essay on one or other aspect of Chesterton's many-sided genius. Karita Motoshi refurbished his article on 'Chesterton no Ningen Gyakusetsu', and Sakai Yoshitaka (now a professor of English at Sophia) wrote a new article on 'Shijin toshite no Chesterton' (Chesterton as Poet). Tagiri Hisazumi wrote on Chesterton's prose style, and Yamagata Kazumi on his Christian faith. From the English Literature department, Yamaguchi Seiji (who had assisted Fukuda Tsuneari in several of his Father Brown translations) wrote on Chesterton as story-teller, Watanabe Shoichi on Chesterton as historian, and Anzai Tetsuo on Chesterton and Shaw. From other departments, Kawanaka Yasuhiro wrote on Chesterton as journalist, and Jacques Bésineau on Chesterton and Claudel. As for the two editors, I contributed Japanese translations of my introductory essays to the above-mentioned editions (with Nakano as translator); and Nakano Kii himself rewrote an article on 'G. K. Chesterton no Juyoshi' (Chesterton's reception in Japan), which had appeared in *Sophia* in 1969. This unique collection of essays, together with a bibliography of Chesterton in Japan prepared by Oda Teizo, was published by Kenkyusha in 1970, with the title *G. K. Chesterton no Sekai*. At the same time, a baby was born to Nakano Kii, and appropriately christened Gilbert!

Soon after the publication of this book, I was approached by another publisher, Shunjusha, with a request to edit a selection of Chesterton's more philosophical writings. After much discussion, in which considerations of the book market were naturally uppermost in the publisher's mind, we decided to begin with *Orthodoxy*, to be translated by Fukuda Tsuneari in conjunction with Anzai Tetsuo, the *Autobiography*, to be translated by Yoshida Kenichi, and *Saint Francis of Assisi* and *Saint Thomas Aquinas*, to be translated and published in one volume by Noguchi Keisuke, an elderly professor of English at Sophia. If these proved financially successful, the publisher expressed his willingness to go on to *The Everlasting Man* and *Heretics*. The first two volumes were planned for spring of 1973, and it was hoped that all five volumes would be out to greet the centenary of Chesterton in 1974.

To conclude this survey, it may be interesting to add some personal comments of unknown Japanese writers, who are all the more typical of their nation for being unknown—I mean, my own students in the English Literature department of Sophia. From their term papers, based on a simple reading of my edition of *Orthodoxy*, I append the following extracts:

After reading this essay, my preconceived idea of orthodoxy was utterly reversed. I felt as if I was attracted by a magician and brought into a bright, mild and startling world of orthodoxy. Through his eyes I almost became able to see this universe with delightful wonder and with such a vast love as Chesterton had, and to feel everything as odd as well as poetic. My prejudice against the world of Christianity was swept away and I could find a not only strict and rigid, but also warm, fierce and magnanimous world which seemed to be quite attractive to me. Chesterton is a true poet and a true scientist who never forgets the children's mind and nature. He uses fresh and familiar metaphors and humour to lead us to his living philosophy of Elfland. By such an extraordinary and living approach to his ideas, we can understand and accept it not only logically but also heartily. It is more persuasive and understandable than any difficult logic arranged before us.

(Shibata Mihoko)

Though I have understood the Christian doctrine vaguely, I felt after having read *Orthodoxy* that I had tried to understand the doctrine by 'criticism' and 'approval'. We must follow a lily to blossom in the field or a bird to fly in the sky, which put their heart and soul into admiring God's glory. Though Nature is everywhere full of God's glory, how lamentable we are not to notice how wonderful they are until we see rivers run with wine! The paradox of Christianity, it releases us from our prejudice!

(Sasaki Kiyomi)

What I felt while reading this book is that it is covered with a very cheerful atmosphere and I have never felt any gloomy one. It seems it is not only because Chesterton himself was a cheerful man, but also because he dared to choose those humorous expressions in order to explain his profound philosophy. . . . After we have read his work being involved in his cheerfulness, we are surprised to find that there was much important philosophy in it.

(Todoroki Naoko)

I enjoyed reading *Orthodoxy*, written by a unique and whimsical yet great philosophical talent, G. K. Chesterton. . . . Throughout his writing I was struck by his wit or his extraordinary manner of saying things and looking at and feeling what are around him. . . . I was so delighted when I came across such a passage as, 'The fairytale philosopher is glad that the leaf is green, precisely because it might have been scarlet'. . . . At such sweet and lovely expressions I cannot help smiling before knowing it.

(Kumagai Mariko)

His criticism is rather severe, but his skilful writing with humour softens the content. His interesting stories and metaphors draw us into his world easily. As his criticism is not rough but soft like medicine with sugar, we must be careful. Because his criticism with humour may be passed over laughing without knowing it is criticism. So when we read his writings, all of a sudden we notice his intent. . . . When we accept his idea, we are able to see the world with different eyes from before. This world becomes a joyful place. With pure childlike minds we are able to discover new things that we have not noticed till now, just as Chesterton does. . . . He is an entirely lovable thinker.

(Ishikawa Mikiko)

G. K. Chesterton has a unique humour and personality. So everybody, including me, reads his works and feels an interest in them.
I think that modern people, especially youth, like him and his
works because of his wonderful humour and thought. And we can
take kindly to his books more easily than to those of others.

(Tsuchiya Atsu)

Notes

'Philosophy in Fiction'—Ian Boyd

1. See, for example, *Gilbert Keith Chesterton* (London: Sheed and Ward, 1944), p.413.
2. 'Notes on the Way', *Time and Tide*, November 9, 1946, p.1070.
3. Ibid, pp.1070-1.
4. *Paradox in Chesterton* (London: Sheed and Ward, 1948).
5. See Maisie Ward, *Chesterton*, p.525.
6. *The Tablet*, June 20, 1936, p.785.
7. Ibid, p.785.
8. 'Chesterton and/or Belloc', *Critical Quarterly*, I, 1959, pp.64-71.
9. 'Notes on Nationalism', *The Collected Essays, Journalism and Letters*, ed. Sonia Orwell and Ian Angus, volume III (London: Secker and Warburg, 1968), pp. 365-6.
10. 'Chesterton', *The National Review* [New York], April 22, 1961, p.251.
11. Ibid, p.252.
12. 'G. K. Chesterton', *Collected Essays* (London: The Bodley Head, 1969), pp.136-7.
13. *Culture and the Coming Peril* (London: University of London Press, 1927), p.18.
14. *Autobiography* (London: Hutchinson, 1936), pp.288-9.
15. Ibid, p.289.
16. 'Old Curiosity Shop', *Appreciations and Criticisms of the Works of Charles Dickens* (London: J. M. Dent, 1911), pp.59-60.

17 Chapter XIV, 'Portrait of a Friend', pp.288-306.
18. Ibid, p.289.
19. January 19, 1929, p.299.
20. M. H. Abrams, *A Glossary of Literary Terms* (New York: Holt, Rinehart and Winston, 1965), p.2.
21. Ibid, p.3.
22. *William Blake* (London: Duckworth, 1910), p.141.
23. Ibid, p.141.
24. Ibid, p.142.
25. *G. F. Watts* (London: Duckworth, 1904), p.65.
26. *The Poet and the Lunatics: Episodes in the Life of Gabriel Gale* (London: Darwen Finlayson, 1962), pp.46-7.
27. *The Victorian Sage: Studies in Argument* (New York: W. W. Norton, 1965), p.12.
28. 'The Crime of a Communist', *The Father Brown Stories* (London: Cassell, 1966), pp.660-74.
29. 'Introduction', *Father Brown: Selected Stories by G. K. Chesterton* (London: Oxford University Press, 1966), p.xv.
30. *The Georgian Literary Scene: A Panorama* (London: Hutchinson, 1938), p.102 and 104.
31. See the dedication to W. R. Titterton in the first edition (London: Chatto and Windus, 1927), p.v.
32. 'Bernard Shaw and Breakages', *Sidelights on New London and Newer York* (London: Sheed and Ward, 1932), p.217.

'The Achievement of G. K. Chesterton'—Stephen Medcalf

1. *The Poet and the Lunatics* (London, 1929), pp.129-30.
2. *Autobiography* (London, 1936), p.329.
3. *The New Jerusalem* (London, 1921), p.188.
4. *The Victorian Age in Literature* (2nd ed., Oxford, 1966), p.111.
5. *The Man Who Was Thursday* (2nd ed., Bristol, 1912), pp.105-6. cf. J. L. Borges, *Other Inquisitions* (tr. R. L. C. Simms, paperback, New York, 1968), 'On Chesterton', pp. 82-5.
6. Borges, op. cit., loc. cit.
7. 'The Purple Wig', *The Father Brown Stories* (10th ed., London, 1963), p.253.
8. *The Man Who Knew Too Much* (Popular ed., London, 1923), p.97.
9. T. S. Eliot, *Collected Poems 1909-1962* (London, 1963), p.208.
10. *G. F. Watts* (London, 1904), p.44. cf. Borges, op. cit., 'The Analytical Language of John Wilkins', pp.104-5.
11. *A Short History of England* (London, 1917), pp.195-7.
12. *Penguin Book of Modern Verse Translations* (London, 1966), p.29.
13. *Collected Poems* (London, 1933), p.179.
14 e.g. the letter to Knox in Evelyn Waugh, *Ronald Knox* (London, 1959), pp.207-8.
15. *The Everlasting Man* (London, 1925), p.11.
16. *Manalive* (London, 1912), pp. 257-8.
17. *The Ball and the Cross* (London, 1910), p.1.
18. *The Everlasting Man*, p.12.
19. op.cit., loc.cit.
20. *The Everlasting Man*, p.35.
21. op. cit., p.27.

22. op. cit., p.34.
23. *William Blake* (London, 1910), pp.129 f.
24. *St Francis of Assisi* (London, 1924), p.32.
25. The suggestion is Miss E. Welsford's, in M. Evans, *G. K Chesterton* (Cambridge, 1939), pp. 33 f.
26. *St Francis of Assisi*, p.101.
27. *Lunacy and Letters* (London, 1958), p.113.
28. *The Man Who Was Thursday*, p.13.
29. *A Short History of England*, p.210.
30. 'The Blue Cross', *The Father Brown Stories*, p.20.
31. 'The Sign of the Broken Sword', op. cit., p.154.
32. T. S. Eliot, 'Baudelaire', *Selected Essays* (3rd ed., London, 1951), p.426.
33. *Heretics* (London, 1905), p.34.
34. J. O'Connor, *Father Brown on Chesterton* (London, 1937), p.41.
35. *St Thomas Aquinas* (London, 1933), pp.217f.
36. *The Man Who Knew Too Much*, p.3.
37. *St Thomas Aquinas*, pp.219-21.
38. op. cit., p.198.
39. 'On Blake and his Critics', *Avowals and Denials* in C. Ricks, *Poems and Critics* (paperback, London, 1972), p.127.
40. *Heretics*, pp.40f.
41. 'The Return', *Rudyard Kipling's Verse. Inclusive edition* (London,1933), p.477.
42. *Chesterton on Shakespeare* (Henley on Thames, 1971), pp.17f.
43. *Fancies versus Fads* (4th ed., London, 1930), p.223.
44. 'On Blake and his Critics', op.cit., loc.cit.
45. *The Everlasting Man*, p.48.
46. op. cit., p.50.

47. op. cit., p.116.
48. op. cit., loc. cit.
49. op. cit., p.118.
50. op. cit., p.114.
51. op. cit., p.156.
52. 'The Donkey' in *Collected Poems* (London, 1933), p.325.
53. *Robert Browning* (Pocket ed., London, 1925), p.151.
54. *William Blake*, p.142.
55. *The Flying Inn* (London, 1914), pp.176-9.
56. *Robert Browning*, p.149.
57. op. cit., pp.150f.
58. *The Napoleon of Notting Hill* (Cheap ed., London, 1904), p.135.
59. Blake, *Jerusalem*, pl. 27, in *Poems*, ed. W. H. Stevenson (London, 1971), p.678.
60. *G. F. Watts*, p.10.
61. *The Napoleon of Notting Hill* (Cheap ed., London, 1904), p.72.
62. op. cit., p.97.
63. op. cit., p.135.
64. op. cit., p.249.
65. op. cit., p.248.
66. *The Man Who Was Thursday*, p.114.
67. op. cit., p.135.
68. op. cit., pp.223ff.
69. op. cit., p.322.
70. op. cit., p.323.
71. op. cit., loc. cit.
72. op. cit., p.329.
73. op. cit., p.330.
74. *Autobiography*, p.102.
75. *The Ball and the Cross* (London, 1910), p.191.
76. op. cit., p.394.
77. op. cit., p.5.
78. op. cit., p.19.
79. op. cit., p.24.
80. op. cit., pp.344f.
81. *St Francis of Assisi*, p.87.
82. *Collected Poems*, p.233.
83. op. cit., p.267.
84. op. cit., p.250.
85. op. cit., p.253.

86. *The Napoleon of Notting Hill*, p.204.
87. *Collected Poems* p.63.
88. *Robert Louis Stevenson* (3rd ed., London, 1929), p.109.
89. *Collected Poems*, p.56.
90. op. cit., p.63.
91. *The Everlasting Man*, p.176.
92. M. Ward, *Gilbert Keith Chesterton* (London, 1944), p.551.
93. Charles Williams, *Poetry at Present* (Oxford, 1930), 'Gilbert Keith Chesterton', p.111—along with Borges' essay, the best criticism of Chesterton known to me.
94. *Collected Poems*, p.230.
95. op. cit., p.257.
96. op. cit., loc. cit.
97. op. cit., p.315.
98. op. cit., p.120.
99. op. cit., p.119.
100. *The Everlasting Man*, p.210.
101. T. S. Eliot, *Ash Wednesday* IV and V: *Collected Poems*, pp.101 and 102.
102. *The Man Who Was Orthodox* (ed. A. L. Maycock, London, 1963), p.43.
103. *Orthodoxy*, (London, 1909), p. 142.
104. op. cit., p.255.
105. op. cit., p.254.
106. W. H. Auden, *G. K. Chesterton. A Selection from his Non-fictional Prose* (London, 1970), p.18.
107. *Orthodoxy*, p.93.
108. op. cit., p.94.
109. op. cit., p.95.
110. op. cit., p.93.
111. *Robert Browning*, p.151.
112. *Orthodoxy*, p.94.
113. op. cit., p.92.
114. 'The Blue Cross', *The Father Brown Stories*, p.20.
115. Introduction to Greville Mac-Donald, *George MacDonald and his wife* (London, 1924), p.11.
116. Borges, op. cit., loc. cit.

117. Arthur Machen, *Far Off Things* (London, 1922), p.123.
118. Charles Williams, *The English Poetic Mind* (Oxford, 1932), ch.1 (pp.1-8).
119. *Orthodoxy*, p.128.
120. *Lunacy and Letters*, pp.183f.
121. *The Flying Inn*, pp.235-7.
122. op. cit., pp.300f.
123. *Orthodoxy*, pp.99ff and 225ff.
124. *The Defendant* (London, 1901), pp.33f.
125. *The Everlasting Man*, ch. V, 'Man and Mythologies' (pp.111-128).
126. S. Kierkegaard, *Fear and Trembling* (tr. W. Lowrie, paperback ed. New York, 1954), pp.49-52.
127. *Manalive*, p.323.
128. *Autobiography*, p.338, quoting Coventry Patmore.
129. *Collected Poems*, p.65.
130. *Hebrews* IV: 12.
131. *Manalive*, p.278.
132. T. S. Eliot, *Little Gidding: Collected Poems*, p.223.
133. *The Poet and the Lunatics*, p.129.
134. Kierkegaard, *Fear and Trembling*, p.131.
135. *Orthodoxy*, p.107.
136. op.cit., p.29.
137. op. cit., p.296.
138. *The Flying Inn*, p.5.
139. G. Janouch, *Conversations with Kafka* (London, 1953), p.57.
140. *St Thomas Aquinas*, p.135.

'Devereux Nights: A Distributist Memoir'—Brocard Sewell

1. For Hilary Pepler and Herbert Shove see also chapter 4 of *My Dear Time's Waste* by Brocard Sewell (Aylesford: St Albert's Press, 1966). Also for Pepler see *The Aylesford Review*, volume XII, number 2, Spring 1965, with articles by Brocard Sewell, Barbara Wall, Edward Walters, Brother David Lowson OP, Fr Walter Gumbley OP, Fr Reginald Ginns OP, and Reginald Jebb.
2. W. R. Titterton, *Drinking Songs and Other Songs* (London: Cecil Palmer, 1928).
3. Marshall McLuhan, Introduction to *Paradox in Chesterton* by Hugh Kenner.

'Chesterton and the Future of Democracy'—Patrick Cahill

1. *Leaflets for Leaguers 3. The League* by G.K.C.
2. *The Outline of Sanity* (London, 1926), p.111.
3. *The Times*, March 17, 1973.
4. *The Outline of Sanity*, p.61.
5. *The Outline of Sanity*, p.62.
6. *Political Parties* (1911), p.189.
7. *The Times*, June 7, 1971.
8. *The Outline of Sanity*.
9. *The Times*, May 11, 1973: Professor Stephen Marglin (Harvard), an economist of participation.
10. *Come to Think of It* (1930).
11. E.g. IBM, Amsterdam; Saab, Sweden; Philips, Holland, etc. Cf also Work Research Institute, Oslo.
12. Publications of the IT Development Group, London.
13. *The Outline of Sanity*, pp.215-16.
14. S. Brittan: *Cuts in Government Spending* (1972).
15. *Britain 1973* (HMSO).
16. *Sunday Times*, March 25, 1973.
17. *Daily Mail*, March 23, 1973.
18. *G.K.'s Weekly*, November 27, 1926.
19. *The Defendant*, No. 12, December 1953.
20. *George Bernard Shaw* (London, 1909), p.33.
21. *Tremendous Trifles* (1909), p.236.
22. R. Michels, p.401.

23. Mr Cyril Smith, elected Liberal MP for Rochdale in October 1972.
24. *Nation*, January 31, 1911.
25. Mr W. W. Hamilton, MP, *The Times*, April 6, 1973.
26. *A Miscellany of Men* (1912), p.37.
27. 'The Secret People' in *The Collected Poems of G. K. Chesterton*.
28. *The Times*, January 4, 1973: Rt Hon. Reginald Maudling, MP.
29. *George Bernard Shaw*, p.31.
30. *The Defendant*, No. 12, December,1953.
31. *Workers' Participation in Western Europe* (IPM, 1971).
32. *The Times*, May 29, 1973: Prof. T. A. J. Nicholson, London, Graduate School of Business Studies.
33. European Commission Report for 1972 on the social situation in the Community.
34. *The Times*, April 30, 1973: Mr Richard Seabrook (Union of Shop, Distributive and Allied Workers).
35. *The Distributist Programme 1934*, p.24.

'Chesterton in France'—Christiane d'Haussy

1. *Tremendous Trifles* (Beaconsfield: Darwen Finlayson, 1968), p.43.
2. Raymond Las Vergnas, *Chesterton, Belloc, Baring*, tr. Fr Martindale SJ (London: Sheed and Ward, 1938), p.134.
3. 'Défense de la Farce', *Revue Universelle*, LXV, 7, July 1, 1936.
4. 'Chesterton raconté par lui-même', *Revue Universelle*, LXX, 1937.
5. *All Things Considered* (Beaconsfield: Darwen Finlayson, 1969), p.51.
6. Charles-Albert Cingria, 'Chesterton', *Labyrinthe*, June 15, 1945.
7. Jacques Lux, 'Chesterton et les

romancières anglaises', *Revue Bleue*, premier semestre, 1914.
8. *Revue Universelle*, July 1936.
9. *Nouvelles Etudes Anglaises* (Paris: Hachette, 1910).
10. *Figures Littéraires* (Paris: Perrin, 1911).
11. *Une Heure avec . . .* (Paris: Gallimard, 1925).
12. Anon., 'L'Oeuvre de G. K. Chesterton, et sa place dans la littérature contemporaine', *Le Mois*, July 1, 1936; and Wladimir Weidlé, 'Chesterton', *La Vie Intellectuelle*, September 10, 1937.
13. *Le Figaro Littéraire*, January 22, 1968.
14. *La France Catholique*, *L'Homme Nouveau*.
15. op. cit., p.296.
16. *Nouvelle Revue Française*, XLII, 1934.
17. Joseph de Tonquedec, *G. K. Chesterton, ses Idées et son Caractère* (Paris: Nouvelle Librairie Nationale, 1920), p.28.
18. *The Uses of Diversity* (London: Methuen, 1920), pp.146-7.
19. op. cit., p.245.
20. *La Vie Intellectuelle*, September 10, 1937.
21. *Nouvelle Revue Française*,XLVII, July-December 1936.
22. *Edwardian Occasions* (London: Routledge and Kegan Paul, 1972), p.80.
23. Pierre Ayraud, 'Père Brown et le Diable', *Témoignages*, April 1952.
24. *Defence of the West* (London: Faber and Gwyer, 1927), pp.6-7.
25. Ibid, p.13.
26. Ibid, p.v.
27. Maximilien Vox, 'Défense de la Farce'.
28. *Anatomie de l'Humour et du Nonsense* (Masson, 1970), pp.58-9.
29. Letter to the author of this essay, January 23, 1968.